W9-ADD-230
WITHDRAWN

Gertrude Stein, Modernism, and the Problem of "Genius"

Gertrude Stein, Modernism, and the Problem of "Genius"

Barbara Will

EDINBURGH
University Press

For Elizabeth Lyding Will
magna mater

Edinburgh University Press Ltd
22 George Square, Edinburgh

Typeset in Stempel Garamond by
Pioneer Associates, Perthshire, and
printed and bound in Great Britain by
MPG Books Ltd, Bodmin

A CIP Record for this book is available
from the British Library

ISBN 0 7486 1198 3 (hardback)

Contents

Illustrations

Acknowledgments

Grateful acknowledgment is made to the Marion and Jasper Whiting Foundation for a research grant to study at Yale University, and to Dartmouth College for a junior faculty fellowship and a generous teaching schedule that allowed me to bring this book to completion. A further thanks is due to Dartmouth College for its financial support in securing permissions for this book. The staff of the Beinecke Rare Book and Manuscript Library at Yale University, of the English Library at the University of Geneva, and Patsy Carter at Dartmouth College have been extremely helpful in their pursuit of sources. I would also like to thank the individuals who helped this project at decisive moments: Leon Katz for his invaluable aid in providing details about Stein's unpublished notebooks; Ulla Dydo for her capacious knowledge of Stein; Sarah Balcomb at Artists Rights for help in locating illustrations; William V. Ganis and Tim McCarthy for unraveling the complexities of Andy Warhol's system of production. Jackie Jones at Edinburgh University Press has been a wonderful editor, and administrative assistant Carol Duncan has also been of great assistance in shepherding this book through its final stages.

I am also pleased to be able to acknowledge with gratitude the colleagues, students, friends, and family who have supported and sustained my work on this project. Dianne Chisholm, Wlad Godzich, Fredric Jameson, Toril Moi, Michael Moon, and Janice Radway provided crucial suggestions and insights at an early stage of the project, while their own scholarly texts remain for me models of critical inquiry. I am deeply grateful to a number of readers who offered detailed comments on chapters of this book: John Blair, Evelyne Ender, Susannah Heschel, Amy Hollywood, Lou Renza, and Roy Sellars. Catharine Stimpson was a generous reader of the first draft of this manuscript, as were my two anonymous readers at Edinburgh University Press. In its later stages, this project was supported and sustained in innumerable ways by many colleagues at the University of Geneva, at the University of Glasgow, and at Dartmouth College

– especially Paul Argenti, Susan Castillo, William Cook, Jonathan Crewe, Martin Favor, Lenore Grenoble, Donald Pease, Gregory Polletta, Matthew Rowlinson, Ivy Schweitzer, Virginia Swain, and Melissa Zeiger. I am also grateful to my students and research assistants at Dartmouth College and at the University of Geneva – especially Nils Arvold, Matt Benedetto, Meg Cashion, Sarah Jackson, Robert Koelzer, Suzanne Leonard, and Carrie Lutz – whose intelligence and enthusiasm for this project have been a source of inspiration for me. A special thanks is due to Brenda Silver, whose unerring sense of style in writing as in life remains a standard.

Thanks also to Hosam Aboul-Ela, Niall Bond, Anita Fabos, Marie-Geneviève Iselin, William Maxwell, and Arthur Tannenbaum for friendship and laughter throughout the life of this project; and to the members of my family for encouragement, companionship, and support. Finally, love and thanks to Michael Ermarth, without whose presence this book would not have been written.

The author acknowledges permission from the following to reprint material under their control: Estate of T. S. Eliot and Faber & Faber, Ltd., for T. S. Eliot material; Farrar, Straus & Giroux and Carcanet Press, Ltd., for excerpts from the poetry of Mina Loy; Harcourt, Inc., for Andy Warhol material (© 1975, 1980 by Andy Warhol); Leon Katz, for Alice B. Toklas material; New Directions Publishing Corporation, for Ezra Pound material (© 1991 by the Trustees of the Ezra Pound Literary Property Trust); New Directions Publishing Corporation, for William Carlos Williams material (© 1931 by William Carlos Williams); Executors of the Virginia Woolf Estate and Hogarth Press; Oxford University Press, for excerpts from the work of Hegel; Estate of Gertrude Stein, for published and unpublished writings, correspondence, and photographs; Yale Collection of American Literature, Beinecke Rare Book and Manuscript Library, Yale University, for material from the Gertrude Stein and Alice B. Toklas papers.

Abbreviations of Works by Gertrude Stein

ABT	*The Autobiography of Alice B. Toklas*
CMA	"Cultivated Motor Automatism"
EA	*Everybody's Autobiography*
FIA	*Four in America*
GMP	*Matisse Picasso and Gertrude Stein (G.M.P.)*
HTW	*How to Write*
HWIW	*How Writing Is Written*
LIA	*Lectures in America*
MOA	*The Making of Americans: Being a History of a Family's Progress*
Narr	*Narration*
NB	Notebooks to *The Making of Americans*
NMA	"Normal Motor Automatism"
P&P	*Portraits and Prayers*
QED	*Q.E.D.*
SR	*A Stein Reader*
TCD	"To Call It a Day"
TI	"A Transatlantic Interview 1946"
TL	*Three Lives*
UK	*Useful Knowledge*
WAM	"What Are Master-pieces and Why Are There So Few of Them"

Introduction

Toward the end of the first decade of her literary career, Gertrude Stein began to realize that she was a genius: "Slowly and in a way it was not astonishing but slowly I was knowing that I was a genius and it was happening and I did not say anything but I was almost ready to begin to say something" (EA, 76). This book asks what "knowing that I was a genius" meant for Stein. Occurring at the moment in which she "begin[s] to say something," after a long effort to authorize a voice and a textual practice that would comply with the modernist imperative to be "absolutely new," Stein's recognition of genius can be seen as the source from which an inventive and original modernist corpus is born. After this recognition, from about 1908 on, Stein's writing would develop in the direction of the rigorous and innovative experimentation for which it is best known today. Yet this crucial and enabling notion of "genius" is far from transparent within the Steinian lexicon. While Stein throughout her life evinced a great interest in the extraordinary or "vitally singular" individual producing masterpieces, she also suggested that "genius" was a capacity anyone reading her texts could share: a decentered and dialogic, open-ended and collective mode of "being." And while Stein often adopted a public stance of self-aggrandizement and self-promotion, referring to herself variously as "the creative literary mind of the century" or "the only one," she just as often made these claims in the context of equally strong claims to being representative of everybody. "Genius," then, seems to name for Stein a contradictory or heterogeneous mode of "being": at once the essential, autonomous authorial subject creating absolutely new and original works of art, and at the same time a way of existing and relating in language that is open-ended, processual, collaborative, and resistant to any final symbolic or authorial containments. "Genius" is the term that differentiates Stein from her audience, and that marks the legitimation of her aesthetic "difficulty"; yet "genius" is also the key term for Stein to describe the relationship between writer and reader as they share in the experience of the modernist composition.

The point of this book is to argue for the centrality of this complex and shifting notion of "genius" to Gertrude Stein's work in particular, and to the aesthetic ideals and contradictory intellectual affiliations of early twentieth-century modernism in general. While many have taken Stein's claim to being a "genius" as either a valid assessment of her capacities or, conversely, as the sign of excessive egotism, such judgments ultimately preclude any substantive analysis of why modernist artists and their coteries were so invested in the notion of "genius," and in how and under what conditions this notion is significant for modernism. The term "genius" is, of course, a construct, a signifier for individual value whose meaningfulness is contingent upon social, institutional and discursive hierarchies and exclusions. Yet precisely because of its association with timeless human originality and transcendence, the notion of "genius" has functioned in such a way as to occlude these social and historical contingencies.[1] The responses to Gertrude Stein's claim to "being a genius" that either charge her with fraud or attempt to rehabilitate her in the face of such accusations only serve to further this occlusion. In the analysis that follows, I will not be asking the question, was Gertrude Stein a genius? But rather, what did the notion of "genius" enable Stein to do or undo? What kinds of possibilities and constraints were signified for Stein by this act of self-naming? And in what sense is the crisis of authority articulated in Stein's discourse of "genius" a problem of general significance for the artist and her audience in the twentieth century?

The investment of Stein and her contemporaries in the discourse of "genius" had an important precedent: for early twentieth-century writers, the question of authority and originality was indebted to Romantic and Enlightenment writings on the subject. The Romantics understood "genius" as both a universal capacity and as a discrete and exceptional figure, as the quintessence of the subject and as the centered, humanist subject incarnate – the ineffable Individual whose capacities were both deeper and greater than those of ordinary mortals. German commentators, with their propensity to synthesize the universal and the particular in one dialectical move, offered the key terms for capturing both senses of "genius." The following description by Hegel in his *Aesthetics* is exemplary:

> Genius is the general ability for the true production of a work of art, as well as the energy to elaborate and complete it. But, even so,

> this capacity and energy exists only as subjective, since spiritual production is possible only for a self-conscious subject who makes such creation his aim.[2]

Hegel's description of "genius" as a universal quality or creative ability is etymologically related to the Latin "gens" or "genus," signifying the generative power of the spirit or the "animus" that inheres in all human beings.[3] Yet for Hegel, only those few artists who have attained a specific degree of self-consciousness, and whose "true power resides in this inner content," can rightly be called "geniuses."[4] Friedrich Schlegel would claim that "[t]o have genius is the natural state of man," for genius represents "[t]he union of the individual with its ideal";[5] yet the genius is also one above others who "carries his centre within himself."[6] Schopenhauer would argue for the physical specificity of the genius, but would also insist that genius as a faculty

> must exist in all men in a smaller and different degree; for if not, they would be just as incapable of enjoying works of art as of producing them; they would have no susceptibility for the beautiful or the sublime; indeed, these words could have no meaning for them.[7]

As a figure, the genius – whose gender is always unquestionably male – embodies energy, creativity, originality, inspiration, and the capacity to bring meaning to matter, to transform the world around him. Hence the importance to nineteenth-century writers of the figure of Napoleon, who seemed to combine in one holistic form vitality, power, originality, and universalism – the very embodiment of a transcendent European culture. Yet "genius" for these writers is both an essence and more than an essence; it is marked by transcendence, by the breaking of rules and laws, and thus cannot be contained by embodiment or even figuration. It is the sign of the divine in a rational and secular Enlightenment world: in works of genius "it is the sacred breath which . . . moves us."[8] For Kant, genius is both mechanistic and "inexplicably" free; it both "gives the rule to art" and serves as "the exemplary originality of the natural endowments of an individual in the *free* employment of his cognitive faculties."[9] Novalis captures this latter sense of "genius" in one of his fragments from the 1790s:

> I feel it within me, struggling
> A genius, feathers smouldering;

> As my sense and heart rise toward the Aether
> The body barely fetters me down.[10]

Novalis's "genius" is something more akin to a "soul," a vital capacity that exists potentially in all humankind and that signifies the subject's aspiration toward transcendence of the material, mechanical, or bodily world. Precisely in transcending rules and transgressing limitations and boundaries, "genius" comes to stand in for the essential freedom of the individual subject, or of the subject as Individual.[11] As the "genie apostle" Johann Caspar Lavater summarizes: "Where action, craft, thought, feeling is, that which man cannot learn – that is genius. Genius – that all perceiving and indescribable thing!"[12]

In a crucial sense, European Romanticism is unthinkable without the concept of "genius"; as Novalis again suggests, the Romantic impulse – "Making absolute – making universal" – must be taken up by those who have the capacity to "renew the world."[13] The same could be said of the period of early twentieth-century modernism, which inherits many of Romanticism's assumptions about "genius" but invests this term with new desires, anxieties, and politics. What is immediately apparent in revisiting the notion of "genius" a century after the Romantics is the degree to which this notion continues to signify "freedom," but a freedom *from* the practical context of everyday life, as from social engagement altogether. The Romantics' insistence upon the capacity of "genius" to "renew" culture or society is given over in high modernism to an emphasis upon the necessary detachment of the artist and the art work from a culture and society marked by humdrum routine and the banalized march of "progress." In part, this development has to do with a change in the perception of "genius" throughout the course of the nineteenth century, from a universal capacity to an embodied type, visibly and measurably distinguishable from non-geniuses through the evidence of discrete physical and mental characteristics: high foreheads, hormonal irregularities, enormous powers of concentration, a tendency to depression.[14] This conceptualization of the "genius" as a rare and unique "personality" would resonate deeply with the aesthetic worldview of high modernism, with its emphasis on abstraction rather than mimesis, distantiation rather than engagement, on the liberation of Art and artist alike from the formal and representational imperatives of a previous aesthetic tradition. High modernist discourses of creativity, originality, and authorial autonomy are thus mutually inscribed in ideologies of formal experimentation and aesthetic "difficulty." As Peter Bürger has noted in *Theory of the Avant-Garde*, the myth of the high modernist genius working in splendid though isolated freedom is inseparable from the formalist idea of modern art as autonomous, hermetic, and self-referential. Perhaps most importantly, the notion of "genius" for high modernism served as a key term in articulating an oppositional stance toward one of the major developments of social and economic modernization from the mid-nineteenth century on: the emergence of an enormous, literate mass that seemed to threaten the very conditions of possibility of modern art.

"Modernism," Andreas Huyssen writes, "constituted itself through a conscious strategy of exclusion, an anxiety of contamination by its other: an increasingly consuming and engulfing mass culture."[15] For an early twentieth-century writer like Ezra Pound, "the masses" signified conformity, contingency, banalization: everything to which the truly creative artist was opposed. In opposition to the eminently aristocratic genius, "the masses" were neither unique, individual subjects nor did they show any tendencies toward transcendence: "Modern civilization has bred a race with brains like those of rabbits," he wrote in 1914, adding with proto-fascistic fervor, "we artists who have been so long the despised are about to take over control."[16] The far more nuanced Virginia Woolf – unlike Pound a vocal anti-fascist – nevertheless found herself firmly on the side of the "highbrows" (as opposed to "lowbrows" or "middlebrows") when chronicling the reticulations of the so-called "Battle of the Brows."[17] Her often acute desire to project herself into the lives of others was counterbalanced by equally anxious descriptions of "the Man in the Street": "a vast, featureless, almost shapeless jelly of human stuff taking the reflection of the things that individuals do, occasionally wobbling this way or that as some instinct of hate, revenge, or admiration bubbles up beneath it."[18] Other modernists felt that the only response to the threat of "the masses" was to withdraw onto an elevated and isolated plane of creativity – the "high" of high modernism. Nietzsche, arguably one of the principal sources for this modernist preoccupation with transcendence, locates the voice of the "genius" in the demiurgic figure of Zarathustra: "Let us live above them [the masses] like strong winds . . . neighbours of the eagles, neighbours of the snow, neighbours of the sun. Their bodies and their spirits would call our happiness a cave of ice."[19] The terms of this passage restage the imagery of Romanticism – particularly the figure of the "mountain-scaling visionary" – by investing this imagery with "a new anti-democratic thrust."[20] Zarathustra's predicament thus frames the distance between Romanticism and modernism, as described by Robert Currie:

> A romantic posits a higher order which is, in general estimation, a better world, and which can be attained. A modernist doubts, almost to the point of disbelief, that the higher order can be attained; and he interprets the higher order in terms so ascetic, or even so objectionable, as to repel all but those who can rise to the austerity of his creed.[21]

The quintessential rendering of this high modernist credo is Mina Loy's self-referential "Apology of Genius," which begins with the elevated sentiment, "Ostracized as we are with God," and manages to add racist imagery to the usual derogatory depiction of the masses ("you turn on us your smooth fools' faces|like buttocks bared in aboriginal mockeries").[22] For Loy as for her contemporaries, genial transcendence is no longer a possibility explored for its own sake, as it was for the Romantics, but a potential means of escape from the "contaminating" rabble below.

Yet this necessary withdrawal of the artist-genius from the social was also seen by many modernists as having an important utopian dimension. Only in "retiring from public altogether," as Clement Greenberg famously put it, can the avant-garde "keep culture *moving* in the midst of ideological confusion and violence."[23] In other words, the "genius" was required to extract himself or herself from "the masses" so that genuinely creative works of art could be produced which would in turn wrest a deadened populace from their habits and stupor. Only through turning away from the clichés and commonplaces of subjective and social experience could the genius effect "the shock of the new." It is for this reason that Ortega y Gasset would call for a "dehumanized" art, or that T. S. Eliot would announce in "Tradition and the Individual Talent": "[p]oetry is not a turning loose of emotion, but an escape from emotion; it is not the expression of personality, but an escape from personality."[24] Eliot's interest in an objective or impersonal aesthetic is based on the belief that the authentic work of art can liberate society from what he saw to be the prevailing conditions troubling modern life: the masses and their assault on "culture," the emerging visibility of non-Western peoples and the politicization of women, the decentering of tradition in the wake of unpredictable and widespread changes in technology and culture. Within Eliot's discussion is a vision of an art that can transform this violent everyday life precisely by creating an alternative or substitutive space where "ideological confusion" and "personality" do not matter, an art productive of a general and universal condition of transcendence. Yet Eliot's ability to pair this attack on "personality" with an equally strong investment in the great artist or "individual talent" producing these modernist masterpieces reveals some of the deep tensions within the early twentieth-century moment. Eliot himself cannot transcend the cult of "personality" even as he claims that high modernism is contingent upon this transcendence; or as he writes in "Tradition," "only those who have personality and emotions know what it means to want to escape from these things."[25] However much identification with the notion of "genius" or even "talent" may justify for Eliot and his contemporaries an assault upon the emotionalism, subjectivism, and other modes of mass false consciousness, the notion of "genius" is also for the modernists descriptive of the *summum* of subjectivity, of the Artist him- or herself, of the heroic Individual toiling in obscure but glorious autonomy. While the modernist art work may in a utopian sense liberate the world from its divisions and differences, the attendant figure producing this work, the "genius," seems intractably rooted during the early twentieth century in an oppositional and hierarchical relationship with a monstrous social Other.

For Gertrude Stein, "genius" would appear to be a term that authorizes, in the Romantic or modernist sense: a term rooted in an essentializing logic and in a conception of the self as intentional and autonomous. It is also, for Stein, an ascriptive term: a name which designates her unique status within the social order, her identity or "type" – something she indisputably "is." As I suggest in Part I of this book, Stein's "knowing that I was a genius" occurs during the process of struggling to identify her own so-called "bottom nature," an effort that had been her central concern since her earliest writings in psychological science. From 1903 to 1911, during the writing of *The Making of Americans*, Stein begins to recalculate the dominant traits of her character type so as to emphasize her "maleness" and homosexuality over her femaleness and Jewishness; this process of self-fashioning allows Stein to reconceive her own "bottom nature" in ways that conform to the gender/sex/race norms "inherent in the individualistic concept of greatness."[26] Out of this process, Stein begins to think of herself as a "genius," a recognition that also arrives at the beginning of her most manifestly experimental period of composition, at the moment in which she "begin[s] to say something"; the assertion that she is a genius would thus appear to be linked to the emergence of this new voice. Viewed from this perspective, "being a genius" appears to be the impetus for Stein to engage in the kind of literary experimentalism that has made her work appear so impenetrable for many readers: the former could be said to justify, to legitimate, even to hallow the latter's seeming difficulty. Only by attending to the genial "inside" and by eschewing the social "outside" can she begin "existing" in and through language.[27] As she would state in 1933:

> Clarity is of no importance because nobody listens and nobody knows what you mean no matter what you mean, nor how clearly you mean what you mean. But if you have vitality enough of knowing enough of what you mean, somebody and sometime and sometimes a great many will have to realise that you know what you mean and so they will agree that you mean what you know... (FIA, 127–8)

Only the "genius" or "vitally singular" individual can know what she herself means; for others, it is enough to know that the difficult high modernist masterpiece was produced by a "genius". Laying claim to "genius" thus seems to describe for Stein an achievement of both identity and authority, of a selfhood creating original works of art uncontaminated by the social, by contingency, by an "outside."[28]

Yet what Stein meant by the notion of "genius" – or whether she meant one thing only – remains at issue here. In her many attempts at self-definition throughout her life, Stein often repeats the same terms in radically different ways. In calling herself a "genius," for example, she often seems to posit a "being" at odds with both Romantic conceptions of the quintessentially centered and self-authorizing self, and with a high modernist emphasis upon the genius as the great individual who must transcend the social in order to engage in the process of cultural revitalization. In the first place, Stein begins "knowing" that she is a "genius" at a moment in which she begins to think of herself less as a bounded "self" and more as a processual and relational "being" emerging in and through textual practice. "Aesthetic has become the whole of me," she writes in 1908, giving voice to a process of complete textual and subjective encryption in which "being" has become synonymous with "writing."[29] Moreover, her earliest work makes clear that this "writing being" is not singular and unified but radically fragmented and dispersed within the text. In scientific experiments that she performed as a student in the 1890s, Stein had already identified in herself the ability to achieve a kind of "self-splitting" through the practice of writing, with one part of her consciousness able to watch herself write without interfering in the writing process. In the 1920s and

1930s, Stein would reformulate this split yet relational textual "being" in terms of "genius": "One may really indeed say that that is the essence of genius, of being most intensely alive, that is being one who is at the same time talking and listening" (LIA, 170). If this is for Stein "the essence of genius," then what she means by "genius" is clearly something other than an extra-linguistic authorial presence or transcendental soul-with-wings. Here, "the essence of genius" is not an essence at all but a process of dialogue, of unstable and shifting language play, of "irreducible plurality."[30] Articulating this process as the "essence of genius" serves to deconstruct both "essence" and "genius" in abstracting both from the province of the centered, unitary subject, and by making both contingent upon open-ended, multiple engagements that are immanent within the text. Hence this "essence," this "being" of "genius," appears to be radically *anti*-essentialist, a "being" that can only be said to exist through a perpetually shifting dialogic exchange. And the text within which this "being" emerges could thus be described as an "emergent phenomenon," a "work in progress" without beginning or end.[31]

In this reformulation of "genius" as an ongoing, anti-authorial, dialogic process, Stein would appear to be contradicting her own early efforts to lay claim to the notion of "genius" as an index of authorial and textual autonomy. "Talking and listening" not only reconfigures the Romantic conception of the "genius" as a pretextual and prerelational transcendental subject but also poses a challenge to the hegemony of high modernism and its strategies of authorial and aesthetic inwardness. Stein's reformulation of "genius" describes a "being" that is profoundly split or doubled, an uncanny "being" that might describe the author "talking and listening" to herself, but could also refer to the open-ended relationship between author/talker and reader/listener. As Stein writes in *The Making of Americans*, "I write for myself and strangers." Thirty years later in *Everybody's Autobiography*, she states that her story, the story of a "genius," is potentially the story of "everybody." By transforming the idea of "genius" into a plural and participatory experience of "talking and listening" Stein not only refuses the centrality of "individual talent" privileged by Eliot and others, but also arguably points the way toward a postmodern moment in which Romantic notions of the autonomous artist and of the absolutely original art work have been replaced by pronouncements about "the death of the author" and by new artistic efforts to blur the boundaries between originality and appropriation, invention and collaboration.[32]

Stein's reformulation of "genius" to describe a multiply engaged textual "being" also anticipates what Marianne DeKoven has identified as "poststructuralist feminist notions of a subversive writing subject that is different from, incompatible with, the identity of the coherent, separate, uniquely individuated bourgeois-patriarchal self."[33] The proliferation of recent feminist criticism on Stein has emphasized that her writing is primarily a "dialogic form, in which difference may enter without being relegated to a secondary position or subsumed under an authoritarian identity."[34] Whether Stein's reader is "anyone" or an intimate and loving Other (specifically Alice Toklas), as Catharine Stimpson suggests, "[a] feature of Stein's more radical texts is their interrogation of the diglottism of conversation and conversation on the page."[35] In locating a multivocal genial "being" in the immediate "conversation" of the text, and by thus "resist[ing] mastery and control over linguistic operations," according to Shari Benstock, Stein both poses a challenge to the coherent, unified self and proliferates the possibilities for textual engagement and signification. Reappropriating the notion of "genius" in this way illuminates Stein's "feminist . . . concern," as Harriet Chessman writes, "for the exposure and transformation of all hierarchies."[36]

This book has been inspired and influenced by the richly varied feminist claims of DeKoven, Stimpson, Benstock, Chessman, and others that Stein wanted her readers to play "active, creative roles" in approaching her texts. These critics have suggested that the issue of Stein's difficulty or hermeticism can be resolved if we learn how to read Stein in the open-ended, processual, decentering ways to which feminist and post-structuralist theory gives access. Their claims would seem to be supported by Stein's own rendering of the idea of "genius" as a dialogic and relational transaction between "talker" and "listener," author and audience. Yet while there are important political and aesthetic dimensions to this reformulation of "genius" as a "general and shared phenomenon,"[37] it is still the case that Stein's effort to undo the authorial position of "genius" was also always accompanied by an effort to redo its hierarchies and exclusions. In seeing herself through the prism of a dialogic, decentered "genius" Stein indeed anticipates "poststructuralist feminist notions of a subversive writing subject that is different from, incompatible with, the identity of the coherent, separate, uniquely individuated bourgeois-patriarchal self." Yet in her contradictory claims to value the "existing inside" over a socially engaged "outside" – as when she suggests about "genius" that "[i]f the same person does the talking and the listening why so much the better" – Stein remains very much a figure of her high modernist age. Always alive to the elisions and gaps of signification, Stein herself continually blurred the signifying boundaries between a revisionary definition of "genius" as a process of defamiliarization and enlightenment shared by writer and reader alike, and a more standard high modernist sense of the term as descriptive of the autonomous artist hermetically sealed off from public understanding; nor was this blurring necessarily always under Stein's linguistic control.

In thinking through the contradictions within Stein's use of the term "genius," I have found Judith Butler's reflections on "the historicity of the name" particularly useful. Butler contends that "the occupation of the name is that by which one is, quite without choice, situated within discourse"; even in the act of self-naming, "there is first a discourse which precedes and enables that 'I' and forms in language the constraining trajectory of its will."[38] Her evocative claim that "speaking is always in some ways the speaking of a stranger through and as oneself" underscores the ways in which language – or its symbolic power – governs both the formation and the self-estrangement of subjectivity and identity. One does not so much use language as be used by it – even in the act of self-naming, which Butler calls the "paradigmatically presentist conceit . . . that language expresses a 'will' or a 'choice' rather than a complex and constitutive history of discourse and power."[39] Through the act of entering into the discourse of "genius," however willfully and subversively, Stein is thereby "quite without choice" interpellated by a particular discursive trajectory which may run counter to other tendencies in her aesthetic.[40] This trajectory allows for certain compositional and creative freedoms, but it raises questions about the recoverability of what is lost by means of this act of self-naming. Stein's effort to recast and redeploy the notion of "genius," to make it resonate with a socially living aesthetic practice – like a piece of putty stretched to form new and previously unimaginable shapes – is nevertheless potentially exceeded by the "historicity" of the term which sets in motion a whole set of ideological, institutional, and discursive affiliations and exclusions, relations and hierarchies.

As Stein states in 1934, "A name is adequate or it is not" (LIA, 210). "Genius" may be a name that for Stein is "adequate or . . . not" in articulating an authorial subject position, and a textual "being," marked by contradictory affiliations. Especially in her early writings, her interest in the "exceptional" individual, her effort to differentiate her "singular" self from the American masses, and her commitment to determining her own "genius type" by identifying with maleness and dis-identifying with "Jewishness" suggest a problematic adherence to the exclusions authorized under this name. Yet these early texts also show Stein experimenting with the splitting and fragmenting of her authorial voice. In her middle and most ostensibly experimental period of writing, during the 1910s and 1920s, Stein like Eliot seems to want to make of the text a space where a renewed, defamiliarized, potentially universal vision can emerge, an alternate "inside" which might revitalize the habitual modes of inscription of the "outside." Yet these are also Stein's most seemingly "hermetic" texts, texts that could be said to dramatize what Wendy Steiner has called the "self-reflexive isolation" of the writer involved in the immediate process of watching herself write: "the writer as the lonely figure locked in [her] own genius."[41] In her late attempts to rethink the relationship between the "singular" individual and the collectivity – whether in terms of the American nation or in terms of public celebrityhood – Stein also registers a desire to make the notion of "genius" signify both an essential, singular subject and a capacity that anyone entering into the work of art could conceivably share. In short, Stein's central claim to "being a genius" is neither elitist nor wholly progressive and democratizing but conflictual, complex, dialectical: both other-directed and self-legitimating, both anti-authorial and productive of authority. The possibilities of this claim represent a vital, enabling "problem" around which Stein's whole textual project can be said to revolve.

As the century in which Gertrude Stein imagined herself "the creative literary mind" recedes from cultural memory, interest in the writer and her work continues to grow; the proliferation of recent artistic and scholarly publications, productions, and exhibits on Stein in America and Europe suggests that her appeal to late twentieth- and early twenty-first audiences is enormous. Yet until relatively recently, much of Stein's work remained unpublished and available only to the archivist, while to this day many of her published texts remain unread and unexamined to any degree by contemporary critics of modernism. Introducing readings of these "forgotten" texts has been one of my aims in this book, as well as suggesting new ways of reading more standard Steinian fare – *Melanctha*, or *The Autobiography of Alice B. Toklas* – in light of their presentation of the figure or notion of "genius." For example, while much has been made of Stein's literary "experimentalism" in the texts that postdate *Tender Buttons* (1914), there has been little sustained discussion of her early experiments in psychological science, conducted while she was a student at Radcliffe and published in two short articles from the late 1890s. Yet arguably, the entire trajectory of Stein's writing during the first decade of her literary career was animated by these early experiments in "bottom natures" and in the possibilities liberated through the doubling of the writing self. In Chapter 1, I read these experiments and the institutional context in which they were performed for their articulation of a complex and contradictory subject position that Stein would carry over into her presentation of the "genial" figure of Melanctha, the African-American protagonist of the middle story in *Three Lives* (composed 1905–6). Chapter 2 continues chronologically by examining the development of Stein's interest in her own "bottom nature" through *The Making of Americans* (composed 1903–11) and of her eventual recognition, around 1908, that she was a "genius." By situating Stein in relation to two crucial events that took place during the eight-year composition of *The Making of Americans* – her relationship with Matisse and Picasso, and her reading of Otto Weininger's 1903 *Sex and Character* – I suggest how this recognition was contingent upon a racialized and gendered calculus of her own authorial exceptionality. Yet Stein's "knowing that I was a genius" also coincides with her readiness to "begin to say something," and what she begins to say carries, paradoxically, a radically anti-authoritarian message.

The first two chapters comprise Part I of this book, "Coming to Terms." Combining close textual analysis with historical contextualization, Part I examines the genealogy that enabled and delimited Stein's act of calling herself a genius. The chronological approach to Stein's work within this section is useful not in showing a progressive "development" but in emphasizing the contradictory affiliations that underwrite the making of Stein's authorial position and textual practice. Moreover, in the act of calling herself a "genius," Stein's relationship to an audience becomes of crucial importance. Part II, "Congenial Fictions" (Chapters 3–5), explores the relationship of Stein's texts from the 1910s, 1920s, and 1930s to three specific audiences: the individual reader, the American nation, and the "masses." While the existence of some form of audience for Stein's work was never really in question, the ways in which Stein mediated her relationship with various audiences through the notion of "genius" is of central interest in allowing us to apprehend the modernist problematics of defamiliarization, difficulty, and "highness."

The subjective dynamics of the reading process as anticipated by Stein's notion of "talking and listening" are first explored in Chapter 3. By making interpretive closure of her texts impossible, Stein enjoins the reader to reconsider the text as a site of generative meaning in which she or he plays a participatory role in the creative process, and can as such potentially share in the "being" of genius, at least as Stein understands this being. Through a series of close readings, this chapter explores the possibilities and limitations of the textual process of "talking and listening." The focus of Chapter 4 lies in the broader arena of national self-identification, and in Stein's late yearnings to plot her conception of "genius" as an "American thing." A lifelong expatriate, and an early critic of American conformity, Stein nevertheless grew to see herself as firmly "American" in character and literary practice, and imagined America to be the fertile ground from which a collective of "vitally singular" individuals could eventually spring. *Useful Knowledge* (1928), a series of writings on America from the 1920s, represents Stein's effort to rewrite the American national myth as an ideal relationship between the individual unit (whether word or human subject) and the collective "whole." *Useful Knowledge* is, indeed, a text that seems most urgently to attempt to substitute for the world, offering itself to the reader as a national "landscape" (Stein's term) in which any "one" is potentially a "vitally singular" one.

The articulation in *Useful Knowledge* of an enlightened American collectivity would continue to preoccupy Stein in the wake of the enormous success of *The Autobiography of Alice B. Toklas* (1933). This latter text, and its companion volume on the nature of "success" in America, *Everybody's Autobiography* (1937), are the subject of Chapter 5. Stein's claims to "being a genius" reach their apotheosis in this seemingly self-promotional, commercially oriented writing, yet the dialogic nature of "genius" is also written into the very structure of these so-called autobiographies. *Everybody's Autobiography* in particular appears to resolve the conflictual relationship between "the genius" and "the masses" by restaging the America of the 1930s as a space in which "everybody" has the potential to be a "successful one." As this narrative tells it, Stein's identity as a "genius" is not the exception but the norm in an America in which everybody seems to be "somebody." To be sure, Stein articulates this vision through blurring the difference between "genius" and "celebrity" in ways that are never entirely free from authorial anxiety; as she herself makes clear in the text, the manufacturing of "celebrityhood" by America's publicity machine is far removed from the idea of "genius" as unique and innate, as original and self-originating. In refusing fully to relinquish this latter idea, Stein's late writings on authority and audience point toward, but do not wholly embrace, a postmodern understanding of the subject as decentered and contingent, as the reiterative effect of institutional and discursive formations. In speaking the discourse of "genius" Stein is always in a sense spoken by its traditional historical and discursive exclusions, as by its cult of "personality." Yet her ability to frame her story as the story of "everybody" suggests once again that for Stein "being a genius" is also largely a relational experience, contingent upon others for its full articulation. It is within the tension between these shifting authorial positions that I locate my own story about Gertrude Stein.

Notes

1. In a postmodern era that heralds the death of the subject, the notion of "genius" has remained largely resistant to an anti-essentialist critique, and in fact continues within both academic and larger cultural discourses to be the sign of a preternatural gift, a gift which springs from internal capacities, not from social and historical contingencies. See the introductory comments to the proceedings of a recent academic conference entitled "Genius: The History of an Idea": "[N]o amount of analysis has yet been able to explain the capacities of those rare and gifted individuals who can produce creative work of lasting quality and value ... For in each age and in each art, genius is that which defies analysis" (Murray, "Introduction," in *Genius: The History of an Idea*, 1). For a response to this collection as being "stuck in a kind of time-warp," and for a stimulating feminist critique of the notion of "genius," see Battersby, *Gender and Genius*, 16–17.
2. Hegel, *Aesthetics*, 283.
3. Nitzsche, *The Genius Figure in Antiquity and the Middle Ages*, 7.
4. Hegel, *Lectures on the Philosophy of World History*, 76.
5. Schlegel, "From *Ideas*," in Simpson, *Origins*, 197; Schlegel, *Philosophische Vorlesungen*, 105.
6. Schlegel, "From *Ideas*," in Simpson, *Origins*, 197.
7. Schopenhauer, *Works*, 116.
8. Schlegel, "From *Letter about the Novel*," in Simpson, *Origins*, 205.
9. Kant, "On Genius," 224; 235.
10. Novalis, "Fragment," *Pollen and Fragments*, 131.
11. See Nahm, *The Artist as Creator*, chs 4–6.
12. Lavater quoted in Kohlschmidt and Mohr, *Reallexikon der deutschen Literaturgeschichte*, 278.
13. "The world must become romanticized. So one finds the original sense renewed" (*Pollen and Fragments*, 56).
14. Contemporary histories of the idea of "genius" credit Francis Galton's 1869 *Hereditary Genius* with changing the terms of the discussion in his focus upon the hereditary and environmental factors distinguishing geniuses from non-geniuses. His connection of "genius" and mental disease would be echoed in Cesare Lombroso's extremely influential *The Man of Genius* (1891). In the same year Lombroso's text appeared,

J. F. Nisbet was arguing for the "degenerate" physiology of the genius in his aptly titled volume *The Insanity of Genius; and the General Inequality of Human Faculty Physiologically Considered*. Ernst Kretschmer, in *The Psychology of Men of Genius*, continues the inquiry into the twentieth century, as do the influential Stanford University/ Binet studies of the 1920s on gifted children, which examine race, heredity, sex, and health in determining intelligence and capacity for "genius" (Terman, *Genetic Studies of Genius*). The most recent and notorious instance of this effort to distinguish the "genius" as a discrete type with identifiable physical and psychological characteristics is Herrnstein and Murray's *The Bell Curve: Intelligence and Class Structure in American Life*.

15. Huyssen, *After the Great Divide*, vii.
16. Pound quoted in Carey, *The Intellectuals and the Masses*, 72.
17. Woolf, "Middlebrow." For the importance of this essay, see Radway, *A Feeling for Books*, 219.
18. Woolf's remarks appear in "The War from the Street," (*TLS*, 9 January 1919); review of D. Bridgman Metchim's *Our Own History of the War: From a South London View* (1918). Woolf takes issue with Metchim's aspirations to describe the Great War from the perspective of an ordinary citizen; it is within this context that her apprehensive reference to "that anonymous monster the Man in the Street" appears. In comparison, Woolf aligns herself implicitly in this review with another citizenry, a "we" that is presumably more individualized and attentive to the subtleties of everyday experience in wartime than Metchim's protagonist. Sixteen years later, Woolf would use a similar metaphor in describing Hitler and the Germans: "And the passive heavy slaves behind him, and he a great mould coming down on the brown jelly" (quoted in Lee, *Virginia Woolf*, 678).
19. Nietzsche quoted in Carey, *The Intellectuals and the Masses*, 74. For Nietzsche's influence on modernist writers, see Schwartz, *The Matrix of Modernism*, esp. 101–2.
20. Carey, *The Intellectuals and the Masses*, 74.
21. Currie, *Genius*, 12. For Currie, "[m]odernism differs from romanticism, according to my definition, not so much in its basic categories as in the *pessimism* with which it understands these categories" (12).
22. Loy, "Apology of Genius," 77.
23. Greenberg, "Avant-Garde and Kitsch," 8. Schwartz discusses the social meaning of Pound and Eliot's "formalism" in *The Matrix of Modernism*, 102–13.
24. Ortega y Gasset, *The Dehumanization of Art*; Eliot, "Tradition and the Individual Talent," *The Sacred Wood*, 48.
25. Ibid., 49.
26. Booth, *Greatness Engendered*, 4. Booth's brilliant analysis of Woolf and Eliot is useful in a larger sense for its articulation of the "challenges to the woman who wishes to become a 'great writer' in a male-dominated literary tradition" (4).
27. "[W]hen the outside is entirely outside that is is not at all inside then it is not at all inside and so it is not existing" (Narr, 39).

28. Bob Perelman, in the only extended study to date of Stein's claims to genius, develops this idea even further: while "Genius was Stein's trademark . . . enabling her to stand out and so survive," it was also the mark of her distance from the social, since "the knowledge a genius possesses cannot be translated outside the precincts of genius." See "Seeing What Gertrude Stein Means," in *The Trouble with Genius*, 129–69; also my Ch. 3, 79–84.
29. Stein, *NB* 14–7. All numbered references to Stein's notebooks in this book accord with the system devised by Leon Katz, who transcribed them and established their chronology. I have retained Stein's original spelling and punctuation in my citations.
30. The term is Rosalind E. Krauss's, from *The Originality of the Avant-Garde*, 181.
31. Adorno, *Aesthetic Theory*, 39.
32. Huyssen, *After the Great Divide*, ix. In his appendix to *Multiple Authorship and the Myth of Solitary Genius* (203–13), Jack Stillinger offers a list of writers from Homer to Ann Beattie whose collaborative efforts contest "the romantic myth of the author as solitary genius" (203).
33. DeKoven, "Introduction" to Gertrude Stein entry, in Scott, *The Gender of Modernism*, 484.
34. Chessman, *The Public Is Invited to Dance*, 3.
35. Stimpson, "Gertrude Stein and the Lesbian Lie," 163.
36. Benstock, *Women of the Left Bank*, 159–60; Chessman, *The Public Is Invited to Dance*, 1; 3.
37. Chessman, *The Public Is Invited to Dance*, 221 note 7.
38. Butler, *Bodies that Matter*, 122; 225.
39. Ibid., 242; 228.
40. Butler employs Louis Althusser's notion of interpellation as an ideological "naming" or "hailing" which "recruits" individuals to take up subject positions within a socially regulated domain. For Althusser's own discussion of interpellation see *Lenin and Philosophy*, 170–7.
41. Steiner, *Exact Resemblance*, 204.

Part I

Coming to Terms

1 In Search of a Subject: Knowledge and Excess in Stein's Early Texts

By this I mean by this I mean, am I in it.
(P&P, 38)

When Gertrude Stein moved permanently to Paris in 1903, at the age of twenty-nine, she was already deeply concerned with problems of subjectivity and knowledge. Are movement, speech, writing, and ideas only the fragmentary external expressions of some underlying, embodied character – what Stein would call "bottom nature"? If so, how is it possible to know this nature? During the last years of the previous century, as an undergraduate at Radcliffe, Stein had conducted psychological experiments on what she called the "human tendency to automatic action." Hoping to determine the degree to which "normal" subjects exhibited this action, Stein tested both herself and other subjects on their proclivity to perform movements "automatically" while their attention was focused elsewhere. In the process, she concluded that an essential nature lies within the subject and emerges through the rhythm of the subject's automatic or habitual actions; and further, that the determination of this nature on the part of the psychological scientist could lead to a larger differentiation of subjects into distinct "types." The observation, compilation, and organization of these varying human types into a synthetic framework would come to occupy Stein's attention for more than a decade, accompanying her intellectual move from psychological science into literary experimentalism. With her eventual effort in *The Making of Americans* to produce a history "of everyone who was and is and will be living," Stein appeared steady in her belief that mapping an exhaustive human typology lay within the realm of textual possibility.

Even while engaged in this early typological enterprise, however, Stein was making a startling discovery that seemed to undermine the epistemological premises of her investigation. While the project of grouping people into "types" rested for Stein upon the assumption that subjectivity could be reduced to a coherent and unified "bottom nature" emerging through automatic, repetitive, or habitual actions over time, the essentialism of this view was problematized when Stein began testing her own proclivity to automatism. In the process, she discovered that she was able to "watch [her] automatic movements without interfering with their complete non-voluntariness" – that she could, in short, perform "automatically" and at the same time remain conscious of this process. This recognition in turn forced her to acknowledge that there exists within the field of automatic motion a certain form of consciousness irreducible to automatism: what she would refer to as "consciousness without memory," since it describes a state of conscious awareness that is immediate and cannot be extended from one moment to the next. Crucially, "consciousness without memory" is unrelated to conscious intention or will, or to self-consciousness, both of which mask automatic or habitual behaviour and provide what Stein calls the "feeling of a personality." Rather, "consciousness without memory" lies outside the persona, as an "extra personal" residuum that emerges through the process of automatic motion. Yet the discovery of this consciousness produced by but in excess of human automatism in turn problematizes the very theory of "bottom natures," since it is precisely the idea of the coherence of the automatic or habitual "bottom" that subtends this theory. One cannot have a "bottom nature" and at the same time have a consciousness in excess of this nature.

Paradoxically, then, what Stein discovers through her study of "bottom natures" is that the subject – and herself *as* subject – is profoundly and irreducibly split. That this discovery would cast into doubt both her position as empirical scientist and her pursuit of a comprehensive typology of human character was not an insignificant problem for the young Stein. Both essentialist and radically anti-identitarian, both inscribed in the discursive tradition of Western scientific epistemology with its attendant subject/object dichotomy and attentive to the limits of such a tradition, Stein's intellectual affiliations and trajectories at the turn of the century register contradictory desires and anxieties. These tensions would circulate within the remarkably heterogeneous texts of her first decade of writing, and across the boundaries of both "science" and "literature." And they would culminate in the formal narrative anxieties and problems of character type in Stein's first major modernist literary work, *Melanctha*.

Fig. 1.1 *Stein as a student in the 1890s, with skull and microscope*

I

Drawn to the psychological laboratory of William James while an undergraduate at Radcliffe from 1893 to 1897, Stein for several years devoted herself to "the master," whom she considered "a man among men; a scientist of force and originality embodying all that is strongest and worthiest in the scientific spirit."[1] If Stein felt alienated by the gendered implications of her words or by James's own references to "the rugged and manly school of science" she did not let it interfere with her ambitions.[2] By all accounts, Stein was a model student (Fig. 1.1), earning the praise of both James and his colleague Hugo Münsterberg, and encouraged to take part in research experiments with an older graduate student named Leon Solomons. Stein produced two articles while working within the Harvard Psychological Laboratory, both of which appeared in the reputable journal

Psychological Review: "Normal Motor Automatism" (1896), coauthored with Solomons, and "Cultivated Motor Automatism; A Study of Character in Its Relation to Attention" (1898). In the co-authored publication, Stein and Solomons write about their effort to blur the distinction between "normality" and "abnormality" by proving that the "normal" subject shows tendencies toward automatic behavior similar to that of the "abnormal" (that is, hysteric) subject. In searching for a "normal" control group through which to measure this hypothesis, the scientists somewhat surprisingly choose themselves, since "[w]e may both as far as we know stand as representatives of the perfectly normal – or perfectly ordinary – being, so far as hysteria is concerned" (NMA, 10). Seemingly untroubled by the questionable objectivity of this assertion, the two researchers proceed to explain their attempts to study automatic movement in one another through a series of experiments in distraction. In one, the subject (either Solomons or Stein) moves a pencil across a piece of paper while the observer reads him or her a story; in another, the subject reads aloud to himself or herself while at the same time listening to another text being read aloud by the observer. Once sufficiently distracted, the subject under observation begins to perform "automatically" and is studied in terms of his specific motor reflexes, his involuntary "writing" or "reading," even his ability to keep his attention off the experiment. In the end, the scientists conclude that the "normal" subject (Stein or Solomons) exhibits "definite motor reactions unaccompanied by consciousness" in proportion equal to the "abnormal" hysteric. While the hysteric's famous "anaesthesia" in relation to his or her involuntary movements represents a failure consciously and willfully to attend to the sensations produced through these movements ("Hysteria . . . is a disease of the attention"), the normal subject as well exhibits a "tendency to movement without conscious motor impulse" (NMA, 10). "Automatism" is, in fact, the "normal" condition of both the normal and the abnormal subject.

Stein and Solomons refer to automatism as "a general background of sound, not belonging to anything in particular," as a kind of bodily habitus or neutral screen of "normal" life against which cognition, imagination, desire, drive, and intention all stand out in relief. A background, moreover, that yields no meaning, for "automatism," as Stein and Solomons repeatedly assert, is something that resists direct apprehension or knowledge, something that lies outside of any signifying system and can be approached only tangentially, through distraction – something like the motorized rumble of daily life. This is what Stein would later refer to as the "bottom nature" of the human subject: the habitual, repetitive, automatic daily actions that collectively point to an essential individual way of being, or "type." In "Normal Motor Automatism," the point is simply to prove that "automatism" is a constitutive element of "normality," and that there is little difference, accordingly, between "normality" and "abnormality" (that is, hysteria).[3] But in the midst of the experiment, a formative difference *does* emerge between the normal person and the hysteric, a difference of "attention" that resides in the former, enabling her or him to perform automatically while, at the same time, being conscious of this process. "Nothing is more difficult than to allow a movement of which we are conscious to go on of itself," the article states, "But as we shall see later it is a habit that can be overcome, and a trained subject can watch his automatic movements without interfering with their complete non-voluntariness" (NMA, 12). "The hysterique," on the other hand, "is *unable* to *attend* to the sensation, attention to which bothered us. It is his anaesthesias which make automatism possible. What in his case is done for him by his disease we had to do by acquiring a control over our attention" (NMA, 18). Hence the "trained" normal individuals in contrast to the hysteric can both be conscious of their automatic movements and at the same time will themselves not to interfere with them. "Training" thus involves the sharpening of one's concentration in order to perform dual and seemingly contradictory functions, achieving what might be termed an *attentive inattentiveness*. In this, "consciousness . . . plays a purely cognitive part" – not controlling but passive and "watchful," for the moment that consciousness "take[s] charge of" something, automatism disappears. Hence, for Stein and Solomons, "Our problem was to get sufficient control of the attention to effect [a] removal of attention" (NMA, 25).

In the "successful" experiments, they note, "[o]ne watched his arm with an idle curiosity, wondering whether or no . . . [a] word would be written" (NMA, 22). Friedrich Kittler, in *Discourse Networks*, has given a suggestive rendering of this scene: "Gertrude Stein watches her hands like separate machines with a modicum of curiosity rather than commanding them to write particular signs."[4] The automatic, machine-like hands of the writer are here coupled with a mildly curious but finally rather indifferent "watchfulness." Stein and Solomons offer the following description of this process:

> This, in fact, was the general condition of things through the greater part of the experiments, after training was well under way. The same sentence might be dictated to the subject over and over

> again, and at the end of the series he would not know what it was. Yet not a single instance of what we have called unconsciousness occurred during the interval. Of course, this is not conclusive, for obviously there is memory of some kind even in this case, though not a memory of what was written. But the important point is that real unconsciousness appeared, not as a last stage of this, but as an altogether different phenomenon coming quite suddenly, and under different conditions. The consciousness without memory seems to *approach as its limit*, simply a condition in which the subject has not the faintest inkling of what he has written, but feels quite sure that he has been writing. (NMA, 17)

"Consciousness without memory" describes a state neither unconscious nor amnesiac but divorced from the "inhibitive or controlling" functions of consciousness, as well as from a sense of temporal continuity that provides what Stein and Solomons, at the end of their article, call "the feeling of a personality." It is a form of consciousness achieved through distraction, in which "the subject has not the faintest inkling of what he has written, but feels quite sure that he has been writing." A consciousness, in short, that accompanies automatic or normal functioning while not arresting or controlling it.

What marks the difference between the hysteric patient and the "normal" Stein and Solomons, finally, is precisely this capacity for dual functioning: to perform "automatically" while at the same time retaining a form of inattentive attentiveness. This duality is of course already inscribed in the authorial positions of the two researchers, who in taking themselves as the objects of their own experiments occupy the two positions of object and agent of the scientific gaze. Yet the split or doubled nature of Stein and Solomons' authorial positions was a fact that eluded, among others, the psychologist B. F. Skinner, who in 1934 famously accused Stein of having spent a lifetime writing "automatically and unconsciously" in the vein of the early Harvard experiments. Coming across the out-of-print "Normal Motor Automatism" in a journal, Skinner claimed to have discovered the "secret" to Stein's later aesthetic – that "the two products have a common origin," or rather, that the literary œuvre was simply a lifelong exercise in "automatic writing." This, for Skinner, explained why Stein's most modernist texts were not only "unintelligible" but "capricious" and "cold."[5] In response to Skinner's assault, Stein would write to her friend Lindley Hubbell, "No it is not so automatic as he thinks . . . If there is anything secret it is the other way . . . I think I achieve by xtra consciousness, excess."[6]

Curiously, here, Stein does not refute Skinner – my writing is "not so automatic as he thinks," she suggests, leaving open the possibility that her writing *is* automatic, to a degree. But she does suggest that Skinner fails to grasp the point of Stein and Solomons' "training" in distraction. It is not the automatism achieved in the experiment which is the ultimate "secret" of Stein's aesthetic, but what goes "the other way": the "xtra" consciousness or "excess" that cannot be reduced to automatism yet remains inextricable from it. To elicit this form of consciousness, one must be simultaneously engaged in the performance of automatism and outside of it, both proprietorial of the self and outside the circuits of automaticity and habit. "Experience is remoulding us every minute," William James has written; this is the process of self-making and unmaking to which the "consciousness without memory" bears witness.

II

It is James, again, who would first plot this dynamic in terms of "genius." In his chapter on perception in *The Principles of Psychology* (1890) – a text which would have been required reading in Stein's undergraduate psychology classes – James sets up a central opposition between "conservative" and "progressive" perception, between "the tendency to keep unchanged, and the tendency to renovate, [the mind's] ideas."[7] On the one hand, he argues, "[m]ost of us grow more and more enslaved to the stock conceptions with which we have once become familiar, and less and less capable of assimilating impressions in any but the old ways."[8] The "old ways" within which knowledge becomes codified are synonymous for James with the notion of "habit" – the "automatic" actions performed in the service of efficiency and expediency, the learned behavior, *idées reçues*, or clichés which enable the world to go about its business. Habit greases the wheel of everyday life, producing efficiency and minimizing disruption: since "habit diminishes the conscious attention with which our acts are performed," it is society's "most precious conservative agent."[9] At the same time, however, habit is what "fixes" our minds into "stock conceptions." Knowledge, once attained, becomes rigid doctrine; creativity and the desire to learn fall by the wayside. This tendency even invades the epistemological domain of science, since "[t]he aim of 'Science' is to attain conceptions so adequate and exact that we shall never need to change them."[10] The result of this perceptual sclerosis is what James quaintly calls "old-fogyism": "the inevitable terminus to which life sweeps us on."[11]

In dynamic tension with old-fogyism, James writes, there is "genius." "Genius, in truth, means little more than the faculty of perceiving in an unhabitual way."[12] "Genius" is a mode of perception, an ability to break away from "stock conceptions" and see the world freshly; it is the antithesis of automatism. James here is reiterating a Romantic and Enlightenment tradition in which "genius," as Kant writes, "is the exemplary originality of the natural endowments of an individual in the *free* employment of his cognitive faculties."[13] James's near-contemporary Schopenhauer extends this definition to underscore the connection between genius and the specific faculty of perception:

> [T]he essence of genius must lie in the perfection and energy of the knowledge of *perception*. Corresponding to this, the works which we hear most decidedly designated works of genius are those which start immediately from perception and devote themselves to perception.[14]

More or less at the same time that Schopenhauer and James were formulating their statements about "genius," other modernists were using similar terms to announce what they took to be the primary role of the avant-garde artist, "to create the vision which results from that deautomatized perception."[15] As the Russian Formalist critic Victor Shklovsky writes in 1917, "Habitualization devours works, clothes, furniture, one's wife, and the fear of war... And art exists that one may recover the sensation of life; it exists to make one feel things, to make the stone *stony*."[16] Interestingly, his words almost precisely mimic Stein's own gloss on her most famous phrase, "a rose is a rose is a rose" – "I think that in that line the rose is red for the first time in English poetry for a hundred years."[17] While contemporaries from Williams to Fitzgerald saw the rose as a symbol of sentimental decay, a "grotesque" and "obsolete" figure incompatible with the austere ethos of modernism, Stein's willingness figuratively to redden the rose can be seen as part of a larger strategy of revitalizing worn or habitual modes of perception.[18] This was also the project of artists on the more radical fringe of high modernism – from the Dadaists to the Surrealists – who felt their primary challenge to be one of perceiving "the marvelous in the everyday."[19]

In James's *Psychology*, references to "genius" appear only in two places: in the above discussion of "unhabitual" perception, and in comments upon "genius and attention." The former is clearly the dominant characteristic of "genius," but the latter is also a commonplace ("Geniuses are commonly believed to excel other men in their power of sustained attention"[20]). For James, then, "genius" is synonymous with unhabitual perception combined with extraordinary powers of attention. And this is precisely the combination that Solomons and Stein privilege in their discussion of normal automatism and its attendant "consciousness without memory." The capacities which they "trained" themselves to develop throughout the course of the experiment are those in which attention is brought to bear upon something that resists attention, one's automatic movements. In the process, "habits" are not simply performed, but perceived anew, *defamiliarized*. That this is a process is crucial, for the point is not to arrest automatic movement, but to allow it to continue while observing it – a process of "sustained attention" which most normal individuals find extremely "difficult" to achieve. In a similar way, Stein's famous "rose" phrase achieves a "defamiliarization" of the clichéd object by placing it within a seemingly endlessly reiterative chain, by in a sense making her noun "automatic." Yet in the course of this process, Stein insists, she is stripping the rose from all of its familiar or habitual associations which have prevented its perceptual apprehension. The reiterations of the grammatical subset "a rose is" both set up *and* destabilize the basic equation of identity. As Judith Butler notes, "reiterations are never simply replicas of the same"; within the performance of reiteration lies the possibility of exposing the "constitutive conventions" of identity.[21] Exposing the performance of reiteration or automatism – exposing automatism *as* performance – is thus the "extraordinary" capacity which the "normal" Solomons and Stein found themselves to have.

Many years later, in a 1935 retrospective analysis of *The Making of Americans*, Stein would relocate this dynamic within the sphere of knowledge and memory:

> [K]nowledge is acquired, so to speak, by memory; but . . . when you know anything, memory doesn't come in. At any moment that you are conscious of knowing anything, memory plays no part. (HWIW, 155)

A "consciousness without memory," then, describes a state of immediate, present-tense distraction where one is "watching what one produces only as it is produced."[22] This is radically opposed to what Stein would refer to as a "nineteenth-century" tradition of epistemological inquiry, where the achievement of "knowledge" is predicated upon a temporally progressive process of experience with and appropriation of the "known" on the part of an objective "knower." In Stein's reformulation of this relationship in the 1930s, "knowledge" based on memory and a domination of knower by known has been replaced by a continuously present process that keeps in play at once two very different activities: production ("motor automatism") and watchful "knowing" or attentive inattentiveness in which "memory plays no part." Stein would ultimately reformulate this process in terms of "genius":

> One may really indeed say that that is the essence of genius, of being most intensely alive, that is being one who is at the same time talking and listening. It is really that that makes one a genius. And it is necessary if you are to be really and truly alive it is necessary to be at once talking and listening, doing both things, not as if there were one thing, not as if they were two things, but doing them, well if you like, like the motor going inside and the car moving, they are part of the same thing. (LIA, 170)

Stein's use of a mechanical metaphor here is highly suggestive. In "Normal Motor Automatism," subjectivity involved a dynamic of "normal" automatism combined with passive, extra-personal watchfulness; in the above passage, this dynamic is reformulated as "genius" or "talking and listening at the same time." The "motor going inside" is similar to the automatic movements of Solomons and Stein in a state of distraction; the "car moving" is the passive, watchful, "consciousness without memory" carried along by its internal "motor." Stein's description of this process as "the essence of genius" diverges strongly from a Romantic and Enlightenment tradition in which "genius" describes a "spiritual power" above and beyond the mechanical or the mechanistic;[23] in Stein's late reformulation, "genius" *arises out of* the mechanical, the automatic, the habitual. As Stein's "rose" phrase again suggests, the "unhabitualizing" faculty of genius cannot function in isolation, separated ontologically from the "habitual" world of the everyday, the ordinary, the generic. Rather, "genius" is for Stein essentially implicated in the habitual, the repetitive, the everyday. Furthermore, Stein's vision of "genius" here is remarkably inclusive: "genius" is a facultative process that anyone can achieve, since it describes the state of "being most intensely alive." Finally, this notion of "genius" is rooted in an immediate, present-tense relationality. As she would later write in *Everybody's Autobiography*, "a genius is some one who does not have to remember the two hundred years that everybody else has to remember"

(EA, 121). Located in a full but never static present, emerging as much from automatic writing as from automobiles, "genius" describes for Stein a universal process of defamiliarizing intimately bound to the familiar, including the most familiar aspects of one's self.

III

It is for this reason that the second of Stein's articles from the 1890s, published in *Psychological Review* under the title "Cultivated Motor Automatism," seems such a departure from the radical developments of the earlier experiment. While Stein claims that this article, written by herself alone, represents a "continuation" of the premises of the earlier article, it in fact registers an important change both in her authorial and scientific position and in her object of study. In 1935, Stein remembers this development of her scientific focus in the following way:

> While I was at college and doing philosophy and psychology I became more and more interested in my own mental and physical processes and less in that of others . . . Then as I say I became more interested in psychology, and one of the things I did was testing reactions of the average college student in a state of normal activity and in the state of fatigue induced by their examinations. I was supposed to be interested in their reactions but soon I found that I was not but instead that I was enormously interested in the types of their characters that is what I even then thought of as the bottom nature of them . . . (LIA, 137)

This remarkable self-history presents the shifting, restless, unstable process of a mind seduced equally by itself and by "the life inside of others," a process that, as we shall see in Chapter 2, underwrites both the conditions of possibility and the potential illimitability of Stein's massive first novel, *The Making of Americans*. What I would like to focus on here, for the moment, is the way this movement animates and also exhausts each step in the process it describes, such that what matters for the experiment of "Normal Motor Automatism" – "my own mental and physical processes" – ceases to be significant in the second experiment, which focuses now upon the automatic responses of an "average" group of Harvard and Radcliffe students "in a state of normal activity." As this passage implies, what differentiates "Cultivated Motor Automatism" from its predecessor is that now a clear divide exists between object of analysis and the scientific "knower" firmly located outside the experimental scene, whose epistemological goal remains the determination of categories of being or "types" of "complete character." In pursuit of this end, Stein offers the following hypothesis: that all subjects can be divided into one of two "types," and that typing can be determined through the tendency of a subject to "cultivate" automatic motion. Simply put, the greater or lesser ease with which a subject reveals a tendency to automatism gives indication of his or her "type." Unlike "Normal Motor Automatism," "Cultivated Motor Automatism" offers no sustained analysis of a subject who seems to combine characteristics from each type; nor is there any interest in developing further the fascinating analysis of "consciousness without memory." Rather, the second experiment seems concerned with constructing a totalizing correlation between automatism and "character": the one leads directly to the other, and it is up to the neutral scientific observer to calculate and organize as many variations on the two types of "complete character" as possible.

That the search for scientific "knowledge" is here coextensive with the determination and organization of types deserves more than passing mention, since it is upon the construction of a "typology" that Stein would stake not only her scientific authority but also the authority of her future literary *magnum opus*, *The Making of Americans*. From Darwin to Lombroso, from Galton to Weininger, major late nineteenth-century inquiries into the science of man, art, religion, criminality, and sexuality were conducted and concluded as typologies. As Foucault has argued, these taxonomies of human kind allowed the scientist the power "of organizing the multiple, of providing oneself with an instrument to cover it and to master it . . . of imposing on it an 'order.'"[24] This order was reflected in the very idea of the "type" as a composite made up of an average of habits, behaviors, or traits abstracted from living representatives. Criminals, women, non-Western peoples, geniuses, and the insane were all defined through "typologies" – calculuses of human variety centering upon an abstract account of typical traits and a list of telling historical "examples." William James, for example – whose philosophy of pragmatism would seem at odds with typological abstraction – would attempt to reconcile his own conflictual epistemologies by creating a typology of religions that would extend to the level of the individual himself. In *The Varieties of Religious Experience* (1902), he proposes "to ignore the institutional branch entirely, to say nothing of the ecclesiastical organization, to consider as little as possible the systematic theology and the ideas about the gods themselves, and to confine myself as far as I can to personal religion pure and simple."[25] For James, "types" of religion are as particular as individual believers, a proposition that would seem to work against the structure of a typology, which could be said to exist only to the extent that it could contain its variable elements within a synthetic "whole." Ignoring these problems of method (although admitting at the end of his weighty volume that he had failed to be comprehensive), James would feel little compunction about identifying such disparate phenomena as hysterical automatism and Christian prophecy as examples of the prototype "religious experience." In the end, what mattered was synthesis rather than difference, "order" rather than miscellanea; as Foucault suggests, the typological imperative inscribes not only a "procedure of knowledge" but also a "technique of power."[26]

Stein's aim in "Cultivated Motor Automatism" is more reductive than that of James, but it foreshadows the enormous ambitions of *The Making of Americans*: to produce a typology of "every one who was and is and will be living." In both texts, Stein's effort is clearly directed toward conforming all possible variations of character into a binary typological framework that will then prove adequate in being applied to everybody. This, despite her recognition in "Normal Motor Automatism" that the subject is by definition fractured, multiply inscribed within contradictory actions of mind and reactions of body, and that frameworks of knowledge and authority are themselves always implicated in the investigations with which they are engaged. As if in reaction to this radical awareness, "Cultivated Motor Automatism" works to underscore authorial "objectivity" and epistemological certainty above all else; an effort that in turn enables Stein to resolve the potential illimitability of the experiment. In a critical culminating gesture, the scientist of "Cultivated Motor Automatism" grounds her classificatory system on the terrain of physiology, as there appears to be "a distinct relation between these two types and the physical condition and blood supply" (CMA, 37). Type I appears to have a "stimulated" constitution; Type II a "sluggish" one.[27] By reading "character" through the body, Stein sets up the latter as a stable and unchanging base or bottom from which "habits of attention" and automatism emanate; it is a base which Stein will again refer to in terms of "bottom nature" during the composition of *The Making of Americans*. As she writes in her retrospective account, this discovery that all human beings could be reduced to an essential "bottom nature" was the real achievement of "Cultivated Motor Automatism."

As contemporary feminist theorists have argued, however, the body is far from a neutral base or ground, a passive or unchanging foundation, but a site of contestation and struggle, of discursive and material inscription.[28] The body may be the "bottom nature" which enables Stein to organize particular characters into two universal categories, and thus to complete her typology; but no body can be typed without also being stereotyped, and without thereby being "stabilized" as a sign which is always exceeded or undermined by what it excludes or represses. And as much as Stein the empirical scientist desired to pin down "complete character," as much as she desired the certainty of complete knowledge, she was above all sensitive to the potential of inscription to undo itself.

IV

Why, given Stein's interest in exploring the self-reflexive, split textual subject of "Normal Motor Automatism," would she take up in turn a radically different epistemological and indeed ontological project in "Cultivated Motor Automatism"? Why would her intellectual interest shift resolutely from an analysis of the "excess" that lies outside the automatic self toward the determination of "bottom nature" or "type," toward the positing of an essential and essentially embodied subject? What might these contradictory projects of the early Stein have to do with an ambivalence over her own authorial position? In the rest of this chapter, I too would like to shift interpretive registers in an attempt to locate these contradictions within a larger cultural habitus that might be seen as both enabling and delimiting Stein's intellectual affiliations and epistemological objectives. Specifically, I am interested in the role that the category of "race" might be said to play in the ambiguities of Stein's intellectual trajectory at this time: in her attention to the self-doubling of "Normal Motor Automatism," and in her investment in typological essentialism in "Cultivated Motor Automatism." As a Jewish woman working in a predominantly Protestant male environment – first Harvard, and then Johns Hopkins University, where she was a medical student from 1897 to 1901 – Stein would perforce find herself located in the interstices between discourses and institutions, a tenuous positioning that would in turn affect the kinds of positionings presented in her two scientific articles. But I am also interested in how the traces of these positionings are inscribed in the problematics of race in Stein's remarkable novella *Melanctha* – the middle story of her collection entitled *Three Lives*, composed 1905–6 – written several years after she had left medical school and America to take up life as a writer and art collector in Paris. To what extent is Stein's portrayal of African-Americans in that work an effect of her early anxieties over the relationship between knowledge, authority, and a racialized "bottom nature"? To what extent is *Melanctha* an effort "to study (the otherness of) oneself by attending to the otherness of an/other Other"?[29]

"Race" is clearly an issue in *Melanctha*, but that this issue might emerge from Stein's fraught relationship to her own racial identity is a potentially contentious point. One could argue that Stein's relationship to her Jewishness is, if anything, notable by its absence.[30] Despite her embeddedness in a close-knit Jewish family at Harvard, in Baltimore, and in the early Paris years, Stein was throughout her life a secular Jew: she was not religiously observant, did not observe dietary laws, and was not interested in Zionism.[31] After her move to Paris and with the start of her literary career, Stein made few explicit references to Jews or Judaism, even in her private notebooks; her occasional nickname for Alice Toklas, "my little Hebrew," suggests that it was Toklas who for Stein carried the "Jewish" traits. Recent revelations about Stein's endorsement of the Vichy regime during World War II further support the contention by many critics that Stein had little interest in Jewish solidarity.[32] This rejection of religion and distancing from community in turn problematizes the extent to which Stein could be said to consider herself Jewish, or to feel herself part of a "racialized" identity. Does race matter for Stein?

In charting Stein's early development as a scientist, an intellectual, and a writer, it is possible to locate the attenuation of her tie to Judaism in the period during the composition of *The Making of Americans* (1902–11) – a text initially concerned with Jewish immigrants, who in successive revisions become "Germans" and then "middle-class."[33] But as a student at Radcliffe and in the Harvard Psychological Laboratory in the 1890s, being seen as part of the "Jewish race" was clearly for Stein both a constraining social reality and a point of pride. As Brenda Wineapple has recently argued about Harvard and Radcliffe during this period, "Jewish students . . . knew they were a group apart."[34] "Allosemitism" – the practice "of setting the Jews apart as people radically different from all the others, needing separate concepts to describe and comprehend them and special treatment in all or most social intercourse"[35] – was widespread within elite American institutions like Harvard. Charles William Eliot, Harvard's president from 1869 to 1909, set the tone by speaking of his desire to greet "all the new races and to do its best for them," Jews included.[36] Although Eliot felt Jews to be "the most resistant and prepotent race in the world," he encouraged "racial" separatism and discouraged intermarriage on the grounds that Jews might well come to "dominate."[37] Many distinguished professors on Eliot's Harvard faculty – including the typologists to whom Stein was so attracted as a young intellectual – also viewed the whole of Jewry as belonging to a discrete and decidedly foreign "race."[38] Their racialist "research" into the nature of "the Jew" was often, although not always, discriminatory. Those who were aligned with anti-immigrant groups used their typological claims to denounce blacks and Jews especially "in an attempt to defend what they considered truly 'American.'"[39] Henry Adams, in *The Education* (recently voted the best English-language book of nonfiction to appear in the twentieth century),[40] referred to the Jew as "reeking," "snarling," and "weird," with "a freer hand than he – American of Americans." His brother Brooks Adams wrote in *The Law of Civilization and Decay* that Jews, in modern economic times, were part of "a favoured aristocracy of the craftiest and subtlest types." Others like Nathaniel Shaler, dean of the Lawrence Scientific School at the turn of the century, used the example of the "typical Jew" to suggest the need for Americans (that is, non-Jews) to recognize qualities of superior intelligence even in an "alien race."[41] As Sander Gilman has recently written in *Smart Jews: The Construction of the Image of Jewish Superior Intelligence*: "the racialist notion of Jewish identity at the turn of the century" was inseparable from concerns over whether the presumed "superiority" of Jewish intelligence was in fact "degenerate": "[W]as their intelligence of the correct quality to enter into the gentility of the American educational system?"[42] Turn-of-the-century critics in Europe and America alike warned that "the greatest number of the decadents are Semites, at least according to their descent, and Jewry today finds itself at the stage of a physical and psychic decadence."[43] Being identified as Jewish, and especially being labeled a "smart Jew," thus carried with it the potential valence of "degeneracy."

Stein's authorial position as a young intellectual was marked by the institutions and discourses of which she was a part, and by their investment in making her visible as a "racialized" Jew. Strongly attracted herself to the typologizing impulse, Stein would largely affirm her own "bottom nature" in the terms provided by her peers and professors. In papers and letters from Radcliffe, Stein would claim that she was "a Jew first and an American only afterwards," insisting that the Jews are "a Chosen People chosen for high purposes," for "noble aims and great deeds." She would aver that Jews have "a covenant with God which has made them endure" and would note the specificity of their "ethical . . . and spiritual nature." And in a passionate essay written for a Harvard forensics course, Stein would champion "race feeling" and Jewish cultural separatism.[44] Yet the young Stein would also resist being interpellated as a "smart Jew." Wineapple recounts a telling anecdote concerning Stein and a non-Jewish Radcliffe student in which the latter claimed "I had never known a Jew; thought they were something different. I remember her [Stein] saying, 'I'm the top of the heap,' and I said, 'The top of your heap.' She was much offended."[45] Stein's taking "offense" is presumably linked in large part to the stigma attached to "Jewish" – that is, "degenerate" – intelligence. Throughout her life, Stein would claim that she was just like everybody, and at the same time "more" than everybody. One need only recall Stein's authorial claim, in "Normal Motor Automatism," to being both "perfectly normal" and capable of extraordinary acts of consciousness at one and the same time. Being "the top of the heap" was not the same as being the top of the *Jewish* heap; asserting Jewish racial difference – especially concerning intelligence – meant that Stein could not lay claim to either representative normality or universal genius.

After abandoning her psychological studies and moving to Paris, Stein would increasingly repudiate racial identification. In the notebooks to *The Making of Americans*, Stein would refer to Jews as having "good minds but not great minds" (NB, A-3). She would refute the presumed essentialism of Jewish character, arguing that non-Jews like Goethe and Frederick the Great could be Jewish "because they persistently and consciously educated themselves, consciously ran themselves by their minds" (NB, C-20). Most problematically, she would embrace as a fellow traveler the anti-Semitic philosopher Otto Weininger, who in his own massive typology argued that both "the Jew" and "the woman" were the negation of the ideal and universal type of "genius." In reading herself through Weininger, Stein imagined herself able to shed the ties of both race and gender and to assert the universality of her own type. Clearly, here, Stein could only be a genius – in the typological terms that made sense to her – by not identifying herself as Jewish. But it is worth considering whether this process of e-racing in order to re-type herself was not already being performed in the composition of a text that Stein wrote two years before she discovered Weininger in 1908 and came to the recognition that she was a genius: *Melanctha*. Written during a hiatus in the eight-year-long composition of *The Making of Americans*, *Melanctha* was a stylistic and thematic departure from the former, which was still at that point a fairly conventional novel of German-Jewish assimilation or American-making. Returning to an early unpublished *roman-à-clef* (*Q.E.D.* (composed 1903)), Stein decided to rewrite this story of a lesbian triangle as a narrative of the heterosexual relationship between two African-Americans. Out of this effort was born Stein's first identifiably "modernist" text, whose noted stylistic strangeness is embodied in the social and semantic "wandering" of its eponymous female protagonist. In the challenge she poses to habitual or automatic action and thought, Melanctha arguably represents the "genius" that Stein would soon lay claim to herself. In her *a*typicality, in her refusal to be "normal" or to act in "regular" or "habitual" ways, Melanctha represents a force of newness, disruption, and modernity. Yet Melanctha is also a racial "type" that would have been instantly recognizable to Stein's readers: the tragic mulatta, drawn by the one-drop rule into an essential (and fatal) association with bottom blackness. In her typicality *and* in her strangeness, Melanctha thus inscribes Stein's conflicted effort – evident in both the early psychological experiments and in her first literary experiments – to think about the human subject as both objectively "knowable" and always already in excess of epistemological and symbolic containments. Crucially, "race" becomes the carrier of these conflicts.

Many critics have focused on the way *Melanctha* treats sexuality and gender, rewriting the homosexual dynamic of *Q.E.D.* as a heterosexual plot yet encoding the otherness of queer desire within Melanctha's mysterious "wandering." Melanctha's refusal of normative femininity and her unconfined bisexuality are thus often read as projections of Stein's own "dissident sexuality."[45] Yet few critics have considered *Melanctha* as a rewriting of Jewish difference or "dissidence" as African-American otherness (it would take the Harlem Renaissance writer Claude McKay to point out that "Melanctha, the mulatress, might have been a Jewess"[47]). This, despite the fact that within *Three Lives* as a whole, *Melanctha* is sandwiched between two non-Jewish German-immigrant stories: *The Good Anna* and *The Gentle Lena*. As the in-between, the liminal, the middleman (a role often played by Jews), *Melanctha* is the story that could be said to supply the "racial" term missing from the German context. Furthermore, as with *Q.E.D.*, Stein makes it clear from the start of *Melanctha* that "race" is central to the character "types" with which both narratives are so centrally concerned. In its effort to render a mathematical proof based upon the relationship between various character types as a naturalist narrative, *Q.E.D.* clearly identifies

Adele – the figure for Stein in the text – as Jewish, and figures Mabel Neathe, Adele's lesbian antagonist, as "a kind of sexual mulatto."[48] Similarly, in the opening pages of *Melanctha* "race" and "type" are inextricable. Intelligence, curiosity, sensuality, and "sweetness" are linked to lighter skin tones, while "real black[ness]" is correlated with coarseness, virility, stupidity, laziness, and childishness. Where these traits are mixed, as in Rose, brought up by a white family, "character" still comes down to a fundamentally racialized "bottom nature": "Her white training had only made for habits, not for nature. Rose had the simple, promiscuous unmorality of the black people" (TL, 60). To be sure, the "excessive literalism"[49] of blackness within the typology of *Melanctha* is problematized by the presence of the mulatto characters, such as Melanctha herself, described as a "graceful, pale yellow, intelligent, attractive negress" (TL, 60). Here, the clarity of an embodied "bottom nature" is obscured precisely because the mulatta's body is seen to be at once white and an imitation of whiteness. Yet Melanctha too is initially presented in naturalistic terms, as living out the inevitably fatal consequences of her "type." While she has a share of "real white blood" that denotes her superiority to Rose, she still bears the mark of miscegenation and thus of degeneration, and despite her "intelligent, attractive" traits, she seems doomed to downward racial and class mobility. In this, she represents the typical tragic mulatta.[50]

Drawn from dominant turn-of-the-century assumptions about the deterministic meaning of blackness, such characterizations have led readers either to condemn Stein as a racist or to forgive her for unthinkingly reiterating "the clichés of her age."[51] Yet one could also argue that the racist clichés in *Melanctha* are the effect of a category crisis for Stein during these early years of authorial self-fashioning, and that what might be called her performance of "blackface" in this text is an attempt both to displace and to resolve this crisis. Stein's crisis about Jewishness, authority, and difference could be both clarified and mediated through projection onto African-Americans, whose racialization was more relentlessly constructed by turn-of-the-century cultural discourses than even that of Jews. As the Yiddish press of the day pointed out, "blacks were in America what Jews were in Europe – the most oppressed, the most despised, and the most victimized segment of the population."[52] "Scientific" racial typing "located signs of contamination on black and Jewish bodies" alike, but the former were seen as even more "alien" than the latter.[53] The Harvard intellectual Nathaniel Shaler, who had advocated Jewish assimilation, would draw the line with Negroes, pronouncing them "ineradicably alien."[54] The anthropologist Franz Boas noted that "The Negro of our times carries even more heavily the burden of his racial descent than did the Jew of an earlier period."[55] Jewish voices, too, contributed to this effort to differentiate their own relative "whiteness" from the resolute "blackness" of African-Americans. Stein's friend Israel Zangwill, Jewish playwright and author of the *echt*-assimilationist drama *The Melting Pot*, a play that emphasized the successful resolution of the Jewish-Gentile marriage plot, would in 1914 note the "justifiab[ility]" of avoiding "physical intermarriage with the negro."[56]

For the young Gertrude Stein desiring epistemological certainty, the African-American Other would have seemed a typologist's ideal subject – primitive, authentic, knowable, *readable*. Yet such problematically unproblematic racial "typing," especially in a writer so sensitive to the complexities of her own racial identification, suggests that Stein's African-American types are also projections and displacements, carriers of her contradictory desires for both identification with and distance from the category of race. In this, *Melanctha* can arguably be located within the long American tradition of blackface minstrelsy: the practice by non-black actors (and some blacks) of darkening their faces in order to perform, in exaggerated and often caricatural ways, "typical" African-American roles.[57] Significantly, Jewish-American entertainers were the main blackface performers at the turn of the century.[58] As Michael Rogin has recently argued in his study of blackface and Jewish-American actors, such performance worked for Jews in two ways: as "appropriative identification" (identifying with and ventriloquizing black otherness) and as dissociation from the category of race altogether (emphasizing through black caricature that Jews had assimilated, that "they were not black"). Blackface, Rogin suggests, serves to "loosen . . . up white identities by taking over black ones, by underscoring the line between white and black."[59] Insofar as *Melanctha* represents the "blacking up" of an autobiographical account of sexual and racial difference (*Q.E.D.*), it can be seen to offer Stein two contradictory modes of compensation. On the one hand, telling her story in African-American terms could allow Stein to emphasize an identification with blackness, its marginality and difference. In this, it is interesting how much Melanctha's "typically mulatta" characteristics could also be seen as "typically Jewish": her light skin, her intelligence, even – or especially – her propensity to "wander."[60] On the other hand, "blacking up" would allow Stein to cast her story as Other, to "loosen" it from self-identification. *As* blackface, *Melanctha* serves to "underscore the line between white and black": if African-Americans embody racial and sexual otherness, then Jewish-Americans do not need to. By performing her story as "black," in short, Stein can mark a distance from the performance of her identity as Jewish.

But if *Melanctha* represents Stein in blackface, then the racial mask that Stein adopts in this text is also what occludes epistemological certainty, including knowledge about "race" and "type." Blackface makes easy stereotypes visible; but as masking it also points to the invisible and the unknowable that lies below the visible surface of the "racial type." What is curious about *Melanctha* is that its African-American protagonist both embodies "racial type" and ultimately resists the gaze that would "know" her *as* a type; she eludes "knowing" even as she is presented as knowable in her racialization. In fact, it is precisely Melanctha's mulatta "melancholy" that marks her both as a "type" *and* as a mysteriously split subject: "melancholia," in Freud's terms, being the condition of "ambivalence . . . in which hate and love contend with each other."[61] Drawn to a bourgeois male lover yet desiring "excitement," Melanctha is "typically" mulatto – the tragic product of mixed blood. Yet she is also the site of ambivalence, of unreadability, of semantic disruption: in short, a mask. She both attracts and unsettles those who watch and analyze her – the narrator, Rose, James Herbert, John, the Bishops' coachman, Jane Harden, and her lover Jeff Campbell. Rose herself laments that "you certainly never can noways learn to act right Melanctha" (TL, 161); Jane Harden claims that "Melanctha Herbert never had any sense of how to act to anybody" (TL, 78); and all men feel her mysterious "power." In the face of Jeff Campbell's middle-class, normative credo – that "being good and careful and always honest and living always just as regular as can be" is best (TL, 85) – Melanctha remains a mystery even to herself: "always she did not know what it was that really held her" (TL, 67). In her changing, desiring restlessness, Melanctha appears to act without intention, will, conscious thought, or the sense of personal identity, and this in turn problematizes any efforts to locate her within a framework of knowledge, of typicality. In this, Melanctha's ultimate narrative function could be said to lie not in proving the veracity of "type" but in confusing and refusing the (sexual, racial, epistemological, narrative) desire of the subjects who would type her.

This refusal is most evident in the protracted passages of dialogue between Melanctha and Jeff which make up the long, middle section of the narrative, and which stage both an epistemological and a linguistic crisis in the text. The Melanctha–Jeff opposition can be understood as a struggle between words that "commit the speaker" and words that work to "undermine the solidity of the name"; between an understanding of signification as productive (of knowledge, meaning, and so on) or as disruptive (resisting the epistemophilic or regulatory gaze).[62] In one dialogue, Jeff enters into a long excursus on the essential difference between "thinking" and "feeling," only to find in Melanctha's response an inversion of his terms of signification:

> "No, I don't stop thinking much Miss Melanctha and if I can't ever feel without stopping thinking, I certainly am very much afraid Miss Melanctha that I never will do much with that kind of feeling . . . I certainly do think I feel as much for you Miss Melanctha, as you ever feel about me, sure I do. I don't think you know me right when you talk like that to me. Tell me just straight out how much do you care about me, Miss Melanctha." "Care about you Jeff Campbell," said Melanctha slowly. "I certainly do care for you Jeff Campbell less than you are always thinking and much more than you are ever knowing." (TL, 92–3)

Jeff expects a clarity from language which Melanctha refuses to mirror: in responding to his request to "tell me just straight out" her feelings, Melanctha reiterates Jeff's words and at the same time implodes the careful semantic structure of his argument. Melanctha's inversion of Jeff's terms deauthorizes the hierarchical relationship between thinking and feeling which his repeated invocation of these terms has attempted to set up, and in so doing reveals that his "sure" definition of reality is itself a shifting discursive construct. Even a slightly altered repetition such as she effects when reordering Jeff's "care about" to the more prosaic (and condescending) "care for" serves to disrupt and expose the direction he attempts to impose upon their mutual discourse, and to call into question the "solidity" of his signifying ground. As Butler writes, "reiterations are never simply replicas of the same"; in reiterating Jeff's words in order to foreground their non-replicatability, their *failure* to repeat "the same," Melanctha implicitly challenges Jeff's belief that one can remain "good and regular" in language as in life. While Jeff represents the regulatory and normativizing forces of habitual or automatic action, Melanctha works to expose this action as a contingent and *in*essential performance whose claim to "goodness" is ultimately repressive and deadening.

As Lisa Ruddick concludes, Melanctha "has what James in a fanciful moment labels genius – 'the faculty of perceiving in an unhabitual way'."[63] Ruddick's dismissal of the significance of the label "genius" as "fanciful" limits her relevance to this analysis beyond the striking fact that she correlates Melanctha with a Jamesian notion of "genius" in the first place. As the *un*habitual, Melanctha embodies James's definition of "genius; as the *un*automatic, constituted through her resistant discursive exchanges with the "normal" Jeff, Melanctha is like the "consciousness without memory" that Stein and Solomons discuss in "Normal Motor Automatism." Significantly, Melanctha "never could remember right when it came to what she had done and what had happened" (TL, 75). Lacking the sense of a past that would enable a "self" to emerge as a consistent presence, signifying desire and resistance toward the automatic, habitual world around her, Melanctha both reinstantiates the "excessive" subject of "Normal Motor Automatism" and anticipates what Stein herself would shortly come to call "genius." Yet precisely in her disruptive, anti-identitarian, genial "wandering," Melanctha also represents a challenge to the typological schema, and to the discourse of "race," which underwrites her story. In arresting Jeff's desire, in resisting "the solidity of the name," Melanctha also dismantles the larger narrative effort to literalize "bottom nature" by locating it in the racialized body. In the end, Melanctha's disruptiveness toward Jeff and others is also a disruption of the entire Steinian typological endeavor and its culminating desire for epistemological certainty through displacement and projection onto "blackness." That Melanctha "all her life did not know how to tell a story wholly" (TL, 70) suggests that the narrative that bears her name also contains an excess that defies both "knowledge" and closure. After over a hundred pages of "wandering," the almost arbitrary ending to this story – Melanctha falls ill and dies within two paragraphs – speaks to the failure of the narrative to resolve its contradictory trajectories; the brutality of this ending suggests Stein's own ambivalence toward a figure too radical and unknowable for its narrative frame. That Stein attributes to Melanctha an unfathomable power that lies outside all determinant characteristics – race, gender, sexuality, "type" – is, however, a sign of something to come.

Notes

1. Gertrude Stein, unpublished ms. from Radcliffe College (25 April 1895), quoted in Miller, *Gertrude Stein*, 146. For critical accounts of

Stein's relationship to James, see Ruddick, *Reading Gertrude Stein*, chs 1 and 2; Chessman, *The Public Is Invited to Dance*, 156–61 *passim*; Ryan, *The Vanishing Subject*, ch. 7; Steiner, *Exact Resemblance*, ch. 2 *passim*; Ashton, "Gertrude Stein for Anyone"; Meyer, "Writing Psychology Over."

2. James, "The Will to Believe," 92.
3. As *The Autobiography of Alice B. Toklas* would later have it, Stein's references to normalcy were *always* embedded in her interest in the strangeness of the ordinary and the everyday: "[Gertrude Stein] always says she dislikes the abnormal, it is so obvious. She says the normal is so much more simply complicated and interesting" (ABT, 102). Priscilla Perkins, in "'A Little Body'," concurs that "Stein's ideologies of . . . normality rarely have a stable value" (530).
4. Kittler, *Discourse Networks*, 229.
5. B. F. Skinner, "Has Gertrude Stein a Secret?", in Hoffman, *Critical Essays on Gertrude Stein*, 64–71. Originally published in the *Atlantic Monthly* 153 (January 1934), 50–7. For an analysis of Skinner's attack within the context of his own "preoccupation with repetition and originality," see Armstrong, *Modernism*, 197–211.
6. Stein–Hubbell correspondence quoted in Meyer, "Writing Psychology Over," 141.
7. James, *Psychology*, 753.
8. Ibid., 754.
9. Ibid., 119 (in italics in original); 125.
10. Ibid., 753.
11. Ibid., 754.
12. Ibid., 754.
13. Kant, "On Genius," 235.
14. Schopenhauer, *Works*, 293.
15. Shklovsky, "Art as Technique," 22.
16. Ibid., 12.
17. Stein quoted in Wilder, "Introduction," FIA, vi.
18. In *The Great Gatsby*, F. Scott Fitzgerald writes "what a grotesque thing a rose is" (169); while William Carlos Williams declares that "the rose is obsolete" (quoted in Quartermain, *Disjunctive Poetics*, 42).
19. Bürger, *Theory of the Avant-Garde*, 65.
20. James, *Psychology*, 400.
21. Butler, *Bodies that Matter*, 226.
22. Armstrong, *Modernism*, 200.
23. Friedrich Schlegel writes of genius, "It is the sacred breath which . . . moves us. It cannot be grasped forcibly and comprehended mechanically, but it can be amiably lured by mortal beauty and veiled in it" (Schlegel quoted in Simpson, *Origins*, 205). But for Kant's correlation of mechanism and genius, see my Introduction, 3.
24. Foucault, *Discipline and Punish*, 148.
25. James, *Varieties*, 29.
26. Foucault, *Discipline and Punish*, 148.
27. Stein's physiological distinctions here originate from and extend contemporaneous work by James and others into the relationship between

mental activity and the blood supply. See James, *Psychology*, 103–5.

28. See Butler, *Bodies that Matter*; Grosz, *Volatile Bodies*.
29. Damon, "Stein's Jewishness," 491.
30. "There has been very little attention paid to Gertrude Stein as a Jewish writer," Linda Wagner-Martin rightly observes, locating Stein's own lack of emphasis on her Jewishness in her desire for "universalism": "The modernist writer aimed to be universal, above political alliances, washed clean in the purity of serious and innovative aesthetics, and Gertrude certainly wanted to play that game well. She would have gained nothing in high modernist Paris by describing herself as a Jewish American lesbian" (Wagner-Martin, "Gertrude Stein," 436).
31. Damon, "Stein's Jewishness," 492. Wineapple also discusses Stein and Jewishness (*Sister Brother*, 56–8, and *passim*).
32. In "Portrait of a National Fetish," Wanda Van Dusen reprints and interprets Stein's "Introduction to the Speeches of Maréchal Pétain" (1942).
33. Richard Bridgman makes this observation in *Stein in Pieces*, 161.
34. Wineapple, *Sister Brother*, 51.
35. Zygmunt Bauman, "Allosemitism: Premodern, Modern, Postmodern," in Cheyette and Marcus (eds), *Modernity, Culture and 'the Jew'*, 143.
36. By the time Eliot stepped down as president, only 2.5 per cent of the student body was composed of students of Jewish descent. Yet Jews under Eliot's tenureship generally fared better socially and institutionally at Harvard than they did under Eliot's successor, A. Lawrence Lowell, who favored admission quotas for Jews. See Townsend, *Manhood*, 92; also Synnott, *Half-Opened Door*, 44–7.
37. Eliot quoted in Synnott, *Half-Opened Door*, 47.
38. Petersen discusses the history of this perception in "Jews as a Race," 35–7.
39. Townsend, *Manhood*, 231. Among the professors Townsend cites are Henry Adams, Charles Eliot Norton, Evert Wendell, Nathaniel Shaler, and Albert Bushnell Hart, W. E. B. DuBois's thesis adviser. Even William James, who called for a "typology" as specific as each unique individual, and who publicly criticized the anti-semitism and imperialism of his colleagues, was less than consistent in his private remarks to students and colleagues (Wineapple, *Sister Brother*, 51). For James's criticism of his colleagues' anti-Semitism, see Townsend, *Manhood*, 236.
40. Smith, "Another Top 100," 45.
41. Henry Adams quoted in Mayo, *The Ambivalent Image*, 58; Brooks Adams refers to Jews in *The Law of Civilization*, 292. Shaler quoted in Townsend, *Manhood*, 232–3.
42. Gilman, *Smart Jews*, 54; 58.
43. Ibid., 133.
44. Wineapple, *Sister Brother*, 57; Linda Wagner-Martin, "*Favored Strangers*", 34. In this essay, entitled "The Modern Jew who Has Given Up the Faith of His Fathers Can Reasonably and Consistently Believe in Isolation," Stein argued that "in the sacred precincts of the home, in the close union of family and of kinsfolk [one] must be a Jew

with Jews; the Gentile has no place there" (quoted in Wagner-Martin, "*Favored Strangers*", 34).

45. Wineapple, *Sister Brother*, 56.
46. For example, see Hovey, "Sapphic Primitivism," 564.
47. McKay quoted in Hindus, "Ethnicity and Sexuality," 73.
48. Adele's Jewishness is marked in the conversational terms through which Stein would later define "genius" ("talking and listening"): "I never seem to know how to keep still, but you both know already that I have the failing of my tribe," she announces to Mabel and Helen, "I believe in the sacred rites of conversation even when it is a monologue" (QED, 57). On Mabel Neathe as "sexual mulatto," see Hovey, "Sapphic Primitivism," 559.
49. The phrase is Sara Suleri's, quoted in North, *Dialect of Modernism*, 65.
50. For a discussion of the figure of the tragic mulatto/a and of the one-drop rule see Sundquist, *To Wake the Nations*, esp. 249–63; also Carby, *Reconstructing Womanhood*, 88–91.
51. Cohen, "Black Brutes," 121. Much has been written since Cohen's formative article on Stein's alleged or actual racism; see especially Cope, "'Moral Deviancy,'" for a brilliant analysis of Stein's work and the politics of interpretation. For other critiques of racism in *Melanctha*, see Saldivar-Hull, "Wrestling Your Ally"; also Hovey, "Sapphic Primitivism."
52. Quoted in Diner, *Almost Promised Land*, 74.
53. Michael Rogin suggests that parallels can be made between racism toward African Americans in America and anti-Semitism directed at Jews in European ghettos (Rogin, *Blackface, White Noise*, 45–70). Yet Jews who came to the United States never shared the same burden of racism as blacks: "in the United States African Americans substituted for Jews as the dominant targets of racial nationalism . . . [t]he people who came to be ghettoized – who had to be stopped from changing their identities, from passing, integrating, and assimilating – were blacks rather than Jews" (ibid., 63).
54. Townsend, *Manhood*, 233.
55. Rogin, *Blackface, White Noise*, 17.
56. Ibid., 6.
57. North suggests as much when he writes of Stein's and Picasso's "racial role-playing" in *Melanctha* and *Les Demoiselles d'Avignon*: "Stein and Picasso act out twenty years in advance the other side of *The Jazz Singer* . . . donning the African mask to make a break with their own cultural past" (North, *Dialect of Modernism*, 66).
58. Rogin, *Blackface, White Noise*, 11.
59. Ibid., 66; 34.
60. I am grateful to Susannah Heschel for emphasizing these points of similarity.
61. "In melancholia, the relation to the object is no simple one; it is complicated by the conflict due to ambivalence . . . [C]ountless separate struggles are carried on over the object, in which hate and love contend with each other; the one seeks to detach the libido from the object, the other to maintain this position of the libido against the assault" (Freud,

"Mourning and Melancholia," in his *Standard Edition*, vol. XIV, 256). See also my Ch. 4, 114–15.

62. The terms of this opposition are taken from North's deft analysis of dialect in *Melanctha* (*Dialect of Modernism*, 74–5).
63. Ruddick, *Reading*, 19.

2 Self-Naming, Self-Splitting: The Making of a Modernist "Genius" in *The Making of Americans* and *G.M.P.*

In the exception the power of real life breaks through the crust of a mechanism that has become torpid by repetition.
(Carl Schmitt)[1]

In many ways, *The Making of Americans* – Stein's massive, 925-page epic composed intermittently between 1903 and 1911 – is a testament to temporal absolutism and self-generativity, to the potential power of the present to resist its own antecedents.[2] The opening scene of the text dramatizes this:

> Once an angry man dragged his father along the ground through his own orchard. "Stop!" cried the groaning old man at last, "Stop! I did not drag my father beyond this tree". (MOA, 3)

The possibility of transgressing the father's own limits of rebellion is clearly suggested here, as it is in the Aristotelian passage from which this parable is drawn.[3] Yet the narrator glosses this parable in terms of repetition and contingency rather than resistance and autonomy. "It is hard living down the tempers we are born with," the narrator continues, stating deterministically that emotion and action are the result of nature, that the process of human life is the rendering of a kind of essential constitution. What Stein would call "bottom nature" is here presented as transgenerational, with sons copying fathers and so on in a reiterative continuum produced, ironically, through the very act of rebellion which is purporting to rupture present from past. Yet the resolution of this opening parable remains significantly open-ended, reminding us of Butler's contention that repetitions need not be "replicas of the same." What *would* happen if the father were dragged beyond the mythical tree – a biblical symbol for limit and taboo – and were shown a world he had himself not dared enter?

In a significant and overlooked passage at the dead-center of *The Making of Americans*, a daughter confronts her father with precisely this issue by bringing him up against the cyclical trauma which is often characteristic of childhood sexual abuse:

> There was a man who was always writing to his daughter that she should not do things that were wrong that would disgrace him, she should not do such things and in every letter that he wrote to her he told her she should not do such things, that he was her father and was giving good moral advice to her and always he wrote to her in every letter that she should not do things that she should not do anything that would disgrace him . . . and then once she wrote back to him that he had not any right to write moral things in letters to her, that he had taught her that he had shown her that he had commenced in her the doing the things things that would disgrace her and he had said then when he had begun with her he had said he did it so that when she was older she could take care of herself with those who wished to make her do things that were wicked things and he would teach her and she would be stronger than such girls who had not any way of knowing better, and she wrote this letter and her father got the letter and he was a paralytic always after, it was a shock to him getting such a letter, he kept saying over and over again that his daughter was trying to kill him and now she had done it . . . (MOA, 488–9)

This passage may have contributed to the outrage the Stein family felt upon reading *The Making of Americans*, and may serve as textual evidence for recent biographical allegations that Stein herself was the victim of sexual abuse.[4] Yet this passage also offers an important thematic parallel to the opening parable of the text. Once again, a child is repeating an action performed by the father but in ways that contradict and threaten to "disgrace" his authority – in this instance, by writing back to him, by using the agency of the letter to resist him. While the father grounds his authority on terms like "morality" and "disgrace" – terms that function to delimit the boundaries of "right" from "deviant" behavior – the daughter indicts his actions by redeploying these same terms against him, showing how his "morality" encrypts the very wickedness it purports to exclude: "when he had begun with her he had said he did it so that when she was older she could take care of herself with those who wished to make her do things that were wicked things . . .". By exposing the immorality of his "moral" deeds, by resignifying and recontextualizing the terms of his discourse, the daughter effectively overturns her father's hononymic association of "right" and "write." Discursive control, domination, and limitation – the thrust of the father's letters – fail at the moment the Other appropriates his language and repeats it in contradictory ways.

I juxtapose these two scenes from *The Making of Americans* in order to emphasize Stein's emerging concern with the dynamic of authority and rebellion during the period of this text's composition. This is a concern that arises out of the contradictory affiliations of Stein's early intellectual period traced in the previous chapter, a concern with the significance and limitations of the scientific and literary models she had inherited from what she called "the nineteenth century." *Melanctha*'s interest both in "typicality" and in a subject who cannot be reduced to the determinants of her "type" – race, femininity, heterosexuality – exemplifies Stein's struggle during this period to write across intellectual boundaries. *The Making of Americans* protracts this struggle, presenting "character" as at once given and essential, compelled to repeat itself in unchanging ways, and as an unexpected and unknowable force whose dimensions are always in excess of a unified "bottom nature." In writing out this struggle, Stein begins to employ repetition as a way of emphasizing both constancy *and* variety, sameness *and* difference; and as a marker of time experienced either chronologically or in terms of a "continuous present." The opening parable of *The Making of Americans*, as we have seen, offers opposing ways to read the function of repetition in this text. On the one hand, the son *must* repeat his father's actions, even in the act of rebellion; hence, repetition could be said to enforce continuity and sameness, as well as an allegiance to the father, however grudging. Repetition as a steady, consistent force which links past, present, and future is, as Jeff Campbell of *Melanctha* might argue, the motor of "normal," decent, "right" living. This understanding of repetition is what seems to be encrypted in the full title of Stein's novel: *The Making of Americans: Being a History of a Family's Progress*. Recalling the fanciful nineteenth-century titles of a Twain or a Melville, Stein's "history" of a "progress" or "making" announces a logic of temporal development wherein the past effortlessly gives rise to some present truth, some better way; and it is the duty of the realist novelist to alert her readers to this transcendent meaning. "History," "progress," and "making" ask us to see ourselves, fundamentally, as our fathers' daughters and sons, as their replicable parts within the great generational machine.

At the same time, as the "queer" and rebellious children in *The Making of Americans* make clear, repetition need not be invoked in the service of continuity nor in the policing of social taboo, but can as easily work to disrupt a logic of sameness. Repetition would function in this way as what liberates difference, as what resembles but is never "exactly the same," as what obfuscates a character "typology"; a "parodic" repetition (Butler's term) that contains within it the possibility for severing the present from the past and from memory, for symbolic patricide, for resignification. As Stein would put it thirty years later, "if anything is alive there is no such thing as repetition" (LIA, 174). This notion of a "repetition" alien to itself emerges not only in scenes of rebellion within the narrative, but on the level of the textual composition itself. "I am writing everything as I am learning everything," Stein announces toward the end of her text, marking her awareness that *The Making of Americans* has metamorphosed from a formulaic reporting of all types of human being into a text *in process*, a text uncertain of its own future direction. Where once repetition had been enlisted as the thematic and linguistic "motor" of the text, something strange and unexpected begins to enter into this machine. That repetition may not link but rupture the present and the past, that it may work against the completion of knowledge, and that it may be deployed against the normalization of individuals into types, is the source of both anxiety and wonderment for Stein as she struggles with her goal, as she puts it, of "describing everyone." Yet once repetition is seen to be a force of *de*stabilization, *The Making of Americans* becomes the site of a shifting, changing, moment-to-moment process that emphasizes sudden, "lively" perceptual encounters over predictable, habitual, "dead" formulations.

I

This latter understanding of repetition is, to be sure, something that emerges gradually through the process of the text. At least in the initial stages of *The Making of Americans* – up to the beginning of the "Martha Hersland" chapter – Stein appears committed to continuing and culminating the search for a "complete" knowledge of character "type" initiated in her earlier scientific project, "Cultivated

Motor Automatism." In "The Gradual Making of The Making of Americans" (1935), a retrospective account of this period, Stein writes that her early textual ambition was to "finally describe really describe every kind of human being that ever was or is or would be living" (LIA, 142). Description, here, is contingent upon a knowledge of character; knowledge of character is in turn derived from an assessment of the consistent, predictable ways in which subjects "repeat" themselves over time: "Repeating then is in every one, in every one their being and their feeling and their way of realizing everything and every one comes out of them in repeating. More and more then every one comes to be clear to some one."[5] In the middle of *The Making of Americans*, Stein rearticulates this process: character "was all there, all always repeating, all always being dominated by the bottom being and all that then was needed was to understand the meaning, that was very interesting, that was what I did by one hard looking" (MOA, 316–17). The terms of this process recall those of the earlier scientific work, with "hard looking" precisely describing the position of the knower who would dominate the known through watching, waiting, noting repetitions and hence determining essences. This epistemophilia, this determination to know all possible human kinds through a gaze which would dominate and domesticate otherness, represents the primary effort of the first three hundred pages of the text. The sheer forward pressure of the taxonomical system which the text imposes onto its study of character, the forceful process of "making" which the text both charts and effects, the commitment to standardizing and normalizing individual difference under the rubric of an inclusive "typology" – all suggest crucial linkages between Stein's early "scientific" work and her first "literary" efforts.[6]

The Making of Americans begins, as we have seen, with the assertion that everyone has within him- or herself an essential "temperament," an idea initially traced through the relationships of a Jewish-American family, the Dehnings, modeled on Stein's New York cousins. In the earliest draft of the novel, begun as notes in 1902 and subsequently put aside in 1903, the focus is clearly upon the "opposition in resemblance" of family members – the struggle between temperament and heredity.[7] Parts of this draft still remain in the first seventy-eight pages, and a brief middle section, of the final version. When Stein returned to *The Making of Americans* in 1906 after writing a series of shorter works of fiction, including *Fernhurst*, *Q.E.D.* and *Three Lives*, she moved into a second phase of textual production, comprising an expanded version of what Ulla Dydo has termed a "fairly conventional nineteenth-century family novel" (SR, 17). Yet in June of 1908, Stein "quite literally threw away almost all of what she had written" and embarked on a new project, what she called in the notebooks "this new thing" (NB, *C-4).[8] Abandoning the specific dynamics of the family plot, this third and final version of *The Making of Americans* begins to focus upon a generalized study of human kinds, stating as its new goal the hope of producing a comprehensive human typology which would include a description of "every kind of human being." Borrowing its terms from "Cultivated Motor Automatism," the narrative now emphasizes two essential varieties of character types: "independent dependent" and "dependent independent," or "attacking" and "resisting."[9] "The way it comes out of them, the way these feelings mix up in them, the way they mix up with other things in them make of each man or woman their kind of man or woman, make them one of the two kinds of men and women, make of them one of the many kinds in each of the two kinds of them" (MOA, 199–200), the narrative states in announcing its new direction. What "makes" a man or a woman into one or the other of the two essential "kinds" is his or her "way" of acting, feeling, thinking – "way" being a crucial term here, implying a consistent mode of repetitive action or automatic behavior which emanates from bottom nature or "temperament," "all there, all always repeating." A person's "way" is his mark of uniqueness or difference, but more importantly for the project at hand, it is the sign of his type or kind:

> Every one has their [sic] own being in them. Every one is of a kind of men and women. There are many very many kinds of men and women, there are many very many kinds of men, there are many very many kinds of women. There are many ways of making kinds of them, this is now a description of all the kinds of ways there are of making kinds of them . . . (MOA, 333)

Once an individual's way becomes apparent to an observer or narrator, it can be categorized as one of two types; and eventually, all possible types will have been calculated and organized within this enormous text. The result, Stein quite seriously imagines, will be a universal typology. Or as she puts it in the midst of her composition: "This is a very certain way of knowing, grouping men and women, understanding, seeing the kind of natures in them, making certain of the resemblances between them. This is then a universal grouping" (MOA, 344).

Yet this ambitious descriptive effort remains increasingly problematic for Stein as the text proceeds, for two reasons. First, the verbal form entrusted with "expressing" this grouping – repetition – starts to mutate, obscuring rather than enlightening the typological enterprise. Second, these expressive difficulties occasion a growing self-consciousness in the authorial voice; this leads to a new immediacy of textual process; and eventually, the struggles of the author watching herself write take over from the typological project as the new, equally limitless, subject of the text.

Repetition is initially presented within the text as performing two central functions for Stein: first, in allowing her to "know" an individual's "way" ("being . . . was all there, all always repeating"), and secondly and subsequently, in allowing her to "describe" this way within narrative time, eventually arriving at a "complete" or "whole" description of everyone ("each one then keeps repeating the whole history of them, this is now some description of my learning to hear, see and feel the whole repeating coming out of some" (MOA, 356)). Both of these enterprises depend upon the idea that repetition is a temporally consistent and predictable mechanism, capable of conveying "bottom nature" to an observer and of being mobilized to convey a character's "drama of emergence" in writing.[10] In examining her subjects for their "bottom natures," and in grouping them into "kinds," Stein assumes not only that repetitive "ways" will consistently illuminate character but also that *repetitive writing* can convey these "ways." Yet as the opening parable of the text makes clear, the present need not exactly repeat the past, and it is this awareness, this essentially modernist problem of temporal disjunction, that both drives the text forward and threatens its underlying pursuit of a complete typology:

> Each one sometime is a whole one to me, then I am hearing or feeling or seeing some repeating coming out of that one that makes a completer one of that one, always then there may be sometimes more history of that one, there may then be never a whole history of any one inside any one . . . Slowly then that feeling is discouraging to one loving having a whole history of every one inside in one. (MOA, 330)

"Always then for such a one there must be many new beginnings," Stein writes, revealing the impetus behind the text's process, as well as its inevitable failure to arrive at an endpoint of "completion." While at an early moment in the text Stein claims that "more and more listening to repeating gives to me completed understanding" (MOA, 291), two-thirds of the way through she acknowledges that

> I have a pretty helpless feeling with feeling all the kinds of ways there are of living, of feeling ways of living, of having ways in living. I feel like one a little beginning and certainly not going to be making very much of progressing. (MOA, 620)

And in a striking figuration during the final, "David Hersland" chapter, repetition appears synonymous with stuttering uncertainty:

> I mean, I mean and that is not what I mean, I mean that not any one is saying what they are meaning, I mean that I am feeling something, I mean that I mean something and I mean that not any one is thinking, is feeling, is saying, is certain of that thing . . . I mean, I mean, I know what I mean. (MOA, 782)

Here, repetition thwarts rather than enables the narrator's desire to "say" what she "means," to forward her "epistemic intention";[11] it is the source of uncertainty, of contradiction, of confusion: "I mean and that is not what I mean."

In the third and final phase of the text's production, therefore, Stein – writing as and out of herself – both enlarges the scope of her typological project and begins to show a growing self-awareness of the recursive limitations of this project, as well as a corresponding interest in the effect of such limitations upon the writing self. From the Martha Hersland chapter on (MOA, 287 ff.),[12] from 1908 to the end of the project in October of 1911, Stein begins to turn her attention increasingly toward the struggles of the writer in the act of writing out her human typology. In "The Gradual Making of the Making of Americans," Stein recounts the attenuation of her typological project and the emergence of a new relationship to both knowledge and to the act of writing as a felicitous experience:

> I found that as often as I thought and had every reason to be certain that I had included everything in my knowledge of any one something else would turn up that had to be included. I did not with this get at all discouraged I only became more and more interested. (LIA, 144)

In the same lecture, Stein correlates the coming out of the artist with a deconstructive opening up of concepts, paradigms, signifiers that had "once to some one had real meaning": "I myself was becoming livelier just then. One does you know, when one has come to the conclusion that what is inside every one is not all there is of any one" (LIA, 150). Becoming "livelier," as Marianne DeKoven has so persuasively shown, signifies for Stein a new way of using language, "dense with multiple, open-ended connections of lexical meaning (image, association, connotation, resonance)."[13] But it also represents a new interest in the "life" animating the authorial voice, a new awareness that there is something "of any one" residing beyond "what is inside every one." "This is what we mean by life," Stein would write in "The Gradual Making" (LIA, 170); "if anything is alive there is no such thing as repetition" (LIA, 174).[14] This "something" that remains irreducible to the repetitive ways of a person's "bottom nature" is what *The Making of Americans* confronts as it turns its focus to the writing self and abandons its insistence upon the eventual achievement of a comprehensive typology of everybody. Hence, she writes: "I am learning but not really grasping these things in me, that is certain" (MOA, 621).

In the early scientific experiment published in 1896 as "Normal Motor Automatism," Stein and her colleague Leon Solomons had written of achieving doubled authorial positions: both engaged and distant, watching themselves perform "automatically" while at the same time remaining conscious of this process. The co-authors described the conscious residue emerging from the process of automatism as a "consciousness without memory," an immediate awareness outside the bounds of automaticity, habit, convention, memory, and "the personal." This discovery of a "consciousness without memory" that resides on the horizon of the personal is equivalent, I would argue, to Stein's recognition during the course of *The Making of Americans* "that what is inside every one is not all there is of any one." In what cannot be traced through consistent repetition over time to a person's "bottom nature" lies an excess, an irreducibility that marks the limit of this "self" or "nature." It is this excess that Stein had begun to explore in *Melanctha*, with her presentation of a character who resists the linguistic and epistemological containments of the "normal" Jeff. It is also this excess that threatens to undermine the typological project of *The Making of Americans*, for it prohibits epistemological "wholeness":

> [A]lways then sometime the one having knowing each one they are ever knowing as a whole one as the living being in that one, such a one then sometimes is having all a wrong meaning to the

> being of some one then seeming to be a real right whole one then inside that one. (MOA, 330)

And it is this excess in *herself* that prohibits the completion of her text:

> It would be an exciting thing to be certain really of this thing having had the complete history of every one already finished in writing. I will not be having it as certain this thing, I will go on being one every day telling about being being in men and in women. (MOA, 684)

What thwarts "certainty" is also what enables the text to continue; what prohibits the writer from achieving a "complete knowledge" of others, or finally of herself, is the fact that neither she nor others is ultimately reducible to the repetitive "ways" upon which a knowledge of type is contingent. The estrangement of the self through the process of attempting to determine the "nature" of this self, of watching herself, thus becomes the potentially illimitable subject of the text.

Many readers have criticized *The Making of Americans* for its length and lack of internal development but have failed to address the issue of why the text might aspire to "nonclosure."[15] Yet in relating the authorial "being" that emerges in the later stages of the text to the split subject explored in "Normal Motor Automatism," one can begin to apprehend *The Making of Americans*'s feeling of illimitability and presentness as "[a] thing not beginning and not ending" (MOA, 701). Once the self is both a "type" and a consciousness in excess of this "type," divided and hence irreducible to itself, the articulation of this "being" in writing becomes a matter of moment-to-moment change with no continuity over time. In the event, what matters is the present, the absolute "now" extracted from a sense of temporality and hence of subjective/linguistic continuity: a present that embodies the structure of "suddenness."[16] The text that records this presentness need not end; there is no depth of narrative time or authorial memory that might bring writing from an insufficient past to "completion," only moments of sudden self-recognition and self-estrangement zooming into temporary focus as the writer engages in the process of watching herself write. Temporal immediacy and language play become the central elements of this process of "being." "At any moment that you are conscious of knowing anything, memory plays no part," Stein would later claim, suggesting that *The Making of Americans* "was one of my first efforts to give the appearance of one time-knowledge, and not to make it a narrative story" (HWIW, 155). That this process of watching herself write takes place in language is, of course, crucial, since it is her signifying medium that now begins to fascinate Stein, especially the uncanny doubling and splitting of signifiers and signifieds.[17] In the moment-to-moment process of writing, the "I" who represents the author "talking and listening" to herself is neither consistent nor extra-linguistic but fragmented, shifting, subjected *to* language and its differential mechanisms. A quintessentially modernist authorial "subject," a "being" in language, emerging out of a text that begins both thematically and stylistically in the nineteenth-century world of the father and becomes – as Stein herself noted later – a work "out of [which] has sprung all modern writing."[18] And a fragmented, modernist, anti-authorial "being" to which Stein would soon give a name: *genius*.

II

In one of a series of French school notebooks she kept to record her working thoughts during the writing of *The Making of Americans*, Stein made an interesting observation: "Picasso and Matisse have a maleness that belongs to genius. Moi aussi perhaps," she notes some time during the winter of 1907–8 (NB, C-21). Here, Stein identifies "genius" as her dominant trait, and the "maleness" that belongs to it as a secondary characteristic, as the necessary condition for "genius." Although doubtfully couched, this claim to authority places Stein on slightly different historical terrain from that occupied by the so-called "mannish lesbians" of her Paris circle, women for whom "maleness" would have been the primary term of identification as the *sine qua non* of intellectual and artistic power.[19] Stein's claim, by contrast, both subscribes to and goes beyond male identification: while undoubtedly she saw in her fellow male modernists a privilege and intellectual freedom denied women, her projection of self seems less concerned with "maleness" as the standard against which she measures herself, than with an exceptionality that lies beyond gender. As Catharine Stimpson notes, "Stein's self-images are more than appropriations of a male identity and masculine interests"; they are reflections of the need "[t]o think of one's self as special."[20]

How Stein began "knowing that I was a genius" needs to be understood within the context of two critical developments during this period. The first was her growing association with Picasso and

Matisse, and her sense of the shared destiny of this threesome. Despite the strained differences between the two painters, Stein remained convinced through the first, formative decade of her writing career that her relationship with Picasso and Matisse had lasting implications for the direction of modern art. Although the "Moi aussi perhaps" of her notebook entry indicates an initial ambivalence toward the terms of this relationship, twenty-five years later Stein's rehearsal of this union is smooth and assured:

> In the long struggle with the portrait of Gertrude Stein, Picasso passed from the Harlequin, the charming early italian period to the intensive struggle which was to end in cubism. Gertrude Stein had written the story of Melanctha the negress, the second story of Three Lives which was the first definite step away from the nineteenth century and into the twentieth century in literature. Matisse had painted the Bonheur de Vivre and had created the new school of colour which was soon to leave its mark on everything. (ABT, 66)

In hindsight, Picasso's portrait of Stein, *Melanctha*, and Matisse's use of color are figured as discrete events which together narrate the progressive story of "modernism," where cultural titans break through the constraint of traditional form into a new world in which there can be no looking back. "Genius" is the concept which best captures the dimensions of these modern artists, as *The Autobiography of Alice B. Toklas* seems to suggest. And "genius" is one of the few categories of identity that answers to itself, seeming to exist outside of all social norms as pure value, and thus avoiding the dual modernist fears of contingency and means–ends rationality.[21] One is born a "genius"; one does not become one. The question of how Stein acceded to the heights of "genius" is never posed in her later autobiographical writing; the certainty of this capacity is taken as a given, as much a fact of Stein's life as her robes and sandals, as her regal bearing (Fig. 2.1). This certainty is also apparent in the notebooks, when Stein presents "genius" as the very ground for her shared artistic effort with Matisse and Picasso: "Matisse, Pablo, and I do not do ours with either brains or character we have all enough of both to do our job but our initiative comes from within a propulsion which we don't control, or create" (NB, B-19). Noted in the midst of her effort within *The Making of Americans* to categorize everybody according to their "bottom natures," this famous comment by Stein represents a self-conscious effort to lay claim to her own bottom nature, to the automatic "propulsion" from which all action, thought, and language repetitively emanate.

The notion of "genius" was ubiquitous in turn-of-the-century Paris, but Stein's specific mobilization of the term to describe herself and her contemporaries was indebted to another important discovery

Fig. 2.1 *Gertrude Stein Genius (1913)*

Fig. 2.2 *Otto Weininger (c. 1903), Author of* Sex and Character

in her early career, a textual discovery that would prove remarkably opportune. The range and character of what Stein was reading during this period – evident in the notebooks, in letters, and in extant volumes of the Stein–Toklas personal library – reveal an enormous interest not only in narrative (Elizabethan dramatists and nineteenth-century realists, as well as in major contemporary American writers and social thinkers from Mark Twain to Henry James to Charlotte Perkins Gilman), but also in philosophy, history, and biography, much of it involving the spectacular feats of "men of mark."[22] Stein approached this latter discussion through readings of Carlyle, Goethe, Schopenhauer, Lombroso, and Nietzsche; their importance for Stein is suggested by her continued concern in the notebook studies to *The Making of Americans* with the nature and possibility of what she calls the "genial type."[23] The greatest contribution to this interest by far was her discovery, in the winter of 1907–8, of the notorious tract *Sex and Character* (1903) by the Austrian philosopher Otto Weininger (Fig. 2.2). As Toklas notes, Stein from the beginning evinced a "mad enthusiasm" for Weininger, whom she thought "the only modern whose theory stood up and was really consistent. Weininger divided people up so completely into parts and that was what she was doing in a different way. And he too was trying to get down to the bottom nature."[24] Initially, with its stated intention of producing a "broad and deep characterology," *Sex and Character* offered Stein a model of inquiry equal in scope and ambition to her own. Yet it was in Weininger's articulation of a type – the "genius" – where his work would have its most lasting effect on Stein, permanently altering her understanding of her own authorial position and its relation to an "outside."

Weininger begins his inquiry with the philosophical query, "Is there in a man a single and simple existence," and like Stein proceeds to answer in the affirmative: "I must set out with a conception of character itself as a unit existence."[25] Where Stein claims in *The Making of Americans* that "every one always is repeating the whole of them" (MOA, 293), Weininger writes that "the whole man is manifest in every moment of the psychical life," a claim – like Stein's own – sanctioned by "science":

> The character . . . is not something seated behind the thoughts and feelings of the individual, but something revealing itself in every thought and feeling . . . Just as every cell bears within it the characters of the whole individual, so every psychical manifestation of a man involves not merely a few little characteristic traits, but his whole being.[26]

Here, "character" or "whole being" is revealed in both psyches and cells, although the relationship between the two remains deliberately vague. That there is a biological basis for human psychology – that "sex" determines "character" – is a proposition *Sex and Character* both forwards and evades, reflecting, as Chandak Sengoopta has shown, a larger cultural ambivalence in the turn-of-the-century scientific community about the significance of the developments of Mendelian genetics.[27] For Weininger, the body is both a physiological ground and an ineffable ideal, both the site of "character" and the manifestation of a yearning toward perfect maleness or femaleness. In an inquiry that shifts rapidly between a rehearsal of dominant theories about the biology of sex and philosophical speculations upon type, the psychology of women and Jews, and "genius," Weininger argues that all humans can be located along a spectrum of sexual difference according to the distribution of "sex cells" in their bodies, yet all manifest an affinity toward either ideal Man ("M") or ideal Woman ("W"). It is this universal continuum of sexual types that most closely resembles what Stein, in her "universal grouping" of bottom natures, was attempting to achieve in *The Making of Americans*.

According to Toklas, Stein's discovery of Weininger gave impetus to her typological project at a crucial moment, for it is after reading *Sex and Character* that Stein finally abandons her limited "family history" and confronts head-on the possibility of "a completed system of kinds of men and women" (MOA, 334). The implications of Stein's reading of Weininger for the new direction of her writing, as for the calculus of her own "type," are thus potentially enormous. Undoubtedly Weininger's attempt to unite physiology and psychology under the rubric of a universal "characterology" would have resonated with Stein's own dominant interest in "bottom natures" which had occupied her attention since the early psychological experiments. With his correlation of sexual types and qualities of character or "mind," Weininger would also have shown Stein a new direction for her study of "bottoms." In her notebooks from 1908, Stein even appears to adopt Weininger's vocabulary as her own.[28] Yet a seemingly intractable problem lies in Stein's identification with a typological system so notoriously anti-Semitic and misogynistic. In establishing his "spectrum of sexual difference," Weininger makes it clear that ideal Man ("M") is associated with the good, the true, and the beautiful, while ideal Woman ("W") is M's dark Other, his negation and antithesis. And in a short chapter on "Judaism," Weininger argues for an essential link between "the Jew" and "the Woman," claiming that they share a deficient moral sense, no real capacity for transcendence, and a "constant close relation with the lower life."[29] For Weininger, these traits reach their nadir in the Jewish woman: "no woman in the world represents the *idea* of woman so completely as the Jewess."[30] How could Gertrude Stein, a woman and a Jew, embrace this perverse logic?

In the previous chapter, I suggested that Stein, in *Melanctha*, displaces her own anxieties about Jewishness by projecting them onto the seemingly readable body of the African-American female Other. In so doing, Stein both emphasizes her own racialization and "loosens" it from self-identification. Yet her African-American protagonist's ultimate resistance to the typological narrative frame that contains her also signals Stein's own conflicted effort to move beyond both "race" and "type." In this complex act of displacement, self-masking, and appropriative identification, Stein creates a "type" who ultimately resists being typed, a figure who resists typicality and even figuration itself. Two years later she would discover *Sex and Character*, which, for all its vile ranting, was equally ambiguous in its presentation of human type as both an essence and a construct. As even his detractors noted, Weininger's most progressive argument was that "character" can be abstracted from the contingencies of race, gender, and sexuality; that an individual born female, for example, can in fact have the "character" of a male. "M" and "W" are but ideal forms on either end of the spectrum of sexual difference, Weininger argues; "actual individuals," comprised of infinitely variable combinations of "sex cells," are always sexually intermediate. "We know, in fact, that there are unwomanly women, man-like women, and unmanly, womanish, woman-like men. We assign sex to human beings from their birth on one character only, and so come to add contradictory ideas to our conceptions."[31] In fact, Weininger claims, "masculinity" or "femininity" can be approximated by anyone regardless of seeming sex, an argument he also makes about Jewishness: "I mean neither a race nor a people nor a recognised creed. I think of it as a tendency of the mind, as a psychological constitution which is a possibility for all mankind."[32] Both Jewish and homosexual himself, Weininger created a pseudo-scientific framework which at once legitimated his own (sexual) difference and enabled him, a convert to Christianity, to justify severing his ties to "Jewishness." By establishing the conditions of possibility for an individual to disconnect his "type" from the contingencies of birth, Weininger brought to the typological enterprise a new de-essentializing trajectory.

Stein's reading of Weininger coincided with the beginning of her relationship with Alice Toklas; arguably, her initial "enthusiasm" for his text may have resulted from its positing of the terms, and the structure, within which her love affair with Toklas could achieve legitimacy.[33] Furthermore, Weininger's contention that lesbianism is linked to a "higher degree" of intellectual development would have led Stein to a new understanding of her own type, one that lay at the opposite end of the spectrum from the problematic categories of "woman" and "Jew": "genius."[34] As Katz has persuasively argued, it is ultimately in Weininger's discussion of "genius" where his influence on Stein is most notable.[35] In *The Making of Americans*, many authorial pronouncements support this correlation. As Weininger's "strongest possible personality," the genius is, like the Nietzschean über-mensch, "characterized by a sense of the whole that enables him to filter experiential data on a large scale into a coherent world view."[36] "To be completely right, completely certain is to be in me universal in my feeling," Stein writes in *The Making of Americans* (MOA, 574). Weininger's contention that "[t]here has never been a genius who was not a great discerner of men . . . the ideal genius, who has all men within him, has also all their preferences and all their dislikes" is also precisely echoed in an early assertion of *The Making of Americans*:[37] "Each one slowly comes to be a whole one to me. Each one slowly comes to be a whole one in me . . ." (MOA, 291). Weininger further argues that "genius" concerns itself with "types and their contrasts" which he "unites in his own mind";[38] Stein's typology of "everyone who was and is and will be living" could be seen as a case-study of this genial effort. Perhaps most importantly, Weininger presents the "genius" as the exceptional being, and as the most de-essentialized "type" conceivable. "The idea is definitely insisted on, that genius is linked with manhood, that it represents an ideal masculinity in the highest form" Weininger writes, in a resolute effort to *embody* "genius."[39] But in a wild culminating chapter on "The 'I' Problem and Genius" he posits "genius" as not a type but a capacity, not an "I" but a universal process:

> Genius is the highest morality, and, therefore, it is everyone's duty. Genius is to be attained by a supreme act of the will, in which the whole universe is affirmed in the individual. Genius is something which 'men of genius' take upon themselves; it is the greatest exertion and the greatest pride, the greatest misery and the greatest ecstasy to a man. A man may become a genius if he wishes to.[40]

In the end, Weininger's greatest influence on Stein lies arguably in his providing her the terms with which to understand her own "type," and thus, paradoxically, to move beyond her own typological project. By laying claim to "genius," Stein is able to type herself, but in a way that allows her to shed the ties of what had earlier constrained her claim to authority: Jewishness, femininity, and the norms of heterosexuality. That this calculus of her "bottom nature" or "type" arrives during the process of *The Making of Americans* is, however, somewhat curious. As I have suggested above, the greater and more illimitable Stein's typological project in that text seems to become, the more she begins to focus on the struggles of the writer in the act of writing. By the later stages of the text, "bottom nature" has been replaced by the idea that "what is inside every one is not all there is of any one"; the search for "complete knowledge" as the subject of the text by an interest in the "being" of the authorial voice "talking and listening" to herself; the idea of narrative progress by a privileging of authorial self-estrangement and temporal "suddenness." *Sex and Character* may have helped Stein rethink her own "characterology" for a time, providing her with new analytical categories and terms, but the lasting effect of Weininger's text lies in enabling her to move beyond her typology. "Genius" may be for Stein her type, but it is a type that transcends the "'I' Problem" and thus enables Stein to think beyond "type" or "bottom nature." Hence for Stein, as for Weininger, "genius" has an intrinsically dialectical dimension. If "kind" or "type" represent a "frozen conception" (James) of the subject which enables the scientist to bring to completion a system of epistemological intentions, then "genius" is what un-freezes these conceptions by approaching the world as an entity in process, infinitely variable, irregular, and enlightening, always repeating itself in contradictory ways. In relation to language, knowledge, memory, and selfhood, "genius" works to negate continuity and reveal the unsubstantiated, the unhypostatized, the unhabitual. Yet "genius" nevertheless can be substantiated, embodied, typed – although always at the same moment resisting this typification. Hence Stein's famous pronouncement that the "genius" is "one who is at the same time talking and listening": both involved in the constructive process of word-making and outside of it, both engaged in the daily, repetitive performance of identity and a force of negation and anti-essentialism. For Stein, appropriating and reworking Weininger's conception of the "highest type" of human being, "genius" denotes both a self and a deconstructive function, a type that cannot be typed, a consciousness or entity alive to the self-splitting presence of the unhabitual.

III

In a series of lectures on the subject of narration given in 1935, Stein would suggest what it means to be a modernist "genius":

> [W]hat is anybody to do about writing well that is the question. I personally think that the solution is that any one must amuse himself with anything and not think to recognize anything beside this thing, beside playing with what he is playing with as he is writing what he is recognizing while the writing is being written by him. (Narr, 58–9)

Here, the textual process of dialogue, of "talking and listening," has become an aesthetic credo, a "solution" to the question of writing in the modernist era. In this simultaneous and multi-layered process, the writer is engaged in the event of producing text ("the writing [that] is being written by him"), in watching himself in the act of production ("recognizing while the writing is being written by him"), and in revising/reinterpreting in the act of watching ("writing what he is recognizing while the writing is being written by him"). Above all, the writer is engaged in *play*. As Wendy Steiner has suggested, play is a "new discovery" for Stein after the completion – or abandonment – of *The Making of Americans* in 1911: a discovery linked to the awareness that there "are discontinuous, disjunctive modes possible in the same person."[41] That this awareness and its playful effects becomes conceptualized through the name of "genius" can be interestingly seen in a literary portrait that Stein wrote at the very end of her struggle with *The Making of Americans*, from 1911 to 1912. *G.M.P.*, also called *Matisse Picasso and Gertrude Stein*, is a remarkable, difficult, and underanalyzed portrait that appears to concern three figures explicitly linked, in the author's imagination, to the quality of "genius." Yet the text is notable less for its representational qualities than for its aesthetic experimentation, less for being a portrait of "genius" than for presenting the *practice* of "genius" – the possibilities and dynamics of which would thereafter provide the impetus for Stein's aesthetic explorations.

G.M.P. has long proved particularly resistant to categorization.[42] Like other works of this period – *A Long Gay Book* or *Many, Many Women* – *G.M.P.* is a massive and heterogeneous text that is neither generically nor stylistically consistent. The two distinct linguistic styles of the text, as well as its two titles – one clearly referential (*Matisse Picasso and Gertrude Stein*), the other refusing nominal specificity (*G.M.P.*) – only further this impression of a text "in process." Initially, to be sure, the text seems to be fulfilling the representational demands of conventional portraiture by foregrounding, through an insistently repeated, reduced language, the relationships, activity, and being of a central but indeterminate "he":

> He who was one and all and all were then, he and he was one and all who were some were then, he and all and he and some, they were all and he was one and all and all were then and he was one, and all and he and all were and he was one, and all were who were and all were, and he was one and he and all, and all were. They were and were not the one who was all that was what it was. He was one and was not all that was what it was. He was one. He and all and he was one. (GMP, 207)

"Although the referents are obscure," Richard Bridgman rightly observes, "throughout the first half , a 'he' is set off from 'they,' as if an innovator were being contrasted with a group."[43] In this, Bridgman adds, *G.M.P.* conveys Stein's desire to "put herself in the company of the two leading modern painters," recalling the privileged terms of association which Stein had previously established in relation to her two contemporaries: "Pablo and Matisse have a maleness that belongs to genius. Moi aussi perhaps."[44] But if Stein's earlier statement of male artistic affinity underwrites the composition of *G.M.P.*, the text itself also "overwrites" this alliance by problematizing the specificity of the figures being portrayed. Both the ambiguous title *G.M.P.* and the insistent repetition of a central masculine pronoun which lacks an antecedent suggest a curious emptying of reference in this text, as though subjectivity – even the most unique and original form of subjectivity, "genius" – can no longer be specified, but functions quite literally within a chain of generic substitutability. Here, repetition works to dismantle and proliferate referentiality. This foreshadows in remarkable ways Stein's assault on male "genius," as on the notion of "completion," in her later, playful portrait of Picasso, "If I Told Him: A Completed Portrait of Picasso" (composed 1923). With an opening repetition evocative of laughter, Stein lets fire a chain of masculine pronouns which finally merge into a kind of generic variable:

> He he he he and he and he and and he and he and he and and as and as he and as he and he. He is and as he is, and as he is and he is, he is and as he and he and as he is and he and he and and he and he. (SR, 465)

As Jennifer Ashton has recently suggested, Stein found "the means of including everyone by creating the formal conditions under which she could include anyone"; these conditions are based upon the principles of substitution and variation, of which pronouns, which have the "capacity to substitute for *anything* named" would seem to be exemplary.[45] By employing a generic "he" to represent "genius," Stein effectively deflates the apotheosis of the latter: "genius" becomes the signifier for a capacity that anyone can share (an idea she would develop more fully in her later "autobiographical" writing). At the same time, this act of deflation, of emptying out the referential act at the moment of describing "genius," can be seen as anticipatory of a larger aesthetic turn.

Halfway through *G.M.P.*, in the midst of a 216-word paragraph, the following lines appear: "undertaking creation is destroying filling . . . and emptying filling is creating action" (GMP, 215). At about the same moment in the text, in anticipation of the style that would find its fullest expression in *Tender Buttons* (composed 1910–12), the text begins to experiment with a proliferating, vibrant, and chaotic admixture of nouns, verbs, and adjectives. A single sentence from the end of the portrait is representative of this shift: "Tooth cake, teeth cake, tongue saliva and more joints all these make an earnest cooky" (GMP, 278). Like a nursery rhyme, the phrase "tooth cake" neither describes nor represents but plays nonsense against the "sense" of the absent phrase "tooth ache," "creating action" through the difference that emerges from variant combinations of phonemes. The same can be said of "teeth cake," a playful variation on "tooth cake" which also insistently foregrounds phonemic metathesis (from \oo\ to \ee\). Both "ungrounded doublings" evoke images of "opaque similarity,"[46] of various and indeterminate pleasures (the sweetness of taste, the satisfying action of mastication, the seduction of a smile, and so on). The same play of differences permeates the unexpected pairing "earnest cooky," a phrase that elicits a variety of associations (alliterative, semantic, syntactic) but that remains irreducible to determinate significance. The effect of this sentence as a whole is not to void meaning or association, but to "creat[e]" semantic, syntactic, and semiotic "action" or "fulfillment" through "emptying filling," a paradoxical idea that denotes both the solicitation and deferral of significance. "Emptying filling" in fact fittingly describes the textual process of "genius," a dynamic process of simultaneous naming and un-naming through which meaning and referentiality are placed in productive, sudden confrontation with the indeterminate. A process, furthermore, whose endpoint is always elliptical: for what can be "filled" can always be "emptied," what can make "sense" can also make "nonsense," and vice versa.

In "Woodrow Wilson" (composed 1920) Stein would announce that "[w]ords are shocks," serving as pointlike eruptions within the conventional structures of grammar, syntax, and meaning (UK, 111). In uncannily proleptic terms, William James in 1890 would also describe the entry of the "unhabitual" into language in terms of *shock*:

> Usually the vague perception that all the words we hear belong to the same language and to the same special vocabulary in that language, and that the grammatical sequence is familiar, is practically equivalent to an admission that what we hear is sense. But if an unusual foreign word be introduced, if the grammar trip, or if a term from an incongruous vocabulary suddenly appear, such as 'rat-trap' or 'plumber's bill' in a philosophical discourse, the sentence detonates, as it were, we receive a shock from the incongruity, and the drowsy assent is gone.[47]

For James, "shock" is the effect of a disruption in the habitual or automatic stream of thought, an event that he elsewhere links to the faculty of "genius."[48] In *G.M.P.*, the shock of a doubling like "earnest cooky" lies in its suddenness, in its negation of the linear stream of "sense" which the structural form of the sentence is meant to convey, in much the same way as the geometric layering of a cubist painting fractures "surface homogeneity." Hence Stein's famous assertion that her portraits were doing in writing what Picasso was doing in painting, a claim that has particular relevance to the second half of a portrait dedicated to the relationship between the two artists.[49] Where the first half of *G.M.P.* may be offering a representation of "genius" – however much this representation may itself be problematized by generality and abstraction – the second half of *G.M.P.* can be said to be engaged in the practice of "genius," that process of "talking and listening," of writing "in the act of being written." The effect of this practice is a text existing always on the borderland of "sense," marked by sudden eruptions of the unexpected, by shock:

> If the best full lead and paper show persons and the most mines and toys show puddings and the most white and red show mountains and the best hat shows lamp shades, if it is the sterns are sterner and the old bites are bulging and the best the very best of all is the sunshine tiny, is the hollow stone grinding, is the homeless wedding worrying. (GMP, 278)

Here, one imagines Stein watching herself as she writes, registering the moment-to-moment changes of this process as new semantic, syntactic, alliterative, and visual possibilities present themselves; "emptying" words of their conventional "filling"; trying to balance "recognition" and "play"; eschewing continuity, direction, and memory; privileging the experience of shock; always "listening" to herself "talking." So ends *G.M.P.*, an ending that suggests the distance Stein has come from the scientific work and the typological enterprise, from the conventions of narrative or poetic structure as from the symbolic and epistemological constraints of paternal law.

Yet in the textual and authorial freedom suggested by the second half of *G.M.P.*, questions of literary hermeticism and of the impenetrability of "works of genius" arise. In the "playful" process of "watching herself write" to which *G.M.P.* bears witness, Stein is clearly taking pleasure in the process of composition as it happens, in the immediacy of writing, in being an audience to herself. Yet where does this leave the reader, the "outside" audience? Perhaps more than with any other writer, Stein's reader enters into this disruptive, unsettling modernist text with a sense of belatedness, of having arrived after the combustive experience of "writing being written" is over. While Stein's most experimental texts continue to this day to shock us with their disjunctions, they also foreground the temporal disjunction between the moment of writing and the moment of reading, refusing the intimacy of revelation through which readers might imagine themselves proximate to an originary moment of inscription. Indeed, such texts relentlessly foreground the fact that "a written sign," as Derrida argues, is "a mark which remains" after the act of writing, a remnant of some moment "irremediably lost."[50] In a crucial sense, Stein's investment in the notion of "genius" to describe her practice of composition only serves to further this impression of belatedness in the reader, as though the process of "talking and listening" were the province of a singular mind in conversation with itself, not with a public or an "outside." By entering into the high modernist discourse of "genius," the problem of audience for Stein becomes crucial. Yet in fact, it is precisely Stein's modernist appropriation and revision of the concept of "genius" to describe an open-ended dialogic process that carves out a new kind of space for the reader, one in which possibility, immediacy, and indeterminacy go hand in hand.

Notes

1. Schmitt quoted in Bohrer, *Suddenness*, 50.
2. While Stein herself claimed that the novel was written between 1906

and 1908, archival evidence suggests that the period of the text's composition was in fact much more attenuated. I am following the chronology established by Leon Katz in his Introduction to Stein, *Fernhurst*, ix-xlii.

3. The source for this parable is Aristotle's *Nichomachean Ethics*; for a discussion, see Bridgman, *Stein in Pieces*, 66–7.
4. Wagner-Martin finds textual evidence in Stein's notebooks for the hypothesis that both Stein and her sister Bertha may have been sexually abused by family members ("*Favored Strangers*", 25). She also notes that Stein's relatives were "angry over her depiction of their family in *The Making of Americans*" (211).
5. Excerpt from *The Making of Americans* quoted in "The Gradual Making of The Making of Americans" (LIA, 140).
6. Wendy Steiner's interrogation of the genre of Stein's work is useful here; she writes that "the early novels [*The Making of Americans*, *Q.E.D.*, and *Three Lives*] are more accurately termed descriptions of character and character relations" (Steiner, *Exact Resemblance*, 162). Steven Meyer also draws a fluid boundary between Stein's "scientific" and "literary" work, suggesting that her intent in *The Making of Americans* to understand and describe "the whole of anyone from the beginning to the ending" represents an effort "which she had been refining since her undergraduate experiments in automatic writing at the Harvard Psychological Laboratory" (Meyer, "Introduction" to Gertrude Stein's *The Making of Americans*, xxiv).
7. The 35-page first draft of *The Making of Americans* is included in Stein's *Fernhurst, Q.E.D., and Other Early Writings*, 137–72.
8. Leon Katz, personal correspondence with the author.
9. "There are then the two general kinds of them, the attacking kind the independent dependent kind of them, the resisting kind the dependent independent kind of them" (MOA, 344).
10. Katz, "The First Making," 285.
11. Derrida, "Signature Event Context," 320. Derrida reminds us that it is the function of repetition to displace rather than to ground authority; repetition indeed demonstrates that "there are only contexts without any center of absolute anchoring" (320). Stein's effort to ground her narrative upon a calculus of "bottom natures" would seem at odds with her Derridean recognition as *The Making of Americans* unravels that the process of repetition disrupts and even *destroys* the fiction of "absolute anchoring."
12. The development of the book after the Martha Hersland chapter is not, however, linear. As Dydo's chronology makes clear, Stein inserted a section from the earliest draft of the text into the middle of this chapter (MOA, 432–41). This section then ends with an apology for its own obsolescence: "[S]ome then have a little shame in them when they are copying an old piece of writing where they were using words that sometime had real meaning for them and now have not any real meaning in them to the feeling and the thinking and the imagining of such a one" (MOA, 441). For a discussion of this episode, see Stein, *A Stein Reader*, 19.

13. DeKoven, *Different Language*, 68. DeKoven's brilliant evocation of Stein's "lively words" has provided a suggestive model for subsequent critics to apprehend the terms of Stein's dissociation from nineteenth-century literary modes.
14. Stein would restate this claim in various forms throughout the 1930s. See also the lucid explanation in "How Writing is Written," an address delivered at the Choate School on 12 January 1935: "The question of repetition is very important. It is important because there is no such thing as repetition. Everybody tells every story in about the same way. You know perfectly well that when you and your roommates tell something, you are telling the same story in about the same way. But the point about it is this. Everybody is telling the story in the same way. But if you listen carefully, you will see that not all the story is the same. There is always a slight variation" (HWIW, 158).
15. This suggestive term is used by Marta L. Werner in an essay on the late Dickinson: "'Most Arrows': Autonomy and Intertextuality in Emily Dickinson's Late Fragments," 56.
16. Bohrer, in *Suddenness*, argues for "the sudden as a central perceptual category of modern consciousness" (45).
17. See Moore, *Gertrude Stein's* The Making of Americans, 77–8.
18. From an autobiographical sketch Stein wrote (for purposes of publication?) in 1923, discovered in the Yale University Collection of American Literature, Beinecke Rare Book and Manuscript Library. In her 1935 lecture "Portraits and Repetition," Stein writes that *The Making of Americans*, alongside "Proust" and "Ulysses," represents "the important things written in this generation" (LIA, 184).
19. Esther Newton has argued that for Djuna Barnes, Radclyffe Hall, Romaine Brooks, and to a certain extent Stein, the adoption of masculine mannerisms and dress were compensatory measures designed to resist Victorian norms of femininity and to signal an eagerness "to join the modernist discourse and be twentieth-century adults" (Newton, "The Mythic Mannish Lesbian," 564).
20. Stimpson, "The Mind," 497–8.
21. Bürger, in *Theory of the Avant-Garde*, articulates two central elements of the problem of autonomy: "the detachment of art from the praxis of life"; and "the obscuring of the historical conditions of this process as in the cult of genius, for example" (40).
22. The phrase is taken from Alvin Langdon Coburn's photographic series, *Men of Mark*, found in Stein's personal library. See Ch. 4, 127.
23. Stein's reading of Nietzsche and Schopenhauer is evident from her unpublished correspondence with Mabel Weeks; her personal library, donated to the Beinecke Rare Book and Manuscript Library at Yale University, contains many volumes by Carlyle as well as Goethe's *Autobiography*. Ulla Dydo discusses Stein's reading of Lombroso, James, and Weininger in light of her "fascination with the idea of genius" in "To Have the Winning Language," 6. References to "genius" or the "genial type" in the notebooks to *The Making of Americans* are numerous, and often accompany lists of selected names: Balzac, Zola, Christ, Lincoln, St Francis, the Cleveland Grant, Pablo,

and of course "me" (see in particular NB, B).

24. Toklas comments from personal correspondence of author with Leon Katz. Curiously, Toklas would later disavow Weininger's impact on Stein, perhaps reflecting, as Katz suggests, an effort to present Stein as an originative genius, unfettered by "influences."
25. Weininger, *Sex and Character*, 81; 83.
26. Ibid., 83.
27. See Sengoopta, "Science, Sexuality, and Gender."
28. "That thing of mine of sexual nature and correlative mind I think works absolutely" (NB, B-25). Katz, however, warns against over-literalizing Weininger's influence on Stein: "Weininger's terms enter into the complexities of Stein's own systematizing terms, which twist and turn his in novel directions" (personal correspondence with author). For Weininger's own "borrowing" of terms from Cesare Lombroso, see Nancy A. Harrowitz, "Weininger and Lombroso: A Question of Influence," in Harrowitz and Hyams (eds), *Jews & Gender*, 90.
29. Weininger, *Sex and Character*, 320.
30. Weininger quoted in Ritchie Robertson, "Historicizing Weininger: The Nineteenth-Century German Image of the Feminized Jew," in Cheyette and Marcus (eds), *Modernity, Culture and 'the Jew'*, 24.
31. Weininger, *Sex and Character*, 2.
32. Ibid., 303.
33. Gertrude Stein met Alice B. Toklas in September of 1907; in the spring of 1908 Stein's notebooks bear witness to the extent of Weininger's influence on the understanding of her future lover: "She is low clean through to the bottom crooked, a liar of the most sordid unillumined undramatic unimaginative prostitute type, coward, ungenerous, conscienceless, mean, vulgarly triumphant and remorseless, caddish, in short just plain low..." (NB, DB-95–6). In *Sex and Character* Weininger had forwarded the idea that W, the category of Woman, could be subdivided into two dominant and opposing types: the mother and the prostitute (215). Both are thoroughly imbued with sexuality, Weininger insists, but the mother is selfless and animalistic, bestowing her love indiscriminately, and "ranks intellectually very low," while the prostitute is of a "higher" form, a "human phenomenon," and almost noble in her shamelessness: "the prostitute has forsworn all social respect and prides herself in her freedom. The only thought that disturbs her is the possibility of losing her power" (228). This difference explains the fact that "[g]reat men have always preferred women of the prostitute type," for "only those men are sexually attracted by the mother-type who have no desire for mental productivity" (226); genius is expressed through intellectual, not physical, issue. While the mother may appear to have more social legitimacy than the prostitute, therefore, the latter type is the fitting counterpart to the great man.

    In the notebooks, Stein repeatedly refers to Alice B. Toklas as the "prostitute type," and equates her with May Bookstaver, Stein's first, fruitless romantic interest: "her sexual base is May, the elusive, finer purer flame of the prostitute" (NB, B-5). In this equation, Stein positions herself as Alice's sexual opposite, as her ideal counterpart: "I think people generally find their sexual kind that is their kind of the two kinds [alike and opposing] the most important to them for friendship, except for the complete passional relation . . . Mabel Weeks more May still more Alice . . ." (NB, J-20). Along with being her "opposite," Alice is also imbued with great powers of conquest: "she cares more about loving than about me, that is she cares more about having completely possession of loving me than of loving me" (NB, H-8), a possibility that Stein "resists" yet reciprocates. For Stein also casts her own desire into a drama of heroic proportions: "My attack on Alice is like Grants on Lee and that is the essential character of the unaggressive complete egotist, always a forward pressure, often suffering fearful loss . . ." (NB, C-46). This epic struggle articulates a relationship which diverges sharply from the conventional, public image of Toklas as helpmate and faithful support to Stein, but one whose dynamic makes sense within Stein's larger, Weininger-inflected framework of self-definition. Alice as prostitute complements Stein as male genius; in accepting the definition of sexual complementarity of types which Weininger promotes in *Sex and Character*, there need be no other rationale for sexual desire, even same-sex desire.

34. Weininger writes, "In all cases of sexual inversion, there is invariably an anatomical approximation to the opposite sex" (*Sex and Character*, 45). Inevitably, therefore, female inverts will in the crucial respects of "sex" and "character" be seen to act like heterosexual men, finding other women sexually desirable, and reflecting a "higher degree" of intellectual, moral, and social development than heterosexual women. In short, "homosexuality in a woman is the outcome of her masculinity and presupposes a higher degree of development" (66).
35. "The whole encrustation of Stein's ideas and feelings in her writing from 1908 to the end of her life emanate from Weininger's envisioning of the highest 'type' of human being" (Katz, "The First Making," 279–80).
36. Katherine Arens, "Characterology: Weininger and Austrian Popular Science," in Harrowitz and Hyams (eds), *Jews & Gender*, 128. Weininger praised Nietzsche as a genius and in particular for his representation of "the woman problem" (*Sex and Character*, 342–3). For Nietzsche's influence on Weininger in general, see *Jews & Gender*, *passim*.
37. Weininger, *Sex and Character*, 110–11.
38. Ibid., 110.
39. Ibid., 113.
40. Ibid., 183.
41. Steiner, *Exact Resemblance*, 41–2.
42. Ruddick notes *G.M.P.*'s failure of "intellectual definition" and its "resistan[ce] to sustained interpretation" (*Reading Gertrude Stein*, 157); Wineapple claims that it "labors under a glut of non-meaning" (*Sister Brother*, 367); and Bridgman, despite acknowledging that it represents the summation of Stein's intellectual and artistic concerns at this period,

categorizes the text as "her soporific work *par excellence*" (*Stein in Pieces*, 119).

43. Bridgman, *Stein in Pieces*, 119.
44. Ibid., 119.
45. Ashton, "Gertrude Stein," 323; 325.
46. I borrow this term from Henry Sayre ("The Artist's Model: American Art and the Question of Looking like Gertrude Stein," in Neuman and Nadel (eds), *Stein and Making*, 30). Peter Quartermain writes that "[t]he energy of this [Stein's] writing comes from the ways in which the tension between referentiality and its lack becomes a structural principle: Indeterminacy of meaning enables grammatical movement and pattern to become a principal means of coherence" (*Disjunctive Poetics*, 26).
47. James, *Psychology*, 253.
48. For a discussion, see Ch. 1, 28.
49. Stein, *Picasso*, 16. But for an important qualifier to this assertion, see Marianne DeKoven, "Gertrude Stein and Modern Painting: Beyond Literary Criticism," in Hoffman, *Critical Essays*, 171–83.
50. Derrida, "Signature Event Context," 317.

Part II

Congenial Fictions

3 "Masterpieces of Yes": Talking and Listening in "To Call It a Day" and "Forensics"

Reading.
Is reading painful.
When one has not the habit of reading reading is not painful.
(UK, 13)

Up to this point, we have explored the dimensions of Stein's early efforts at naming and defining her authorial position, however much this position is ultimately marked by change, process, and nonclosure. Through a chronological analysis, we have seen that Stein's act of naming herself a "genius" also signals the emergence of a mature modernist aesthetic marked by the dynamic process of "talking and listening." In the chapters that follow, we shall consider the implications of this emergence for what Stein often referred to as "the outside": her perceived or imagined audience, as well as the social and national context within which she was writing. If "high modernism" is, as Fredric Jameson has suggested, characterized by "strategies of inwardness, which set out to reappropriate an alienated universe by transforming it into personal styles and private languages,"[1] then Stein's adoption of the label "genius" to mark her move into a complex and difficult aesthetic is highly significant. For to call herself a "genius" would therefore seem to authorize not only an authorial position but a mode of expression disengaged from the alienated world of the everyday, as from the conventions of ordinary language. "Genius" thus would come to stand in for the aesthetic demands and dimensions of a high modernism in which, as Bob Perelman writes in *The Trouble with Genius*, "to be an artist means using a separate language."[2] Extending the implications of Jameson's point, Perelman implies that the idea of "genius" functions for the modernist artist as "an alibi for full social participation,"[3] effecting and indeed sanctioning the estrangement of the artist's voice from any but herself; for "[t]he knowledge a genius possesses cannot be translated outside the precincts of genius."[4] Outside these precincts lies "the world as audience" but *not* "the world as phenomena"; with Stein's work "questions of its social trajectory remain."[5] Or as Mike Gold put it rather more harshly in a review from the 1930s, "In Gertrude Stein, art became a personal pleasure, a private hobby, a vice."[6]

To mark Stein as "disengaged" and "unreadable," or to dismiss her as "hermetic," an "egotist" placing untenable demands on the reader, is nothing new; even a cursory glance at reviews of her work as it began to reach an American audience around 1913 reveals a public response amounting to outrage.[7] For a more sympathetic contemporary reader like Perelman, "[d]espite her insistence that the meaning of her work was as obvious and immediate as the words of her explanations, her writing was obviously unusual and obscure."[8] The texts of Stein's most fertile and experimental period, beginning with the portraits produced during the final years of *The Making of Americans* and culminating in the lyrical works of the 1920s and 1930s, prove particularly intractable, leading Perelman to ask whether "understanding was finally a very significant issue" for Stein. Adopting the label of "genius," Perelman suggests, freed Stein "from ordinary occupation . . . from ordinary senses of size . . . from ordinary sequence."[9] Ironically, this self-distancing from the "ordinary" can itself become a form of public distinction, as the critic Susan Schultz has recently suggested. For Schultz, Stein courts linguistic "obscurity" as a form of "self-advertisement":

> The unreadable text is less a text, in the usual sense, than an icon – less an act of communication than of bravado . . . [It] becomes a commodity through which Stein can buy the label of genius, and become famous less for what she writes than for the fact that she writes so obscurely.[10]

Jameson's contention that the institution of high modernism becomes "visible" at Stein's moment is telling here: what matters is less the meaningfulness of the text itself than the fact that the text reflects modernist "difficulty," as well as the heroic "struggle" of the writer against the banalizing forces of social modernity.[11] From this perspective, Schultz's argument makes sense: Stein's cultivation of "unreadability" accompanies her claims to "genius"; both create a market value that insures fame and the circulation of a (difficult, complex, anti-bourgeois) "image," if not a dedicated readership.

"Above all," Wayne Koestenbaum writes, "one must remember this about Stein: *she did not care.*"[12] Koestenbaum wants to register a sense he gets from his reading that "Stein is so assured of her genius . . . that she can rest content with platitudes, with vague phrases that point to objects but don't plumb or describe them"; her goal is not to represent the world to the reader but to reside within her own, hermetic universe, "the flat, non-undulating geography of contentment."[13] In a statement that seems to summarize these various accounts of Stein's disconnection from the social, Janet Flanner comments retrospectively that Stein "wrote for no one but herself. Why she didn't consider anybody else on earth. You might as well have been illiterate as far as Gertrude was concerned. She was writing for Gertrude Stein."[14] Interestingly enough, Flanner's words echo in contradictory ways a phrase from the very text through which Stein arrived at the recognition that she was a "genius," *The Making of Americans*. There, at the beginning of the Martha Hersland chapter, Stein notes famously that "I am writing for myself and strangers. This is the only way that I can do it" (MOA, 289). For Stein, Flanner may be half right: hers is an aesthetic founded upon the pleasures that attend the construction of the self in writing, the pleasures of penning "some history of me" (MOA, 662). At the same time, Stein notes, "I want readers so strangers must do it" (MOA, 289), announcing unabashedly her eagerness for a public outside the bounds of the familiar or the familial. And while Stein's appeal for readers may seem disingenuous, or simply self-serving – as the comments of both Koestenbaum and Flanner suggest – many readers have taken issue with this assessment, finding Stein's most *un*familiar texts to be remarkably open to interpretation precisely in their seeming inaccessibility.

The difficulties experienced by Koestenbaum, Flanner, Perelman, and others can be contrasted with the following assessment of one of Stein's most seemingly "hermetic" works by contemporary critic Peter Quartermain:

> [T]he writing is remarkably accessible. To figure out what's going on in works like 'A Little Novel' [1926] the only thing you need besides a knowledge of the language (as you might have got it from learning to speak it) is to have been to a social gathering of some sort. The writing, that is to say, demands very little acculturation of its readers.[15]

The "knowledge" of an unacculturated subject "learning to speak" a language: what could be simpler, less "obscure" than this? For Quartermain, Stein's writing, precisely in its refusal to foreground authorial intentionality, is a model not of obscurity but of all-embracing democracy:

> [F]or if the work of art, the writing, is to be of the twentieth century and American, available to everyone in that land of immigrants, no matter what their education, culture, origin, or acculturation, then the work must carry within it its own history, and there can be no hierarchies of meaning except for those that reside within the text itself . . . By this logic there cannot be a single meaning of the text, for to provide that is to empower the author over the reader, and to falsify experience.[16]

The poet John Ashbery puts the matter more succinctly: Stein's texts, he suggests, provide "a general, all-purpose model which each reader can adapt to fit his own set of particulars."[17]

General and democratic; or the "private language" of "genius"? Like the apocrophyl figure of Melanctha, the Steinian text refuses the gaze that would know it. Stein's act of calling herself a "genius" to describe a seemingly coherent authorial position only redoubles the confusion. When Stein announces in *Portraits and Repetition* (1935) her aesthetic credo – "One may really indeed say that that is the essence of genius, of being most intensely alive, that is being one who is at the same time talking and listening" (LIA, 170) – a radically demotic version of "genius" emerges, of an authorial position, and a textual practice, that is decentered and dialogic, open-ended and collective. But when in the same breath Stein writes that "[i]f the same person does the talking and the listening why so much the better" (LIA, 170), then the opposite vision emerges of the artist engaged in a solitary and hermetic conversation with herself. Here, as Albert Cook has recently noted, "'dialogue' bears the mark of obsessive monologue."[18]

In the end, the problem of "genius" for Stein lies in its capacity to authorize contradictory authorial positions. On the one hand, "genius" provides *the* term of legitimation for aesthetic "autonomy" and an attendant social withdrawal; "talking and listening to oneself" by definition is a process that needs no confirmation from an "outside." It is also an immediate and immanent process, one which happens as the writer watches herself write: a process linked to Stein's lifelong emphasis upon the "continuous present" and to her notable indifference toward revising her texts after they had been written.

Insofar as it emerges at the instant of writing, the "being" of "genius" must presumably wither once the process of composition is over, just as the text that formed this immediate experience must, once made, represent for the "outside" only the trace of an originary achievement. From this perspective, the high modernist text and the high modernist "genius" can be seen as mutually constitutive, both coming into "being" at the moment of composition, yet both thus ceasing to exist in any vital way after this moment has passed. Stein acknowledges this temporal, linguistic, subjective problematic in "What Are Master-Pieces" (1936): "nothing could bother me more than the way a thing goes dead once it has been said" (WAM, 154). On the other hand, as the previous chapters have tried to suggest, Stein always imagined her unhabitual acts of perception and linguistic revitalization to be in dynamic tension with the everyday, the typical, the habitual, the "normal." As such, her description of the "being" of "genius" as "talking and listening," as a fluid and inconclusive conversational dynamic – even as a hermetic conversation – by definition foregrounds the possibility of "outside" engagement, of the dispersal of the text that articulates this "being" across boundaries and hierarchies. Despite the temporal and spatial disjunctions which this engagement poses to the modernist writer, "talking and listening"has the potential to inscribe the reader into its dynamic: as, for example, when the reader "listens" to the text and "talks back" to it in the act of interpretation. To this extent, the Steinian text can be seen as a heteroglossic meeting-point between different categories of "being," performing, signifying: the site of plural, shifting, and ongoing engagements in which anyone, potentially, can "be in it."

Interestingly, this idea of "genius" as a potentially shared capacity recalls the Romantic definition of the term. For despite its relationship to originality and uniqueness, to the transcendent individual, the Romantic notion of "genius" was also invariably associated with the idea of transmission – both receptivity and expressivity. Weininger at one point refers to "genius" as an extraordinary receptivity to sensation akin to impregnation, an idea indebted to Hegel's discussion, in "Imagination, Genius, and Inspiration," that "one usually understands 'genius' as meaning the self-centered totality of the mind, in so far as it exists on its own and consists of the subjective materiality of another who is only delimited externally as an individual."[19] Kant, too, would employ the maternal metaphor in describing "genius" as an "innate mental aptitude" upon which nature impresses the rules of fine art.[20] These accounts of the essential receptivity of the capacity of "genius" are often linked in Enlightenment discourses to the figure of the educator and exemplar, as when Friedrich Schlegel describes the genius-artist as

> someone who carries his centre within himself. Whoever lacks such a centre has to choose some particular leader and mediator outside of himself, not, to be sure, forever, but only to begin with. For a man cannot live without a vital centre, and if he does not yet have one within himself, then he can only seek it in another man, and only a man and a man's centre can stimulate and awaken his own.[21]

Like Schlegel, Kant would characterize "genius" as an exemplary faculty "which others may use to put their own talent to the test, so as to let it serve as a model, not for *imitation*, but for *following*."[22] And Nietzsche, in "Schopenhauer as Educator," would write that every human being "bears a profound yearning for the genius within himself"; but the recognizable genius is one who

> reveal[s] to you the true primordial sense and basic stuff of your being, something that is thoroughly incapable of being educated and cultivated, but something that in any event is bound, paralyzed, and difficult to gain access to. Your educators can be nothing other than your liberators.[23]

Hence despite the fact that the notion of "genius" remains to this day the privileged signifier for an essential, original (and self-originating) individuality abstracted from the realm of the social, certain philosophical writings on the subject suggest that "genius" is also a term of contingency, defined within a relational framework and through networks of receptivity and transmission. As we shall see in Chapter 5, Stein would eventually come to focus almost wholly on the contingent and transmittable aspect of "genius", describing it as a capacity or faculty or even an identity that "everybody" could share. This latter notion is located in a conception of the text as radically open, in which any reader can find his or her interpretive and re-visionary way through an infinitely suggestive web of signifiers. From this perspective, simply to enter into the Steinian text – simply to read – is perforce to share in the experience of "genius."

I

Among a series of attempts in the mid-1930s to define what she meant by "being a genius," Stein would offer the following:

> Nothing makes any difference as long as some one is listening while they are talking. If the same person does the talking and the listening why so much the better there is just by so much the greater concentration. One may really indeed say that that is the essence of genius, of being most intensely alive, that is being one who is at the same time talking and listening. It is really that that makes one a genius . . . I say I never repeat while I am writing because while I am writing I am most completely, and that is if you like being a genius, I am most entirely and completely listening and talking, the two in one and the one in two and that is having completely its own time and it has in it no element of remembering. Therefore there is in it no element of confusion, therefore there is in it no element of repetition. (LIA, 170; 180)

In this description, Stein deconstructs the singularity of "being," the uniqueness of "genius," and the univocality of linguistic production. "Being a genius" describes a textual "being" that is split, decentered, and processual, a "type" that is always in excess of typological containments. The model for this idea of "genius" is clearly the conversation: that "some one is listening while they are talking." As with a conversation, "being a genius" is fundamentally relational – "the two in one and the one in two" – and is realised through an immediate, potentially limitless linguistic exchange; this relationality is in turn, paradoxically, "the essence of genius." The parallel construction of Stein's formulation plays on the double senses of "being" as noun and participle, as at once the state and the ongoing process of existence, and "genius" as both type and what eludes typification. This parallelism suggests that "genius" represents something one "is," but only dialogically and in process. Whether one achieves this "being" through exchange with another subject or through "talking and listening" to oneself, the result of this process is to exist within a unique temporal and textual framework that "has in it no element of remembering . . . of confusion . . . of repetition," free from the subjective demands of memory or repetition which attempt to harness the self into a coherent entity and which provide, as "Normal Motor Automatism" puts it, the "feeling of a personality."

In commenting upon Stein's work, Jean-François Lyotard offers a way to describe this shifting, fluid process of Steinian "genius":

> No "subject" receives it [the Steinian phrase], in order to interpret it. Just as no "subject" makes it (in order to say something). It calls forth its addressor and addressee, and they come take their places in its universe.[24]

For Lyotard, there exists no substantive "subject" outside the site of enunciation who precedes and controls, or receives and "understands," signs.[25] Rather than the text being the effect of transcendental authority, the inverse pertains: the Steinian text viewed through a postmodern, Lyotardian lens is a discursive structure which "calls forth" reading/writing positions, calls them forth as arbitrary and contingent effects of *its* processes. M. M. Bakhtin's account of dialogue as the fundamental "orientation" of language is also applicable here. For Bakhtin, any rhetorical act is always already inscribed in a relationship to another: "every word is directed toward an *answer* and cannot escape the profound influence of the answering word that it anticipates."[26] Feminist critic Harriet Chessman has shown what this means for Stein, arguing that the Steinian text offers "a poetics of dialogue, where dialogue presents an alternative to the possibility of patriarchal authoritarianism implicit in monologue, reliant upon the privileging of one voice, one narrator, or one significance."[27] In Chessman's view, Stein's modernist rehabilitation or subversive citing of the quality of "genius" as "talking and listening" suggests "a general and shared phenomenon";[28] the implication is that Stein's invocation of "genius" poses a challenge to the power structure of "patriarchal authoritarianism" in which univocality predominates over polyvocality and difference. Finally, Ellen Berry has shown how Stein's texts invert a conventional hierarchy of active writer/passive reader by encouraging exploratory readings that are both open-ended and multiply layered; her texts solicit the reader, not through appeal to conventional modes of "listening" – for mastery, for meaning – but by encouraging the reader to participate in the pleasures of indeterminacy, possibility, and the suspension of knowledge:

> Rather than approaching the text with our critical distance intact, expecting it to yield a solution, we must relinquish a position of mastery, linked to the affirmation and preservation of meaning, and give ourselves to the text . . . agreeing to wander where it takes us, submitting ourselves to language as Stein herself did. On the other hand, we must attempt to read carefully, alertly, with the utmost attention to every detail . . . Reading Stein's texts, then, requires a paradoxical or split act of attention – a relaxed hyperattention, an unconscious hyperconsciousness, a borderline state of awareness a little like insomnia.[29]

Berry's point suggestively recalls the central scene of authorial self-doubling recorded in "Normal Motor Automatism": the scene in which Stein writes "automatically" and at the same time watches herself engaging in this performance. By putting these automatic motions or habits on "display" – by turning them into a performance – Stein also displaces their priority and implicit authority, effectively decentering the "bottom," habitual, automatic self. Stein's most identifiably modernist writing during the 1910s and 1920s continues this dialogue with herself, exploring within an aesthetic field the self-deconstructive process of "talking and listening" initially explored in "Normal Motor Automatism." But for Chessman, Berry, Lyotard, and others, this process also defines the "relaxed hyperattention" of the *reader* of Stein's texts, who must remain both engaged and committed to the text, pursuing its indeterminacies, creating a dialogue with its disruptions, "talking" to the words on the page "as Stein herself did," while at the same time "listen[ing] very carefully to the other woman's desire."[30] The reward for this process, Berry suggests, is "the possibility that something radically different might speak," something beyond "the limits of what is currently possible, licit, or readable."[31]

Within such interpretive frameworks, Stein's somewhat unorthodox notion of "genius" as dialogue ("talking and listening") appears commensurate with a post-structuralist and feminist agenda, encompassing a critique of the fiction of the author as transcendental (phallic) signifier and of the reader as passive receptacle for a fixed meaning. Stein would often suggestively associate this dialogic process with the modernist masterpiece, as in a phrase found in one of her working notebooks: "masterpieces of yes, Oh yes masterpieces oh yes, master pieces, oh yes."[32] The idea of "genius" as dialogic appears to level textual hierarchies and circumscribe a poetics that says "yes" to any reader's interpretation. Ashbery, too, reminds us that Stein's texts serve as exemplary, "general, all-purpose model[s] which each reader can adapt to fit his own set of particulars." For Ashbery the Steinian text stands as a model, displacing the expectations that adhere to both the writing and the reading process, speaking to us through *example*, not through precept, character, direct appeal, or authorial directives. Like Berry, Ashbery shows us that the position required of the reader within the Steinian universe – "a paradoxical or split act of attention" – is a position that reproduces the position of the author herself while she is engaged in the act of writing. Again, for both Ashbery and Berry, the possibility that Stein's most experimental work holds out to the reader is one of exemplarity: like

Stein, the reader too can share in the experience of "being a genius" by "talking and listening" to the text, exploring its possibilities and indeterminacies, and transcending habitual modes of perception. In an undated note to herself, Stein wrote the following words about her reader: "Being old fashioned purblind and slow the reader is often dazzled often caught in a whirl of mist often bewildered. But then again he has insights which seem more like intuitions of genius than any homelier process."[33] By allowing ourselves to be "bewildered," to be led, literally, off the straight and narrow path of habit, might we too share with Stein "intuitions of genius"?

"Any of you try it," Stein encouraged an audience in one of her 1935 lectures on narration,

> and you will see what a difficult thing it is to listen to anything and everything in the way any one is telling anything and at the same time while you are listening to be telling inside youself and outside yourself anything that is happening everything that is anything. That is what genius is to be always going on doing this thing at one and at the same time listening and telling really listening and really telling. (Narr, 34)

In the rest of this chapter, I would like to take up Stein's challenge, to "try it," responding less to the inevitable seductions of (over-) identification with the faculty of "genius" than to Stein's claim that *any* reader might perform the textual dynamics she associates with precisely this capacity.[34] And to suggest that the texts I am examining, largely unread and "experimental," are both shockingly open-ended and profoundly available, approachable from a variety of perspectives: semantic, grammatical, narrative, historical, even visual or spatial. If "listening" closely to these texts while "talking" back with possible, partial interpretations, doubts, queries, insights is what it means to "be a genius," then anyone, as Stein suggests, can "be in it."

II

"To Call It a Day" (composed 1924), a text from early in Stein's "landscape" period,[35] begins like this:

> A description of the scarecrows and monuments of the war in and near Belly [sic] which is in Bugey, which makes part of the department of the Ain, a department in the East of France and equidistant from Chambery Lyon Grenoble and Bourg in Bresse,

> Bresse is the department which has become famous for chickens. (TCD, 243)

Seemingly straightforward, if somewhat prolix, this statement on closer inspection serves as an unsettling introduction to the text. While presenting itself as a "description," the text rather appears to be posing the question: what is a description? Conventionally, to describe is to transpose into words a clear visual or mental image of something: here, the landscape of a certain area in southeastern France. But the restless movement within this paragraph – its symphonic pileup of dependent and independent clauses punctuated by a single comma – suggests that the transposition of a primary object (the landscape) into a secondary form (the literary description) is neither straightforward nor hierarchically fixed. Rather than *representing* the landscape, the text in fact appears to be *generating* it through a syntactic logic which quickly forces the reader's attention to the movement of signifiers rather than to the production of significance. This logic is based upon syntagmatic relations (which bear on the possibility of combination), and can be diagrammed in the following way: every place-name (Belly – significantly misspelled in the printed text – Bugey, the Ain) must be followed by a preposition which situates the place within another system of relations; hence, Belly is "in" Bugey, which is "part" of the Ain, which is "in" the East of France and "equidistant" from four other places. This logic appears to have an infinite range, for the possible systems of relations between a place and its surroundings could continue indefinitely – as the final clause seems to be suggesting. With "Bresse is the department which has become famous for chickens," Stein abandons the strictly geographical matrix of reference and invokes another relational context (reputation rather than location), in so doing opening out the conditions of possibility for continuance (chickens are known to peck, pecking is a form of eating, etc.). As Stein would put it in *Lectures in America*: "And so description is really unending" (LIA, 156).

But it is worth noting as well that the last clause of this paragraph disrupts the strict terms of a previous syntagmatic logic, as though the text had suddenly refused to continue according to its "habitual" descriptive pattern. We are suddenly wrenched from greater to smaller things, from geography, monuments, and war to birds and their concerns ("scarecrows"). Peter Quartermain refers to this kind of "shocking" disjunction in the text as a moment in which "the writing begins to comment on its own procedures."[36] One could also see this disjunction in the terms with which this study has been concerned: as part of the process of "genius," in which the writer, having "listened" to herself develop a syntactic pattern verging on the automatic, begins to "talk" back to herself. The sudden reference to poultry which appears at first to be a digression from the main subject of the paragraph (geographical location) can thus be seen instead as a "suddenness" that arrests the continuance of the prior subject.[37] It is this kind of immediate and necessarily emphemeral resistance to the habitual or automatic in language that Stein so clearly wants to enshrine as the primary practice of "genius." Yet this is also a radically open-ended practice. "Description is really unending" since there will always be a "listener" ready to take up the task of "talking" back to the text, of leading the text in a direction different from its habitual paths – whether this listener be a reader or the split-subject of the writer "watching herself write."

That this text is centrally concerned with the disruptive, unhabitualizing, open-ended process of "genius" is exemplified by its richly layered title. "To Call It a Day" initially evokes the clichéd expression "let's call it a day," meaning "let's finish what we're doing," or "let's go home." For Stein, however, clichés – habitual, codified uses of language; signifiers of the daily – are always the springboard for imaginative rearticulations, for sudden explosions of the unhabitual. Thus in the *carnet* which Stein used during the composition of "To Call It a Day" one finds interspersed between literary text and love notes to Alice the following shopping list (Fig. 3.1):

> Rousset
> Vernis Copal and brush.
> Camel yellow and kitchen matches.
> flowers. 5.80
> say it with flowers.
> 1 lb. of papers.
> letters.

Stein's *carnets* frequently include such marginal jottings: addresses, reminders, shopping and "to do" lists. As such, the *carnets* reveal a blurring of the lines between composition and rumination, the artistic process and the process of daily life. Under "flowers. 5.80" Stein writes "say it with flowers," an advertising slogan that has no place in this list other than being called up through association with the thought of flowers. Yet some seven years later, this phrase would appear again in a text with a title of the same name.[38] What this

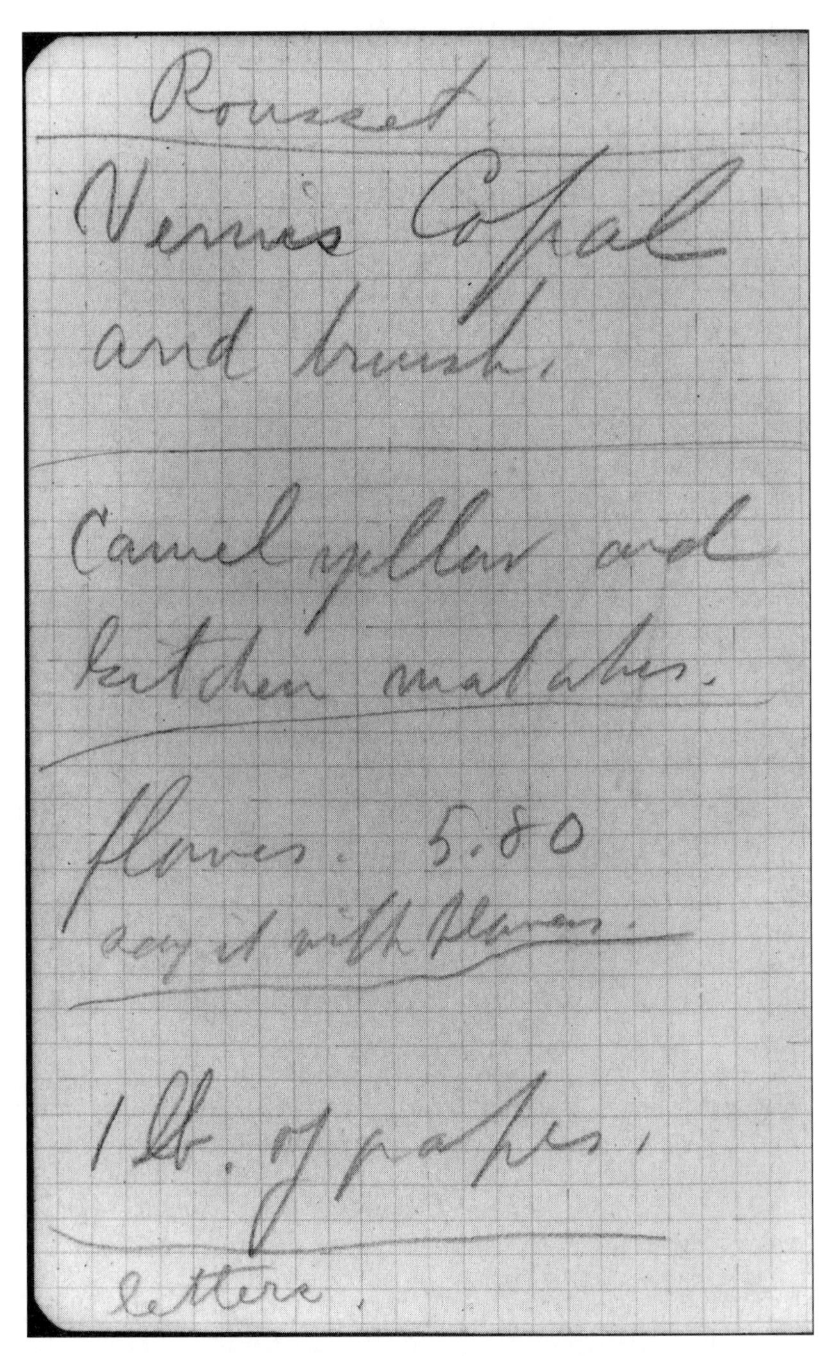
Rousset

Vernis Copal
and brush.

Camel yellow and
kitchen matches.

flowers. 5.80
say it with flowers.

1 lb. of grapes.

letters.

Fig. 3.1 Carnet *with shopping list (1924)*

suggests is not only the retentiveness of Stein's mind but that the material for her literary investigations often arises out of the "habitual" or "automatic" background of everyday life – advertisements, household objects, the exchange of clichés that makes up the texture of the quotidian. In *Everybody's Autobiography* (1937), Stein writes of her trip to America, "There on the road I read buy your flour meal and meat in Georgia. And I knew that that was interesting. Was it prose or was it poetry I knew that it was interesting" (EA, 254). Like "buy your flour meal and meat in Georgia," "Say it with flowers" belongs to the the world whose features were beginning to dominate the twentieth-century American landscape, the world of advertising and consumption which was also the world of women's work and pleasures, as Stein was well aware.[39] Stein's achievement is to reappropriate these worn clichés for the modernist aesthetic, and – as many critics have shown – for women, by revitalizing the terms of daily life. Hence the "objects," "food," and "rooms" of a work like *Tender Buttons* belong both to the "feminine" realm of the domestic and of shopping, *and* to the realm of desire, language, and the body. For Stein, then, the quotidian constitutes the material out of which the unhabitualizing, dialogic, open-ended practice of "genius" can emerge; it is the ordinary, the everyday or the normal that contains within it the potential for the extraordinary, the queer, the singular.

From this perspective, the effort "to call it a day" becomes highly complex. What *is* a "day," and what multitudes does "it" contain? What kind of transformations can be brought to bear on dailiness by the practice of "genius"? Joyce's *Ulysses*, a narrative that takes place over the course of a single day, had presented "dailiness" as the site where the habitual and the unhabitual merge, the site of banality and transcendence, triviality and myth. In "To Call It a Day," written two years after the 1922 Paris publication of *Ulysses*, "dailiness" is also at issue, conceivably as the fulcrum through which Stein grasps the impact of the recent World War on the landscape of Belley, France: "dailiness" as a way to encompass "scarecrows" and "monuments of war" within the same physical and textual space. Such, arguably, would also be the point of Stein's later memoir on daily life in occupation France, *Wars I Have Seen* (1945). Yet such contextualization need not and indeed cannot be definitive, as the second paragraph of the text suggests:

> To call it a day is it necessary is it necessary to call it a day in order that there was nearly such a description that before it had been ascertained that the direction in which she was looking and at a

> distance, in that case in the other direction there might easily be three. Three or more makes a hundred as four are nearly equally there. In this way no doubt. (TCD, 243)

In the phrase "to call it a day," "it" appears to function in a semantically neutral way, as in the conventional sense of "let's call it a day"; the same could be said of "it" in the propositional phrase that follows: "is it necessary." Each of these phrases, taken separately, has an entirely normative status in the English language; each comprises a semantic cluster within which the signifier "it" has a purely empty function. Yet when these two phrases are combined along a syntagmatic axis ("to call it a day is it necessary"), lexical and syntactical complexities begin to proliferate. The second "it" now seems no longer part of a propositional phrase but a pronoun with an anaphoric function: that is, pointing backward in the sentence to a correlated antecedent. But to which antecedent? The first "it"? The phrase "to call it a day"? The complete text that bears the same title? Meaning lies in the antecedent we choose to privilege; yet each choice is *potentially* viable. If we take the second "it" to be pointing to the first, then the text seems to be asking whether the signifier "it" is "necessary" for the act of calling or naming something (such as "a day"); the implication is that "it" perhaps gets in the way of naming, that because of its multiple functions, "it" obscures reference, blurs meaning. The paradox is that we arrive at this interpretation through the anaphoric specificity of the second "it." Likewise, if we take this second "it" to be referring back to the expression "to call it a day," the issue then becomes one of the specificity of "it." Why call "it" a day? Why call "it" anything other than what "it" is? "To call it a day is it necessary" pits paradigmatic relations (governing the selection of words in a sentence) against syntagmatic ones (governing the combination of words), by presenting an act of substitution (it/day) whose necessity is simultaneously called into question by the text.[40] Stein would later articulate her need to "know that [things] were there by their names or by replacing their names" (LIA, 235) paradoxically suggesting that language is both mimetic and generative, that language both substitutes for the world and *is* the world. Yet this paradox in turn unsettles any coherent position from which words can be spoken/received or written/read; meaning or representation works both within and against syntax and grammar.

The phrase "to call it a day," like the quotidian itself, becomes in the Steinian text the source of multiple possible meanings which each reader can reread anew, can "adapt to fit his own set of particulars."

As the paragraph proceeds, these possibilities only further multiply. "[I]s it necessary to call it a day in order that" sets up the expectation that whatever follows this phrase will in some way illuminate the necessity of "call[ing] it a day." What follows, however – "there was nearly such a description" – suggests that the necessity of calling or naming "it" is no longer the point; rather, what now seems to matter is the fact that description *almost* occurred (when? in the first paragraph?) and that this fact had bearing upon what happened "before" a spatial orientation that remains indeterminate ("it had been ascertained that the direction in which she was looking"). This orientation, in turn, becomes the point of both departure from and contrast to the following phrase: "and at a distance, in that case in the other direction there might easily be three." Here, the text seems to have come to a tentative conclusion again through some indeterminate act of choosing ("in that case"), a conclusion that affirms what an earlier text (*G.M.P.*) had denied: "there is not a number that is three." In "To Call It a Day" "there" might be "three" if we imagine the former to be a misspelling of the latter; or "there" might be "three" if "there" is taken as an pronoun used to introduce a clause (*there* might be *three* (scarecrows? monuments?) standing in the field). Given Stein's proclivity for playful self-referentiality, this phrase might be seen as an ironic response to the composition entitled *G.M.P.*: "there might easily be three" monuments/geniuses, but if we look at these monuments "in the other direction," the three might appear to be scarecrows. Or this final phrase may be an internal response to the orthographic variation of "Belly": "Belly" might be "Belley" if we want to read this text as a "description" of place, although "in the other direction" – in the direction of otherness – "Belly" might be a private reference to the topography of the lesbian body ("Lifting Belly").[41] In any event, the text suggests, the possibilities of mutation from one signifier to another (there to three) can take place only "in the other direction," in the direction of the Other; for the text itself refuses to illuminate interpretive directionality.

It is perhaps appropriate to refer to the Steinian experimental text as "a blur of indeterminacy."[42] This is an indeterminacy of meaning – the significance of these sentences simply cannot be definitively determined, although the text seems to accomodate us however we approach it – and of structure, for the really interesting aspect of this second paragraph, like that of the first, is the abstract syntactical pattern it develops and then "suddenly" drops as it proceeds. Following the opening structural palindrome ("to call it a day is it necessary is it necessary to call it a day"; a complete pattern in itself[43]), the text proceeds through rhythmic shifts of semantic register which follow the conjunction "that" ("is it necessary to call it a day in order that"; "there was nearly such a description that"; "before it had been ascertained that"). What disrupts this rhythmic, visual, and syntactic pattern is the conjunction "and" ("and at a distance"), after which "that" ceases to function as a conjunction but as a pronoun ("in that case"). Consequently the text announces that a new direction has been perceived in relation to the mutation of signifiers ("that" changes from a pronoun to a conjunction; "there" changes to "three"). What is liberated by the disruption of the pattern of "'that' clauses" is "otherness" – as though Stein had tired of the "direction in which she was looking," and indeed needed to put this word-patterning "at a distance." This development echoes the development of the first paragraph, which established a syntactic pattern of dependent clauses only to find its progress arrested by the "sudden" final clause. In the second paragraph, similarly, Stein "listens" to herself "talking" until a pattern has been established, then disrupts this pattern by a series of syntactical, grammatical, and lexical moves which signal "the other direction" she is preparing to take.

In reading the first two paragraphs of "To Call It a Day" this closely, I have attempted to suggest how complex the process of "reading" becomes in a text which supposes, as Rachel Blau DuPlessis puts it, "just about any language manipulation that can be postulated."[44] Admittedly, to read with the kind of concentrated attention demanded by the Steinian text is perforce to read extremely slowly; hence to attempt a "full" reading of a text like "To Call It a Day," which is less unique than representative within Stein's œuvre, would easily fill an entire critical study. This, despite the fact that the piece is only eight printed pages long. Yet every word requires the same degree of deliberation from the reader that Stein has clearly enlisted in the act of composition; every word that we "listen" to asks that we "talk" back to it by exploring the semantic plurality and lack in the absence of any controlling authorial presence. In the *carnet* containing the earliest version of the text only the first two paragraphs are written out, as though the author herself could approach the open-ended text in microcosm only (Fig. 3.2). Containing this text, exhausting it, writing it out fully, is impossible; the only "whole" that this writing proffers is the linguistic unit (the word, the sentence, the paragraph) within which, as we have seen, description and reference remain both multiple and indeterminate.

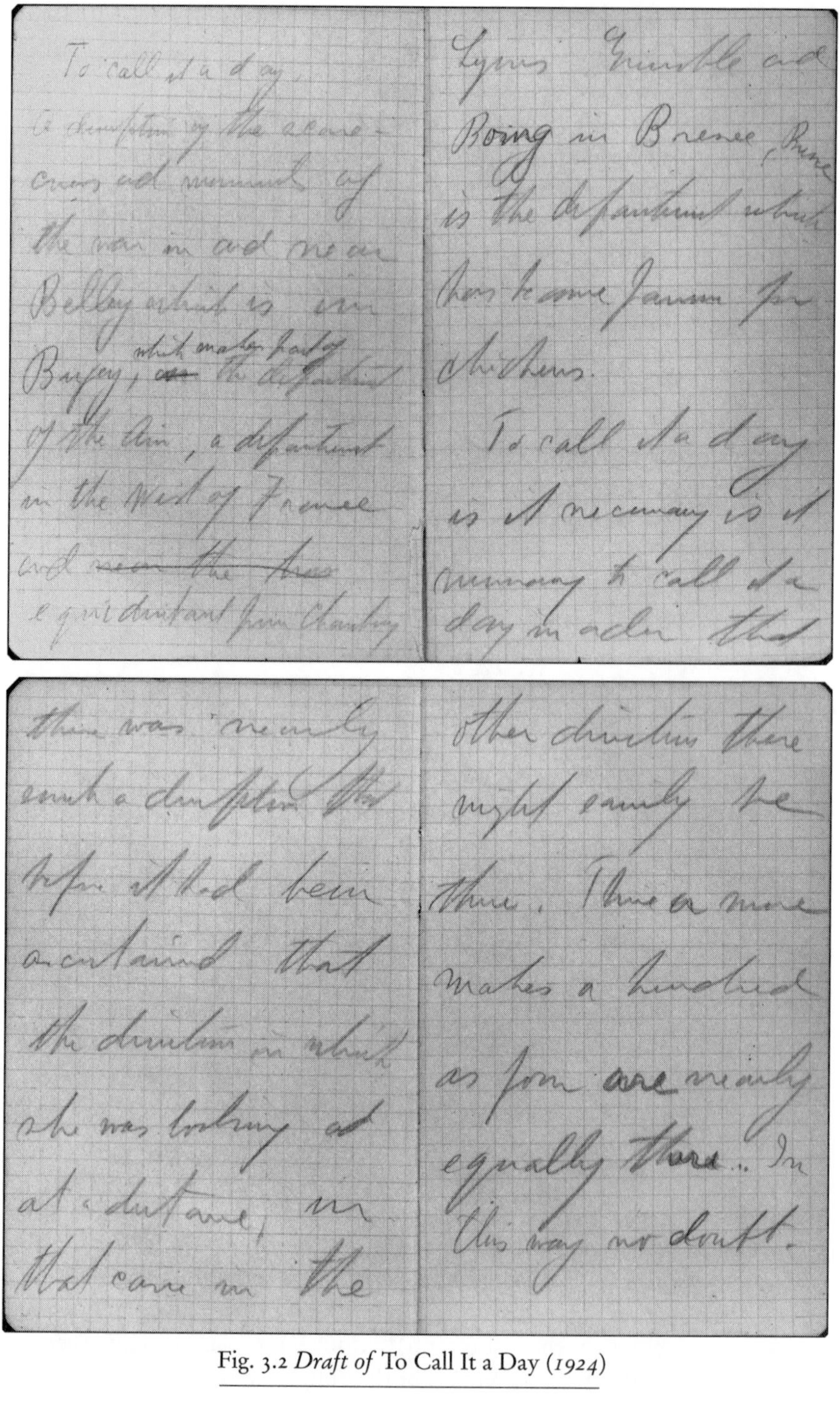

Fig. 3.2 *Draft of* To Call It a Day (*1924*)

In the last chapter, I argued that Stein, in the midst of *The Making of Americans*, begins to take as the subject of the text herself engaged in the act of writing. The self-estranged, de-essentialized authorial subject that emerges from *The Making of Americans* has much in common, I have argued, with the subject that is the focus of Stein's early scientific work: a subject divided between "automatic" behavior and a passive, watchful "consciousness without memory." And it has much in common, as well, with the dynamic interchange that Stein would later call "genius," an interchange between the productive yet unrestrained generator of text ("talking") and an "extra" consciousness that is engaged and critical, watching and "listening." Yet while in *The Making of Americans* "talking and listening" seems to entail the recursive practice of simultaneous functions on the part of a single subject (as in Wendy Steiner's suggestive description of "someone talking into a microphone connected to ear phones which he is himself wearing"[45]), the question I have raised in this chapter is how the reader fits into this immediate and self-reflexive process. Stein would herself struggle with this issue in "Composition as Explanation" (1926), noting that "[t]he quality in the creation of expression the quality in a composition that makes it go dead just after it has been made is very troublesome." This, she writes in indirect acknowledgment of the problem of audience, "is always a fear a doubt and a judgement and a conviction" (SR, 502). Yet arguably what a text like "To Call It a Day" insists upon is that the reading reader *replicate* the process experienced by the writing writer; that in reading the experimental Steinian text readers must perforce both "make" and "unmake," both "talk" and "listen" to what they are reading, precisely because the text refuses to register any single symbolic containment. "Anybody can say so" reads the last sentence of "To Call It a Day" – a declaration that the text belongs as much to us as to Stein, and as much to anybody else as to us. By "listening and talking" to the Steinian text, the reader too can participate in its composition, though not with any finitude; indeed, this is the demand the text places upon the reader. But this demand has its rewards as well: "that is if you like being a genius" (LIA, 180).

III

Given the profound resistance to directing the reader's gaze in "To Call It a Day," Stein's decision several years later to entitle a collection of eight short pieces *How to Write* (composed 1927–31) seems more than a little surprising, as though her textual experiments could be distilled into a series of easily applicable rules, principles, and formulas. By invoking a popular American genre (the self-help or "how-to" book), Stein's text purports to offer a straightforward guarantee – buy this book and you too can be a modernist genius![46] Yet while the "how-to" formula is contingent for its success upon the transmission of expertise, Stein's text unseals this pact with the reader by voiding the centered authorial position from which "knowledge" can be delivered. In this, *How to Write* represents another form of the paradoxical "explanations" of her work that Stein was beginning to offer the public in the late 1920s. Written in the same period as such "explanatory" texts as "Composition as Explanation," *The Autobiography of Alice B. Toklas*, and the lectures that would be delivered in America, *How to Write* is a text that works to decenter the authorial position while taking on the guise of a popular explanatory handbook.

Yet Stein's "how-to" book has much in common with the genre to which it makes reference if one considers that the origins of this genre lie in the production of models of living from which the reader can learn to better or "make" himself. From John Bunyan to Cotton Mather, Benjamin Franklin to Thomas Jefferson, early modern writers and intellectuals influenced by Reform and Enlightenment ideals had sought to convey the value of individual effort through texts which offered personal exhibits as exemplary testaments to worldly and spiritual achievement. An instance of this genre from colonial America is George Fisher's oft-reprinted volume, *The American instructor: or, Young Man's best companion* (1748), which billed itself as a complete manual for how to perform all the necessities of life "without the help of a master":

> Containing, spelling, reading, writing, and arithmetick, in an easier way than any yet published; and how to qualify any person for business, without the help of a master. : Instructions to write variety of hands . . . How to write letters on business or friendship. Forms of indentures . . . releases, &c. : Also merchants accounts, and a short and easy method of shop and book-keeping. : Together with a method of measuring carpenters . . . and painters work . . . : Likewise the practical gauger made easy . . . and some general observations for gardening every month in the year. : With instructions how to pickle and preserve; to make divers sorts of wine; and many excellent plasters and medicines, necessary in all families. : A compendium of the sciences of geography and astronomy. Also some useful interest-tables.[47]

Fisher's book offered a range of practical advice; his contemporary and publisher Benjamin Franklin extended this model to the particulars of the self in his enormously popular *Autobiography* (1794). Franklin encouraged the reader to apprehend not only the "considerable Share of Felicity" in Franklin's past, but "the conducing Means I made use of, which, with the Blessing of God, so well succeeded" in order that the reader "may find some of them suitable to their own Situations, & therefore fit to be imitated." Franklin's text in fact blurs the distinction between "autobiography" and "how-to" guide in presenting the self, including the personal past, as something to be remade, recreated, shaped and improved through the will of a controlling authority. This possibility is encoded in the function of the "I" in Franklin's text, which is presented both as the central term around which all lived events circulate, and as a literary device subject to continual revision.[48] As such, the *Autobiography* underscores both the singularity of the self and its mutability. The rationale behind this dual emphasis is not necessarily narrative but rather a function of pedagogical imperatives: that his text prove *useful* for the reader; that it function as a secular version of the life of Jesus, one of the historical personnages Franklin most desired to emulate.[49] In keeping with this goal, the *Autobiography* positions the "I" as a link on a chain of emulation, both singular and generic, a model "fit to be imitated" to which anyone can apply himself.

How to Write represents a modernist version of Franklin's *Autobiography*, both grounding itself in authorial exemplariness and refusing in turn the essentialism or exceptionalism that would substantiate the exemplar. As this chapter has suggested, the Steinian text offers new ways to think about the role of the literary "model" in the experience of writing/reading, one not contingent upon a central or centering authority that would ensure the transmission of expository advice and knowledge. Here, again, Stein's affiliation with and transformation of the notion of "genius" to describe not the transcendental, unitary "I" but a modernist process of "talking and listening" is crucial. If "being a genius" might be seen as what gives Stein the authority to write *How to Write*, then it is also for Stein descriptive of the process whereby this authority becomes decentered and divided, hence potentially available to anyone. As I have suggested throughout this chapter, any "listener" or "reader" of the Steinian text is also by definition a "talker" or a "writer," helping to create and mold the text's interpretive possibilities.[50] Where Stein departs from the Franklinian model is in her refusal to locate her text in the experiences of a central "I" who precedes and authorizes textual articulation. Rather, as Lyotard has argued, the Steinian experimental text itself precedes and determines the voices of "authority" – "authority" which is thus contingent, multiple, and shifting. In this, a text like *How to Write* seems to be prefiguring another kind of literary model, the vertiginous, postmodern version of the "how-to" guide: hypertext, in which readers are compelled to find their own, necessarily partial interpretive way through an open-ended web of signifiers or "links," and in which the very structure of the medium forecloses the possibility of any final interpretive "containment."

"Forensics," the last piece in *How to Write*, both exemplifies and theorizes the pleasures of multivocality and even argumentation: "Forensics are the words which they like"; "Quarrels may wear out wives but they help babies" (HTW 387; 385). Stein, describing the dynamics of her domestic arrangement, often referred to herself as "baby" to Toklas's "wife," suggesting that the composition may have originated with recriminations between Stein and Toklas, and that it may be the source of productive feelings for the writer ("Quarrels . . . help babies"). What this argument is about remains unspecified, as do the various singular but indeterminate figures who quarrel in this piece (I/you; he/she; I/she). References to an invitation, a date, and a parlor where "they feel that they had rather not gather" suggest a dispute concerning a party and perhaps the composition of a guest-list, a dispute possibly encrypted in the text's title (forensics = four and six). Later, the dispute is located not only in the doubling of the title but in titular authority itself: "Forensics are double./They dispute a title and they dispute their trou-/ble./A title is made for defense. It did not defend/him nor did I" (HTW, 387). One possible point of "Forensics" is that anything, even the title itself, can be doubled and hence disputed; that argument, in short, renders authority or entitlement impotent. Yet while the differences evident in quarreling may cause "inconvenience and disgrace," they may also produce not entitlement, but "Enlightenment./Forensics is an argument" (HTW, 388). Here again, "talking and listening," even in the course of an argument, describes an open-ended process characterized by grammatical and syntactical disruption, representational play, and the fragmentation and multiplication of the authorial voice.

Yet the text ends with an intimation of threat on the horizon of the utopian textual world of "talking and listening": the threat of a nameless and authoritarian "they" that supplants the voices of difference through "union and organisation," "win[ning] in fusion," and a "thirst for gold" (HTW, 391; 393; 395). "Forensics is a distribution unequally," the text reads, and while this statement is one of a variety that self-reflexively posit a definition of the text's central term, its appearance close to the end of the text accompanies a turn away from inconclusive and ongoing "quarreling" and toward a grammatical and syntactical "detachment." The ending of "Forensics" follows a similar development in an earlier piece of *How to Write* entitled "Sentences," which begins "Part V" with the word "disengaged," alone and unqualified on a single line (HTW, 210). The later text seems to register a recognition that the goal of forensics is not simply the practice of ongoing debate but the triumph of one position over the other, a triumph the text figures in terms of military conquest and staccato issue: "They have authority. For all. That they want. As Their. Treasure" (HTW, 395). The "treasure" fought for and won may be that of being "in unison," of transcending division and particularity and merging into a "they" – a possibility already projected in the very first line of the text: "They will have nothing to do with still" (HTW, 385). The indeterminate "they" refuses either to be contained or to sit "still" and, if we consider "still" as an adverb, refuses to brook debate. "Advanc[ing] in volume" as the text nears its end, "They" also seal the fate of the "it" that had proved so suggestively open-ended in "To Call It a Day": "It is better to have it lost than if it had remained two." This loss of doubling is also registered within the text as a loss of possibility and of the potential of indeterminacy: "This may not be there and they will not venture not to dwell in this way more upon it." Ultimately, possibility is replaced by negation and hesitation, and by the disappearance of productive argumentation. Hence "Forensics may pale" (HTW, 394).

Stein herself had practiced the skill of forensics during her junior year in college, in a required course for all Harvard and Radcliffe undergraduates geared toward the production of "a written thesis maintaining one side or the other of a given question."[51] The turn-of-the-century Harvard writing courses, as Priscilla Perkins has recently noted, were characterized by an "uncertainty of mission" that sought to privilege the conventions of *belles-lettres* while at the same time encouraging students' rhetorical mastery over "the languages of business and the professions."[52] As the two discourses were not necessarily compatible, a central question remained: "Why and how should an educated, perhaps well-to-do, American citizen learn to write?"[53] Thirty years later, Stein would answer this question with

How to Write, a guide that parodies the Harvard fundamentals (grammar, syntax, rhetoric, argumentation) by deploying them in the service of a radically anti-authoritarian screed, an exemplary account of textual engagement "without the help of a master." Yet in the text's final, dirge-like pronouncements about "authority," "destruction," "unison," and "death," Stein's early education in forensics may serve as something like the return of the repressed. Just as arguments must be won and authority reassert itself, so must texts come to an end and the utopian project of "talking and listening" cease. *How to Write* suggests that "to write" – or "to read" – entails maintaining ad infinitum *both* sides "of a given question"; the ending of its final piece, "Forensics," suggests the patent limitations of such a project.

IV

"Let the word-man in you come forth, dance for a time," Gertrude Stein is reported to have said to friends in encouraging their active participation as readers of her texts.[54] In her 1917 work "The King or Something. (The Public Is Invited to Dance)," Stein clearly extends this invitation to the public at large. The possibility of achieving the "intuitions of genius" that Stein herself felt during the process of composition, was, she believed, also available to any reader of her texts who might be willing to explore the pleasures of the "unhabitual," to "dance for a time." In this chapter, I have attempted to trace these congenial dance-steps, to suggest how open Stein's dialogic notion of "genius" is to multiple identification and appropriation.

Envisioning the capacity of "genius" inherent in her texts as a potentially general and shared phenomenon ("talking and listening") does not necessarily differentiate Stein's aesthetic project from that of other high modernist writers. Even the very spokesman for "individual talent," T. S. Eliot, criticized in 1919

> our tendency to insist, when we praise a poet, upon those aspects of his work in which he least resembles anyone else. In these aspects or parts of his work we pretend to find what is individual, what is the peculiar essence of the man. We dwell with satisfaction upon the poet's difference from his predecessors, especially his immediate predecessors; we endeavor to find something that can be isolated in order to be enjoyed.[55]

In contradistinction to this view of isolated creative originality, Eliot famously poses the modern poet at the end of a great, interconnected chain:

> Whereas if we approach a poet without this prejudice we shall often find that not only the best, but the most individual parts of his work may be those in which the dead poets, his ancestors, assert their immortality most vigorously... No poet, no artist of any art, has his complete meaning alone. His significance, his appreciation is the appreciation of his relation to the dead poets and artists. You cannot value him alone; you must set him, for contrast and comparison, among the dead.[56]

Contemporary critic Frank Lentricchia has noted in Eliot's argument a "social hunger," a "desire for community-in-history" in which "to lose one kind of isolate, disconnected 'self' in order to find a self organically connected to a whole."[57] Such, it might also be claimed, lies behind Stein's imperatives to link the notion of herself as "genius" to a larger group or "whole" toward which she might be seen as both representative and aesthetic guide. Unlike Eliot, however, whose tortured poet dances among the tombstones and monuments of the dead elite, Stein wanted to "dance" with a living, contemporary audience liberated through her texts into an enlightened congeniality. Stein also increasingly wanted what Eliot could not abide: a "public," an audience composed of "everybody," including the great American masses and their counterfeit "culture" which both writers had left behind in expatriate flight many years earlier. Reviewing Stein's "Composition as Explanation" for *The Nation and Athenaeum* in 1927, Eliot wrote of his contemporary:

> [H]er work is not improving, it is not amusing, it is not interesting, it is not good for one's mind. But its rhythms have a peculiar hypnotic power not met with before. It has a kinship with the saxophone. If this is of the future, then the future is, as it very likely is, of the barbarians. But this is the future in which we ought not to be interested.[58]

For Eliot, Stein's "peculiar... power" lies in her affinity with the masses, and particularly the racialized masses, as his dismissive reference to the instruments and rhythms of jazz makes clear. His description reiterates the familiar, often derogatory view "that a special Jewish/black interaction had given birth to jazz."[59] Yet in sounding the same alarm about racial difference and the threat of miscegenation that his distant relative Charles William Eliot had done in discussing Jews at the turn of the century, T. S. Eliot ironically transforms Stein into the figure she herself had once created in anxious displacement: the figure of Melanctha, queer, peculiar, powerful, both "complex, desiring" and "simple[,] . . . vulgar."[60] For Eliot, Stein/Melanctha's racial primitivism heralds the dawn of a new age, an age in which "we" – fellow Europeanized expatriates and bohemian elites – "ought not to be interested": the age of an emerging, powerful, racially mixed American mass culture which would change the way both "tradition" and "individual talent" could be articulated. Increasingly, Stein herself would seek to locate the idea of "being a genius" in relation both to America and to that nervous-making modernist monolith called "the masses."

Notes

1. Jameson, *Fables of Aggression*, 2.
2. Perelman, *Trouble with Genius*, 138.
3. Gilbert, "Review of *The Trouble with Genius*," 600.
4. Perelman, *Trouble with Genius*, 150.
5. Ibid., 153; 169.
6. Michael Gold, "Gertrude Stein: A Literary Idiot," in Hoffman, *Critical Essays*, 77.
7. For an excellent review of the early public response to Gertrude Stein in America, see Curnutt, "Parody and Pedagogy." For a later response, see the embittered comments by the art collector Alfred Barnes, who felt poorly served by his representation in *The Autobiography of Alice B. Toklas*, and who wrote to Leo Stein in 1934 that Gertrude "is meat for the newspapers here and nearly always with ridicule played to the limit" (unpublished correspondence (2 November 1934), Gertrude Stein and Alice B. Toklas Papers, Yale Collection of American Literature. Beinecke Rare Book and Manuscript Library).
8. Perelman, *Trouble with Genius*, 150.
9. Ibid., 142; 154.
10. Schultz, "Stein's Self-Advertisement," 86.
11. See Jameson, "The Ideology of the Text," 56–71.
12. Koestenbaum, "Stein is Nice," 313.
13. Ibid., 308.
14. Flanner's comments appear in an unpublished typescript of filmed interviews conducted by Perry Miller Adato for a 1970 NET program on Gertrude Stein. Located in the Gertrude Stein and Alice B. Toklas Papers, Yale Collection of American Literature. Beinecke Rare Book and Manuscript Library.
15. Quartermain, *Disjunctive Poetics*, 41.
16. Ibid., 43.
17. John Ashbery, "The Impossible," in Hoffman, *Critical Essays*, 105.

18. Cook, "Some Notes," 100.
19. Hegel, *Encyclopädie der Philosophischen Wissenschaften*, 353 (paragraph 405). Weininger writes, "The woman is impregnated not only through the genital tract but through every fibre of her being. All life makes an impression on her and throws its image on her child. This universality, in the purely physical sphere, is analogous to genius" (*Sex and Character*, 233).
20. Kant, "On Genius," 224.
21. Schlegel, "From *Ideas*," in Simpson, *Origins*, 197–8.
22. Kant, "On Genius," 226–7.
23. Nietzsche, "Schopenhauer as Educator," 190; 174. See also John Stuart Mill's *On Liberty* (1859): "Originality is the one thing which unoriginal minds cannot feel the use of. They cannot see what it is to do for them: how should they? If they could see what it would do for them, it would not be originality. The first service which originality has to render them, is that of opening their eyes: which being once fully done, they would have a chance of being themselves original" ("On Liberty," 92).
24. Lyotard, "Gertrude Stein Notice," in *The Differend*, 67.
25. "[T]he very prinicple that one ought to treat a work as an object of ownership may constitute a wrong (as when it is not recognized that the 'author' is its hostage)" (*The Differend*, xi).
26. Bakhtin, *The Dialogic Imagination*, 280.
27. Chessman, *The Public Is Invited to Dance*, 3.
28. Ibid., 221, note 7.
29. Berry, *Curved Thought*, 18.
30. Ibid., 25.
31. Ibid., 27. Cyrena N. Pondrom similarly notes in Stein's "experimental" period "the loss of immediately paraphrasable meaning for the traditional reader; Stein's texts of this type bear the burden of quite literally teaching the reader a new reading practice. It is this new reading practice, with its absence of linearity or climax, its polyvocality, its lack of an authoritative paraphrase outside of the act of reading, and hence its immediacy (as it is re-created differently in each new reading) that is of critical importance for Stein" and clearly, also, for the reader ("An Introduction to the Achievement of Gertrude Stein," in Stein's *Geography and Plays*, xxxvi).
32. Stein, Carnets. In a late lecture entitled "What Are Master-pieces and Why Are There So Few of Them" (1936), Stein would further deconstruct the essentialist notion of the "masterpiece" by stressing its graphic fragmentation ("master-piece"). In questioning "why [there are] so few of them," Stein argues for a difference in degree, not kind, between the "master" and "anyone" – a difference of the former's ability to exist within the immediacy of the text, "to be able to talk and listen to listen while talking and talk while listening" (WAM, 148–56).
33. Unpublished ms., Gertrude Stein and Alice B. Toklas Collection, Yale Collection of American Literature. Beinecke Rare Book and Manuscript Library.
34. For insightful comments on the fantasy of identification with Stein, see

Brian Selsky, "I Dream of Genius," in Doyle, Flatley and Muñoz (eds), *Pop Out: Queer Warhol*, 180–90.

35. The term is Stein's, arising, according to DeKoven, "from her involvement with the Rhône valley country around Belley, where she and Toklas began to spend their summers in this period, and also, of course, from her intimate acquaintance with landscape painting. But the literary principle of 'landscape' has less to do with landscape painting, or with the quality of the Rhône valley countryside, than with Stein's notion of intensity of movement as the central interest in genuine twentieth-century writing . . . A landscape is an integrated whole, all its parts existing, as Stein says, 'in relation, one thing to the other'" (Dekoven, *A Different Language*, 123–4). For a discussion of American "landscape" writing, see also my Ch. 4, *passim*.
36. Quartermain, *Disjunctive Poetics*, 34.
37. See Ch. 2, note 16.
38. Stein, "Say it With Flowers. A Play." (1931), *Operas and Plays*, 331–43.
39. In "Flirting at the Bon Marché," an early portrait written during *The Making of Americans*, Stein notes the seductions and illusions of shopping for middle-class women: "[the] shop is a place where every one is needing to be finding that there are ways of living that are not dreary ones, ways of living that are not sad ones, ways of living that are not dull ones, ways of living that are not tedious ones . . . [C]ertainly shopping is in a way interesting, certainly it is not changing the living they are having, the way of living in which they are living" (Stein, "Flirting," in her *Two*, 354).
40. The paradigmatic/syntagmatic distinction is further elucidated by Jonathan Culler: "syntagmatic relations bear on the possibility of combination; paradigmatic relations determine the possibility of substitution" (Hawthorn, *Glossary*, 185).
41. Belley is spelled correctly in both the *carnet* and the *cahier* of "To Call It a Day." Whether Stein authorized the later "misspelling" in the printed text is indeterminate. In other places, "Belly" is clearly an erotic nickname for herself or Toklas: "Belly is leaving/her home or at/any rate where she is." (Stein, Carnets.)
42. Quartermain, *Disjunctive Poetics*, 36.
43. This pattern has an additional spatial dimension in the manuscript text of "To Call It a Day." There, Stein creates a chiastic alignment, visually reinforcing the uncanny doubling (and undoing) of the original proposition.

    To call it a
    day is it necessary
    is it necessary to
    call it a day in

44. DuPlessis, "Woolfenstein," in Friedman and Fuchs (eds), *Breaking the Sequence*, 102.
45. Steiner, *Exact Resemblance*, 44.
46. The 1975 Dover edition of *How to Write* in fact markets the book as part of its "Language Books and Records" series, among such titles as "Learn Dutch" and "German: How to Speak and Write It." Patricia

Meyerowitz's "Preface" attempts to set the unsuspecting reader straight while also articulating an important statement about Stein's mode of composition: "this book will have no immediate meaning to you because it certainly does not tell you how to write. What it does tell you is how Gertrude Stein was writing at the time that she wrote it . . . [I]ts meaning is contained within its method and moment of creation" (HTW, v).

47. Fisher, "Advertisement," in his *The American instructor*.
48. "[W]ere it offer'd to my Choice, I should have no Objection to a Repetition of the same Life from its Beginning, only asking the Advantages Authors have in a second Edition to correct some Faults of the first" (Franklin, *Autobiography*, 3).
49. "Moral Virtue 13: Humility. Imitate Jesus and Socrates" (ibid., 92).
50. This in turn allows us, as Jacques Lezra perceptively writes, "to construe the expression 'How to Read How to Write' appositionally, as . . . two parallel, infinitive expressions" (Lezra, "How to Read," 117).
51. "Forensics," *Oxford English Dictionary*, 621. The *OED* makes a specific notation about this "college exercise" at Harvard.
52. Perkins, "'A Little Body'," 531.
53. Ibid., 531.
54. Stein cited in an unpublished clipping by Sherwood Anderson, Gertrude Stein and Alice B. Toklas Papers, Yale Collection of American Literature. Beinecke Rare Book and Manuscript Library.
55. Eliot, *Sacred Wood*, 40.
56. Ibid., 41.
57. Lentricchia, *Modernist Quartet*, 278.
58. Eliot, "Charleston, Hey! Hey!," 595.
59. Rogin, *Blackface, White Noise*, 58.
60. According to Manju Jain, Charles William Eliot was the third cousin once removed of T. S. Eliot's grandfather (*T. S. Eliot*, 25).

4 Genii Locorum: Expatriate Resolutions in *Useful Knowledge*

No use for Stein to fly to Paris and forget it. The thing, the United States, the unmitigated stupidity, the drab tediousness of the democracy, the overwhelming number of the offensively ignorant, the dull nerve – is there in the artist's mind and cannot be escaped by taking a ship. She must resolve it if she can, if she is to be.

(William Carlos Williams)[1]

Enlightenment and Romantic discourses on "genius" were often inseparable from the emergent modern European discourse of nationalism. Exhibiting a heightened degree of intellectual and cultural development and potency, the "genius" could serve as the standard-bearer of collective consciousness, as the enlightened representative of a people's aspirations. Hegel wrote of the "world-historical individual" that "the nations flock to his standard, for he reveals to them and carries out what is already their own immanent impulse" (1830).[2] Schlegel referred to the man of great character as having "[t]he power and the tact, not merely to attach men to himself, but also to unite them among themselves in a new political creation; to communicate and impart to the being thus united and new formed, a life of its own . . ." (1796).[3] Mme de Staël merged woman, "genius," and nation into the mythical firgure of "Corinne, or Italy" (1807), whose "flights of genius" mirror the glory and strength of her nation. And in 1798, Novalis referred to the nation simply as "Genius to the second power."[4]

For the young Gertrude Stein, however, the nation – and specifically, America – was precisely what needed to be transcended in order for "genius" to emerge. After abandoning her medical studies and leaving America in 1903, Stein would find in the European metropolis a space of freedom from nationalist imperatives, a place of difference, shock, and discontinuity in the interstices of which new identities could be experimented with, new social arrangements formulated. In the modern metropolis, as Raymond Williams has argued, "there was at once a complexity and a sophistication of social relations, supplemented in the most important cases – Paris, above all – by exceptional liberties of expression."[5] The impact of this environment would prove exhilarating to artists and writers: "[l]iberated or breaking from their national or provincial cultures, placed in quite new relations to those other native languages or native visual traditions, encountering meanwhile a novel and dynamic common environment from which many of the older forms were obviously distant."[6] In 1940, Stein herself would put the matter more succinctly: "and so there is the Paris France from 1900 to 1939, where everybody had to be to be free."[7]

The text which Stein began writing at the time of her decision to take up permanent residence in Paris – and the text through which she discovered that she was a "genius" – is, of course, *The Making of Americans*. In Chapter 2, I suggested that we read this text as a self-reflexive story of textual discovery, of the authorial "making" of Gertrude Stein over the course of several formative years of narrative exploration. But it is also crucial to attend to the place of national discourse in this process of self-emergence. As Priscilla Wald has recently argued, *The Making of Americans* "has been read in all kinds of aesthetic contexts but almost never in a cultural context, almost never in terms of her [Stein's] own relentless efforts to tell a story in and about America."[8] This "story" – the story of Americanization, of the "making of Americans" – is of more than passing interest in the text, Wald suggests, and in fact serves as a central node of "anxiety" out of which Stein's aesthetic experimentation could be said to emerge. Insofar as the opening pages of the novel present the immigrant experience as a struggle with "incomprehension," with a language and a narrative that does not fit into an officially sanctioned middle-class American narrative of assimilation, then what follows after this plot has been abandoned – the hundreds of pages of discursive struggle against the structures of grammatical and narrative coherence[9] – could be seen as a forcible extension of, rather than a departure from, this opening. The "different language" that grows out of *The Making of Americans* can, in short, be seen as the language of immigrant experience, animated by the terror and freedom of an "incomprehensibility" that is also the mark of unassimilated selfhood.

Yet if *The Making of Americans* – conceived in 1902 in London; begun in 1903 in New York; completed between 1906 and 1911 in Paris[10] – is a narrative of immigration, then it is also, patently, a narrative of expatriation: of the constraints of the American middle class not only upon foreign emigrants but also upon their first- and second-generation offspring, like Stein herself, who were looking to Europe as a place from which to escape Americanization. From this perspective, it is significant that during her struggle to complete the novel Stein's intellectual allegiance would shift away from the American "master" William James to the echt-Germanic Otto Weininger, a shift accompanied by Stein's immersion in the rich tradition of European writings on "genius," within which she would subsequently attempt to position herself.[11] Such self-transformation is prefigured early on in the novel, when the narrator melodramatically warns her readers against identification with either the family patriarch or the national *patria*:

> Brother Singulars, we are misplaced in a generation that knows not Joseph. We flee before the disapproval of our cousins, the courageous condescension of our friends who gallantly sometimes agree to walk the streets with us, from all them who never any way can understand why such ways and not the others are so dear to us, we fly to the kindly comfort of an older world accustomed to take all manner of strange forms into its bosom and we leave our noble order to be known under such forms as Alfred Hersland, a poor thing, and even hardly then our own . . . (MOA, 21)

Stein's voice, in these early passages from *The Making of Americans*, earnestly underscores the heroic nature of the turn-of-the-century American expatriate, a type characterized by Leon Katz as "the noble breed who have the courage to go their singular way,"[12] "fleeing" an America which in its emphasis on material production and consumption is seen to be stultifying to imagination and creativity. To be "singular," to lay claim to "genius," was not, for the ambitious, eager, well-traveled Stein, commensurate with languishing in the bourgeois parlors of Cambridge and Baltimore.[13] Indeed, Stein's claim to "being a genius" could only be articulated through a language – and a literal self-transplantation – in excess of America and its middle-class, late Victorian, feminine mores. It is telling that Stein's first claim to "genius" – the "Moi aussi perhaps" that she appends to her description of the genial Picasso and Matisse – is uttered in a foreign language; while English is firmly the sign of American assimilation, the French *bon mot* can inscribe a different narrative of selfhood, one that lies outside the limits of the American mind.[14] Understanding the early Stein in this way is even more relevant if, following Lisa

Ruddick, we read the term "singular" as "a cover term for her [Stein's] lesbianism,"[15] whose outward expression would find little support in the assimilationist-minded Jewish immigrant community with which *The Making of Americans* is initially concerned. The appeal to "brother singulars" can thus be seen as a call to other mannish queer friends to abandon any attempts to replicate the conformity and heterosexuality of their parents, and to follow her singular way across the Atlantic.

Yet as Ruddick has also convincingly argued, these early sections of the novel present "a collision of incompatible self-images" which problematize seemingly unambiguous distinctions between "the good" (queer, foreign, immigrant/expatriate singularity) and "the bad" (heterosexual, middle-class American conformity).[16] The following passage from the beginning of the text, for example, presents "singularity" not as something that must transcend the American context but as a capacity encoded *within* American typicality, if only potentially:

> Yes real singularity we have not made enough of yet so that any other one can really know it. I say vital singularity is as yet an unknown product with us, we who in our habits, dress-suit cases, clothes and hats and ways of thinking, walking, making money, talking, having simple lines in decorating, in ways of reforming, all with a metallic clicking like the type-writing which is our only way of thinking, our way of educating, our way of learning, all always the same way of doing, all the way down as far as there is any way down inside to us. We all are the same all through us, we never have it to be free inside us. No brother singulars, it is sad here for us, there is no place in an adolescent world for anything eccentric like us, machine making does not turn out queer things like us, they can never make a world to let us be free each one inside us. (MOA, 47)

Stein multiplies the possibilities for reading this passage through a complex doubling of her narrative voice, a grammatical blurring in which the "we" can encompass both conformist, standardized, mechanical "Americans" and eccentric, free, "queer things." The narrator (and her audience) appear to be not one or the other, but both: "[w]e all are the same all through us," yet "machine making does not turn out queer things like us." On the one hand, Americans can be said to exemplify type, to embody typicality: in their "habits" and repetitive, automatic ways of living, moving, and thinking,

Americans are like the machine-made products they covet and consume. A typology of Americans, such as *The Making of Americans* on some level aspires to be, is thus a redundancy: for to talk about Americans is by definition to talk about "type." Mark Seltzer has noted a similar logic at work in Henry James's *The American* (1876–7), a text which pre-dates *The Making of Americans* by several decades and which confronts "not so much the idea of the typical American as . . . of the American *as* the typical – of Americans as typical, general, and reproducible."[17] Turn-of-the-century Europeans had a term for this type: *homo Americanus*, produced on a great national citizenship assembly-line.[18] And within this framework "there is no place" for queer singulars who yearn for a liveliness that falls outside a mechanized, prescriptive world.

On the other hand, standardization and mechanization also function within the contrasting term of this passage, "singularity": "Yes real singularity we have not made enough of yet so that any other one can really know it. I say vital singularity is as yet an unknown product with us . . .". Surprisingly, here, "vital singularity" is figured as a "product," like "dress-suit cases, clothes and hats" – something not yet within the capacity of American manufacturing to "make" but potentially a viable American good. This is far removed from a more Romantic notion of singularity as what must transcend the American context in order to thrive; here, the economy of the market and of industrialization mirrors the economy of subjectivity, each structured according to a logic of mass production. The irony of this representation – an irony that neither James nor Stein misses – is that, after all, the "singular" self is in many ways synonymous with the "typical" American – the self-realizing, rugged individualist. But if Stein is suggesting that the "singular" American is the "typical" American – if, in short, singularity is a "type" potentially able to be mass-produced like suitcases or hats – then this in turn problematizes any neat distinctions between the "noble" expatriate who turns to Europe in order to become a "genius," and the conformist American who stays behind and becomes "a dead one."

The singularity/conformity dynamic is doubly problematized by the expatriate narrator's own implication in the mechanized, standardized system of production she is ostensibly criticizing. In this regard, her reference to "the type-writing which is our only way of thinking, our way of educating, our way of learning, all always the same way of doing," is highly suggestive. As opposed to the "natural" character of handwriting, which seems to arise as a spontaneous emission from the creative depths of an individual, the mechanics of typewriting suggest a soulless copying of text, an inscription divorced from the body, a standardized repetition of signifiers – everything that Stein, in her expatriate flight from America, may be said to have left behind in order to find her authentic self in Europe, the world of Romantic inspiration. We might recall that Stein employed a variety of women (including, most famously, Toklas) to type her texts after she had written them out by hand; while handwriting is the mark of (male, European or expatriate) "genius," typewriting is the mark of the (female, American) amanuensis. Yet the critique of typewriting in this passage is at odds with its position at the forefront of a text which will attempt to conform "every human being" into one of two kinds or types. To write about "types" or to write about Americans – which may be the same thing – is to become in a sense a type-writer, to become the *homo Americanus* of whom Stein writes in *The Making of Americans*, conforming her observations into standardized formulas and categories. In this sense, the typewriter is a central metaphor for what *The Making of Americans* is performing in its typological process: the repetitive motions and habits that reveal one's "type" are analogous to the typewritten marks on a page which conform thought into a standardized system of inscription. "Our writing materials contribute their part to our thinking," Stein's contemporary Nietzsche wrote;[19] in writing of types, and in deploying repetition as the consistent mechanism of typological essence, Stein could be seen as echoing in *The Making of Americans* the mechanical work of inscription performed in the daily typewriting ritual of Alice Toklas. But this in turn unsettles the hierarchical distinctions upon which a high modernist critique of mechanization and massification can rest.

In short, where the opening pages of *The Making of Americans* might at first glance appear to function within a melodramatic, manicheistic logic that pits "good" singularity against "bad" bourgeois conformity, "Europe" against "America," handwriting against typewriting, and the Romantic genius against the mechanized masses, these binarisms are continually undermined through a series of self-reflexive doublings and ironic reversals that preclude any single reading of what "America" means to the writer of this text. Again, the central and unanswered question of these opening pages appears to be the following: what is the relationship between the "queer," "singular" individual and the national, American context? Is this relationship one of mutual exclusion or one of mutual constitution? Stein leaves both possibilities open, and this in turn affects the text's later, densely articulated attempt to describe "everyone who was and is and will be living." For while the text subsequently metamorphoses from an explicit discussion of America and Americans into a more universal study of "everybody," it does not accordingly abandon its emphasis upon nation but simply incorporates it, as Wald suggests, into the process of narration. Where initally "America" had served as the site within which individual singularity or "difference" struggled against national and familial conformity, eventually this struggle carries over to the composition itself, with the effort by Stein to bring her typology of everybody to completion warring against her recognition of the elusiveness of individual "being," an idea that threatens to make her text "a thing without ending" (MOA, 521). Viewed from this perspective, the "different language" that emerges in the later sections of the novel can be seen not so much as the language of the unassimilated immigrant as the language of the melancholic exile – one who, in the words of Edward Said, "exists in a median state, neither completely at one with the new setting nor fully disencumbered of the old, beset with half-involvements and half-detachments, nostalgic and sentimental on one level, an adept mimic or a secret outcast on another."[20] For Stein, writing in exile about the making of Americans, the American nation is both a physical boundary and a "spiritual principle"[21] that needs to be transgressed only in order to be remembered and resignified time and again; a place of melancholic identification that in its ambivalent significance remains the source of continual (self-)discovery.

That "America" is for the young Gertrude Stein the site of melancholic identification is an interesting proposition, given Stein's notable resistance to understanding herself – or anyone else – in psychoanalytic terms. As Alice Toklas recalled, "After Gertrude read Freud on Hamlet she refused to read any more. We both read the thing in Freud on Hamlet, and that was the beginning and the end for Gertrude."[22] The "thing in Freud on Hamlet" probably refers to a passage from *The Interpretation of Dreams* (1900) that appears immediately after Freud's first description of the Oedipus complex, and in which Freud discusses Hamlet as a "repressed" version of Oedipus.[23] Freud would also in time come to see Hamlet as the epitome of the melancholic, one whose reaction to the loss of a loved object results in a degree of anxiety and obsessive self-criticism that extends beyond simple mourning: "an extraordinary diminution in his self-regard, an impoverishment of his ego on a grand scale."[24] This response, Freud writes, results from a refusal by the ego to accept the loss of an object and the corresponding attempt to "incorporate this object into itself" through identification, a process that is also intrinsic to the Oedipal phase; hence melancholia is in a sense a foundational condition in the development of identity.[25] Yet melancholia is also marked by a profound "ambivalence": "In melancholia, the relation to the object is no simple one; it is complicated by the conflict due to ambivalence," wherein "countless separate struggles are carried on over the object, in which hate and love contend with each other; the one seeks to detach the libido from the object, the other to maintain this position of the libido against the assault."[26] It is precisely this "ambivalence" that makes melancholia so hard to overcome – if indeed melancholia is not always already "constitutional" – since it reflects not only an unwillingness to accept object-loss but also an unresolved relationship to this object, now "incorporated" into the ego: "[the melancholic] knows *whom* he has lost but not *what* he has lost in him."[27]

While it is difficult to imagine Gertrude Stein on Sigmund Freud's couch, it is not so hard to see in a text like *The Making of Americans* the work of internal psychic processes – in this instance, the struggle by Stein both to "maintain" and to "detach" her libido in relation to the object lost during the process of writing the text, "America." This is apparent in the early sections of the novel, where the narrator urges expatriate flight on her "brother singulars" but also implicates her literary practice in the "typewritten" culture of which she is so ostensibly critical. It is equally apparent in the later sections of the book, composed after Stein had become an expatriate, which retain the terms of ambivalence of the earlier sections as well as their melancholic tone:

> I am all unhappy in this writing. I know very much of the meaning of the being in men and women. I know it and feel it and I am always learning more of it and now I am telling it and I am nervous and driving and unhappy in it. Sometimes I will be all happy in it. (MOA, 348)

Fluctuating between the desire to arrive at "complete knowledge" of "the being in men and women" and the difficulty and discomfort of "telling it," the narrator's ambivalence can be seen as a displacement of her earlier uncertainties over national identification and subjectivization. For it is precisely the way "the being in men and women" can be seen as both singular and conformist, as both utterly unique and conformable into "types," that so confounds the project of *The*

Making of Americans: "Every one is separate then and a kind of men and women" (MOA, 292). As we have seen in Chapter 2, *The Making of Americans* is finally caught between the ambition to conform "every one" into a type or "kind" and the recogntion that such "complete knowledge" is impossible. Uncertain, searching, endless, *The Making of Americans* speaks the position of the expatriate, "beset with half-involvements and half-detachments," as Said writes, "outside the mainstream, unaccommodated, unco-opted, resistant . . . happy with the idea of unhappiness."[28]

I

In the texts that postdate *The Making of Americans*, Stein seems resolute in her avoidance of the American theme. After 1911, Stein turns her attention to intimate literary portraits of daily life and relations in Paris, to the exploration of syntax, repetition, and "movement," and to the revisionary process of "talking and listening" engaged in by the writer watching herself write. Texts like *G.M.P.* or "To Call It a Day" effectively deconstruct the position of the singular authorial individual around whom text and meaning are seen to revolve; what emerges in the void is a matrix of "lively words" that multiply meaning and reference, allowing for a plurality of readings, a plurality of "authorizations." In "A Transatlantic Interview 1946," Stein retrospectively describes this shift away from *The Making of Americans*:

> I began to play with words then. I was a little obsessed by words of equal value . . . You had to recognize words had lost their value in the Nineteenth Century, particularly towards the end, they had lost much of their variety, and I felt that I could not go on, that I had to recapture the value of the individual word, find out what it meant and act within it. (TI, 504)

"Value," Stein writes, was a term she borrowed "largely from Cézanne," referring to the particularity or difference of an object; in her notebooks from 1909, she writes that Cézanne makes "the reality of the object count, what I might call the actual earthyness of the object the object for the object's sake" (NB, B-1). In "A Transatlantic Interview," Stein elaborates on Cézanne's breakthrough:

> Up to that time composition had consisted of a central idea, to which everything else was an accompaniment and separate but

> was not an end in itself, and Cézanne conceived the idea that in composition one thing was as important as another thing. Each part is as important as the whole. (TI, 502)

A dispersed vision, here, correlates with a separation of means from ends: while a previous realism had conceived the composition as a "means" of producing a certain, meaningful "end" ("a central idea"), in Cézanne's aesthetic all parts of the composition are meaningfully weighted. As Randa Dubnick observes, the Cézanne painting is "decentralized, with corners having as much importance as the center of the canvas," its elements functioning autonomously and in isolation from one another, as "ends" or absolute values in themselves.[29] For example, in one of the ten canvases of Cézanne's last, great series, *Le Mont Sainte-Victoire* (Fig. 4.1), painted between 1902 and 1906, there is no central, organizing perspective around which the painting revolves, despite the work's seeming commitment to the very symbol of Romantic sublimity, the mountain. Far from directing and focusing the viewer's gaze upon the Mont Sainte-Victoire, Cézanne's canvas disperses this gaze by blurring the outlines of the landscape's shapes and contours through repeated patchy brushstrokes of color. The effect is one of layered abstraction rather than "realist" representation. Gertrude Stein's "lively words" clearly share with Cézanne's work a similar decentralized vision. In the texts that postdate *The Making of Americans*, Stein writes, "I took individual words and thought about them until I got their weight and volume complete and put them next to another word" (TI, 504). The effect of this process is a work in which each word has autonomous "value" ("weight and volume") yet also exists in an endless shifting, mutating relation as part of a whole, or a "composition."

Stein's acknowledgment of her debt to Cézanne and his notion of "value" is useful in purely aesthetic and formal terms, in allowing the features of modernist "experimentalism" to be traced across various signifying media. Yet it is also possible to argue that Cézanne's influence may extend for Stein beyond the realm of the purely aesthetic and into the symbolic register of national identity. As one of Stein's earliest critics commented, "[i]t is perhaps not wholly fanciful to discern in this [Stein's] doctrine of verbal equality a remote variation upon the theme of sturdy American democracy."[30] Indeed, one could claim that the emphasis of the later work upon the "value" of each individual "part" of the composition is parallel to the emphasis in *The Making of Americans* upon the potential "vital singularity" of each American. Stein herself would make this parallelism explicit in

Fig. 4.1 *Paul Cézanne,* Le Mont Sainte-Victoire vu des Lauves *(1902–6)*

1946, in discussing her aesthetic breakthrough after *The Making of Americans*:

> I tried to convey the idea of each part of a composition being as important as the whole . . . After all, to me one human being is as important as another human being, and you might say that the landscape has the same values, a blade of grass has the same value as a tree . . . [t]here are of course people who are more important than others in that they have more importance in the world, but this is not essential, and it ceases to be. (TI, 502–3)

In this account, the relationships between Cézanne, Stein, the decentered art work and the human collectivity become more distinct. Through a series of homologies, Stein equates the object, the word, and the human being as all "part[s] of a composition": landscape, text, and nation. The modernist composition is what can contain this democratic ideal within its anti-hierarchical, decentralized frame. Since "each part is as important as the whole" in her compositions, the struggle between the singular "one" and the larger "whole" need not take place; and this has implications that for Stein extend

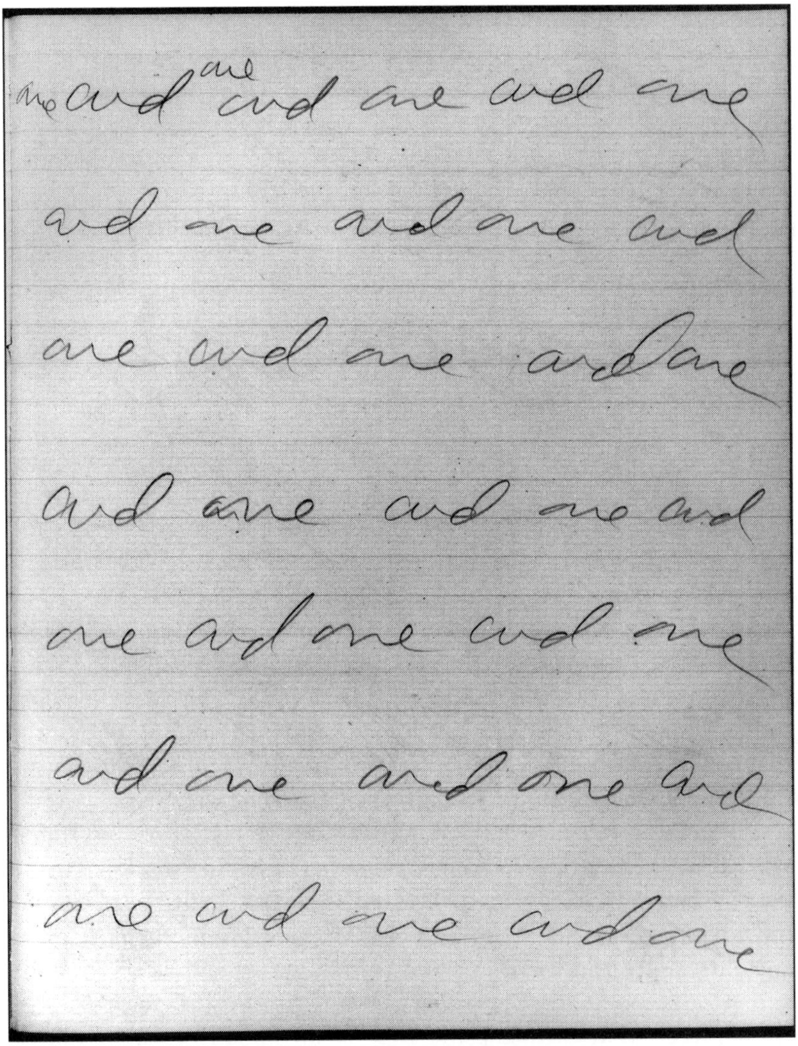

Fig. 4.2 *Draft of "An Instant Answer or A Hundred Prominent Men (1922)*

beyond the text itself. In this statement of aesthetic and ethical purpose, finally, Stein seems to be reimagining and indeed resolving the problematic she had struggled with in *The Making of Americans*: to present the "vitally singular" individual as both unique in his or her individual history and part of a larger historical framework of national or textual "making."

What this would suggest is that Stein, in her experimental work, has not abandoned her early effort to tell a story about Americans –

their conformity and their singularity – but rather transplanted these concerns into the body of the modernist text itself. One could say that Stein's concern moves from a text called *The Making of Americans* to the textual process of making her own Americans, of creating through her doctrine of verbal equality a "national text" in which each "one" is a vitally singular one and in which "each part is as important as the whole." The modernist text thus becomes a kind of ersatz nation, a "landscape" (Stein's term) that contains within its structure an ideal dynamic of individual "value" and communal inclusiveness – precisely what had been lacking in Stein's actual, lived experience. Within the modernist text, then, the "promise" of America encrypted in *The Making of Americans*' lament over "vital singularity" can at last be realized.

There are historical reasons why Stein would begin, around 1920, to revise her ultimately critical assessment of America put forward in the early pages of *The Making of Americans*. Notably, there was the impact of the Great War on Stein's own relationship to politics, national discourse, and personal identity. In "The War" chapter of *The Autobiography of Alice B. Toklas* Stein is presented in heated debate with critical European intellectuals, positioning herself as spokesperson for "understand[ing] America" (ABT, 188). *The Autobiography* hints that it was English assumptions about America's role in the war that led Stein to begin to comment upon such ideas as "the disembodied abstract quality of the american character" (ABT, 187). And while Stein's criticism of American conformity had never interfered with her efforts to find an American audience for her work, after the war she began to justify her work to disinterested editors in increasingly nationalist terms. Taken as a whole, these developments suggest a departure from the earlier stance of ambivalence toward America and Americans. And they point forward to a remarkable series of short pieces written during the 1920s, published in a 1928 volume entitled *Useful Knowledge*, which show Stein returning to the American theme with a fresh interest in rewriting the singularity/conformity dynamic.

Described by Stein in *Everybody's Autobiography* as "all the poetry and prose I had at that time done describing America" (EA, 225), *Useful Knowledge* offers many possible points of entry for an investigation of how and what "America" has come to mean for the late Stein – as a discussion of national differences ("The Difference Between the Inhabitants of France and the Inhabitants of the United States"); as an exploration of American English ("Scenes from the Door"); or as an account of war's effect on national identity ("Or

More (or War)"). But it also suggests Stein's idealized resolution of the earlier concerns that had plagued *The Making of Americans*. Where before America was presented as stifling to "vital singularity," as what needed to be abandoned in order for "genius" to emerge, in *Useful Knowledge* "America" serves as a utopian "landscape" which neither subsumes individual "value" nor abandons the larger frame that is integral to the collective. In this "national text," every "part" – whether it be a state, an individual, or a word – is as important as "the whole"; every "one" is a genial "one"; and this, Stein writes in her "Advertisement" to the text, "is the American something."

II

"Wherein Iowa Differs from Kansas and Indiana," one of the pieces in *Useful Knowledge*, resignifies the singularity/conformity problematic of *The Making of Americans* as a geographical dynamic between individual states and the larger nation that "contains" them. Like the "vitally singular" American, the state of Iowa is profoundly "different" from Kansas or Indiana; yet all three states are clearly linked to one another and thus by implication to a larger unity, "America." In a 1935 article entitled "American States and Cities and How They Differ from Each Other," Stein would clarify this idea:

> Seeing the actual territory of them of each state that is different makes you feel differently about them it is the same as meeting any one who comes from them. The people make you feel what the state is what the city is in one way and seeing the actual physical ground and country and building of the cities and the color and the lay of the land and the things growing on it and the way the city is built and the amount of water lakes rivers marshes and ponds or sea connected with it makes you feel each state as completely inside in it, it really has nothing to do with the state next to it although all of them are alike in having what they all have connected with it that is with them the habits and character of being American. (HWIW, 79)

Where in *The Making of Americans* Stein had attempted to determine the specificity of an individual as well as the larger "type" into which said individual might be grouped, here she attempts to measure the specificity of each state as well as "what they all have connected with it that is with them." While each state has "value" as an autonomous unit, having something "completely inside in it," it also is indubitably connected with something larger and more general: "the habits and character of being American." The essential point for Stein in formulating these paradoxical equations is that "difference" can exist within a larger national unity; or as she writes of a trip through America, "It is still for me a romance to be starting for all points East or West or South or North and each one of them a different city and a different state and all of them American" (HWIW, 78).

The stress on difference is evident from the opening statement of "Wherein Iowa Differs from Kansas and Indiana": "Otherwise seen and otherwise see and otherwise seen to see, to see otherwise." Locating its voice in the gap between subject and object of desire, the text seems almost a case study for post-structuralist theories of subjectivity in/as language and postmodern definitions of the nation as an "imagined community." "Seeing otherwise" might be taken, in Julia Kristeva's terms, as the process wherein the foundational negativity of signification is reinvested as a process of visual and linguistic disruption, a process that foregrounds the internal alterity of representation itself. In the development of the speaking subject, Kristeva writes, this negativity is both forgotten (in the effort, as Kristeva states, "to express meaning in a communicable sentence between speakers"[31]), and constantly reinscribed as a semiotic votility through the heterogeneity of the signifier. In modernist poetics, Kristeva writes without ever making explicit reference to Gertrude Stein, this negativity is absolutely foregrounded. Modernist writers "see otherwise" by remembering this negativity, soliciting it, stressing within language not symbolic coherence (meaning, or communication) but semiotic difference (the "gap" or incommensurability between signifier and signified). Kristeva's theory of the subject-in-language has much in common with contemporaneous postmodern notions of national identity as "an artifact rather than a tacit assumption, a purely contingent social construction rather than a meta-social universal."[32] It is the nineteenth-century French intellectual Ernest Renan who has provided an elegant equation for many contemporary discussions of national identity when he writes that "the essence of a nation is that all individuals have many things in common, and also that they have forgotten many things."[33] Imagining themselves part of a single, meaningful unity, a "nation," groups of individuals "forget" that they are in fact a collection of differences: states, cities, families, individuals, in relation to which the nation functions as a suture. To "see otherwise" within a national context, therefore, would require a mnemonic act of remembering, of reinscribing the destruction that enabled one to define conceptually "the nation" (or the state, the city, the family): the "brutality," Renan writes, that is always a prerequisite for "unity."[34]

Stein's achievement in "Wherein Iowa Differs from Kansas and Indiana" is to "see otherwise" in a complex act of remembering that liberates the internal differences within both nation and language:

> Iowa means much.
> Much much much.
> For so much.
> Iowa means much.
> Indiana means more.
> More more more.
> Indiana means more. As more.
> Kansas means most and most and most and most.
> Kansas means most merely.
> This is the difference between those three. (UK, 38)

"Meaning," here, appears to lie at the heart of "the difference between those three," although Stein's "this" is characteristically ambiguous in its lexical function. More specifically, it is the degree of meaning that seems to constitute difference – "much," "more," and "most" – and it is clearly these adjectives or adverbs or pronouns that the text wants to underscore. To claim that all states are equivalent is therefore to repress, or negate, the individual "meaning" (bottom nature?) of the essence of "Iowa," "Indiana," and "Kansas" – a meaning that the text seeks not only to remember but to emphasize through repetition ("Much much much"). Yet there is also a second order of difference in these lines, a difference of language or a "différance" that is liberated at the moment Stein's text leaves indeterminate its own signifying process. For it is precisely the fact that "much," "more," and "most" can function *variably* as grammatical and syntactical units that problematizes the text's simultaneous claims to "meaning." The function of these qualifying terms as parts of speech within conventional (non-poetic) language is usually signified through contextual markers ("much merriment"; "more than usual"; "at most"), markers that repress or "forget" the votility of the signifier, its heterogeneity as well as its materiality, and serve to deliver in place of this votility a "communicable meaning." Furthermore, Stein's text emphasizes the *materiality* of the signifier, what Kristeva would call its "musication": to liberate the lyrical qualities of "much much much" is to substitute the "brutality" of symbolic meaning for the forgotten echolalias of infancy. In Stein's text, "much," "more," and "most" are invoked precisely so as to foreground this forgotten votility: each signifier both solicits referential meaning and remains resolutely heterogeneous. As I attempted to show in Chapter 3, there is, finally, no way to bring interpretive closure to such a text; or rather, the point of such a text is to emphasize interpretive possibility, illimitability, nonclosure.

All this is demonstrable within "Wherein Iowa Differs from Indiana and Kansas." Yet if the text stresses difference and *différance* over unity and determinant meaning, it also, seemingly paradoxically, strives to underscore the "wholeness" of both nation and composition. As Renan reminds us, the essence of a nation is not only "forgetting" but also "hav[ing] many things in common"; both sides of this equation are arguably present in Stein's text. As the text proceeds, for example, isolated sentences about individual states begin to be replaced by longer, more fluid descriptions of shared qualities:

> Not continued as Iowa, not continued as as continued as Iowa, as continued Iowa as continued and Indiana as continued as Indiana and as Kansas as Kansas as continued.
> The next makes a meeting between Iowa, to notice, the next makes a meeting between Indiana a notice the next makes a meeting between Kansas or makes a between Kansas or makes a meeting, Indiana makes a meeting, Iowa a meeting, Iowa a meeting, makes a meeting Indiana, makes a meeting Kansas. Meeting Kansas meeting Indiana meeting Iowa, next meeting Iowa next meeting Indiana next meeting Kansas. (UK, 41)

The terms "continued," "next," and "meeting," all repeated insistently throughout this passage, serve to foreground proximity and contingency. As opposed to the terse descriptions of single states in the first passage quoted above, this passage generates a lengthy accumulation of clauses punctuated only by commas, as though to emphasize the fluidity of movement between states and statements. Even more strikingly, this description employs signifying units internal to the state names (the "as" of Kansas; the "a" of Iowa) as conjunctions that textually link isolate states, and individual statements, to one another. Here borders of geography and signification do not prohibit but *forge* relationships of resemblance and similarity: being "next" to a state or a word can "make . . . a meeting" that in turn multiplies meaning and association.

As Stein suggests throughout this piece, American states can be both singular and similar, both unique and part of a larger nation;

likewise, "statements" can be seen as graphic and phonetic units of profound internal "value" and infinitely complex heterogeneity, yet they are always part of a larger "whole," whether this whole be a sentence, a paragraph, or what Stein calls "the modern composition." In a series of lectures that Stein gave during her American tour of 1934–5 she provides several key theorizations of this dynamic of state and statement alike. For instance, Stein writes of American English in terms of "words that move as the Americans move with them move always move and in every and in any direction" (Narr, 14); the multi-directionality of signification is itself "part" of a larger "American thing." Containment as a mode productive of "movement" is also suggested by Stein's memorable analysis of America as a "space of time that is filled always filled with moving" (LIA, 161). In this, Stein seems to be conceiving of nation or text as a differential equation – a calculus that requires both a quantity ("nation," "text," "whole") and the rate of change of that quantity (as affected by the movement of variables, including the shifting differences of its internal parts). This equation expands, shrinks, and shifts in relation to the temporal and spatial change and difference of the elements that comprise the given quantity, but the equation must also retain the givenness of the original quantity; hence the "whole" can remain integral, "complete," even with internal difference. Again in 1935, Stein uses similar terms to describe what she saw throughout her career as the quintessential "modern composition," *The Making of Americans*:

> And so it was natural that in writing The Making of Americans I had proceeded to enlarge my paragraphs so as to include everything. What else could I do. In fact inevitably I made my sentences and my paragraphs do the same thing, made them be one and the same thing. This was inevitably because the nineteenth century having lived by phrases really had lost the feeling of sentences, and before this in English literature paragraphs had never been an end in themselves and now in the beginning of the twentieth century a whole thing, being what was assembled from its parts was a whole thing and so it was a paragraph. You will see that in The Making of Americans I did this thing, I made a paragraph so much a whole thing that it included in itself as a whole thing a whole sentence. (LIA, 159)

As "end[s] in themselves," whole sentences, whole paragraphs, and by implication the "whole" text of *The Making of Americans* exemplify the difference between twentieth-century writing and nineteenth-century efforts, which had come to be "no longer full of any meaning." Stein writes that "wholeness" serves "to include everything," whether this refers to semantic, grammatical, syntactical, or narrative possibilities, just as the American nation includes within it a potentially infinite variety of states, cities, families, and individuals. Yet the variability of these internal elements does not in turn invalidate the givenness of the "whole."

To be sure, this kind of composition presents immense spatial and temporal difficulties, as Stein admits in the same essay:

> [A] great deal of The Making of Americans was a struggle to do this thing, to make a whole present of something that it had taken a great deal of time to find out, but it was a whole there then within me and as such it had to be said. (LIA, 147)

"Wholeness," then, has a temporality, a presentness that is at odds with the past effort that precipitated its emergence; the implication, here, is that a "whole present" (sentence, paragraph, body of knowledge, or national body) must needs repress, subsume, or "forget" the heterogeneous "parts" which allowed it to emerge and which it "includes in it." This is the "struggle" of *The Making of Americans*, Stein suggests, a struggle of incorporation ("a whole there then within me") that is also, as I have suggested previously, productive of melancholia. Yet Stein's imaginative reconstruction of "America" in *Useful Knowledge* moves beyond this melancholia by recalibrating the whole/part dynamic of *The Making of Americans* in new terms that also define the conditions of possibility for her aesthetic. Simply put, Stein makes it possible in *Useful Knowledge* to imagine a "whole" – a nation, a text, or any formal unity – composed of variable and shifting "parts" that are ultimately irreducible to the whole. In so doing, she offers a way of thinking about the text, or the nation, that also makes room for individual difference, singularity, or finally "genius."

III

This, to my mind, is the point of arguably the most interesting piece in *Useful Knowledge*, "An Instant Answer or A Hundred Prominent Men." As its disarmingly straightforward introduction suggests, the "question" to which this text is offering its answer is that of the relationship between selected examples and a larger composition, or between "part" and "whole": "I will select a hundred prominent men and look at their photographs hand-writing and career, and then I will earnestly consider the question of synthesis" (UK, 144). In this parodic invocation of such popular books of her day as Alvin Langdon Coburn's *Men of Mark* (1913), a collection of photographs of well-known men that was found in her personal library, Stein makes reference to the "synthesizing" effort to identify "genius" out of a mass of individual particulars such as handwriting, facial or cranial characteristics, and the achievement of fame.[35] (In preparation for a never-realized book on prominent women, Coburn had Stein sit for him; the result was a series of photographs including the famous 1913 "genius" shot that emphasized Stein's power, authority, and regal bearing (Fig. 2.1).)[36] Coburn's photographs were meant to focus the viewer's attention on shared traits – high foreheads, asymmetrical features, intense gaze – that cumulatively build up a larger understanding of the concept of "prominence" or "genius." "Synthesis," accordingly, describes the combination of individual traits or "parts" so as to form a whole. Yet "An Instant Answer" makes it clear that the opposite effort is the concern of Stein, who indeed never manages to arrive at her "earnest" considerations despite the initial promise to do so. As the text's title suggests, "the question of synthesis" is answered, instantly, by the concept of "a hundred prominent men": an answer which in fact undermines the very notion of "synthesis" since it posits a "whole" that precedes a prior, cumulative analysis of individual parts. Indeed, there is nothing in her subsequent list of unnamed individuals that identifies them as either "prominent" ("the fourth one illustrates plentifully illustrates the attachments all of us have to what we have"; "the thirty-second is an irresistible pedestrian"; "the ninety-ninth who is the ninety-ninth, as for me I prefer to call tissue paper silk paper") or "men" ("The tenth one the tenth one feels traces of terror... He can be a king or a queen or a countess or a Katherine Susan"; "The fifty-fifth is very pretty in any language"). Each of these individuals is described through a mode of linguistic indirection that multiplies identification, and indeed comes to include even the reader herself in its scope:

> The fifty-fifth is very pretty in any language. How do you do is one way of looking at it. He minds it the most and the shape of it very much. He is very easily offended and he believes in a reference. I refer to you and to you and to you. I always refer to you. (UK, 152)

As this passage suggests, the cryptic "fifty-fifth" could also "refer to you," a supposition emphasized repeatedly throughout the text by a running commentary between two unidentified interlocutors that thoroughly undercuts the specificity of the "hundred prominent men" purportedly being described. To this extent, "An Instant Answer" offers an unusual combination of elements: a formal "whole" (the list of one hundred individuals) and a heterogenous series of "parts" marked by variability and indeterminacy.

This combination is encapsulated within a remarkable sub-series from the middle of the text:

> The forty-sixth prominent man is the one who connected them to their country. My country all the same they have their place there. And why do you tell their names. I tell their names because in this way I know that one and one make a hundred. It is very difficult to count in a foreign language. (UK, 150–1)

A *mise-en-abyme*, an internal, condensed, self-reflexive rendering of the artistic whole, this iteration of a hundred "ones" joined together by "and" enacts in microcosm the larger dynamic of the text it mirrors. Like the Cézanne canvas, this passage proceeds through a "flattening of climaxes"[37] in which the central figure, the "one," is multiplied and dispersed across an unchanging textual plain. Stein's handwritten manuscript of "An Instant Answer" makes it clear that the "one"s of this passage are meant to occupy equal visual and textual space (Fig. 4.2). The two works of art are striking visual analogues, suggesting yet once again Stein's sensitivity to the non-signifying aspects of her medium, her attraction to modes of textual performance that fall outside the purely literal. Yet one must also heed Marianne

DeKoven's warning that for Stein "writing and painting are different means for expressing [the] twentieth-century vision," that Stein is not simply producing "literary cubism," and that her relationship to Cézanne lies in an affinity of aesthetic vision rather than in artistic mimicry.[38] For it is the notion of "value" that Stein claims to have taken from Cézanne which is largely relevant here. As with the different "parts" of the Cézanne canvas, the list of one hundred "ones" is presented in a way that each "one" appears distinct from any other "one," and while collectively this grouping "make a hundred," this fact does not occlude the individual "value" of each. In other words, there is an effort in this passage to create a numerical, spatial and visual whole in which each "one" will "have their place there," and in which the absence of a single "one," whoever this might be, would be unaccountable. Furthermore, the textual "whole" created by this series of "ones" is explicitly linked to the issue of nationality in this paragraph, as to the "difficulty" of foreignness. As the last sentence of the paragraph suggests, among the reasons Stein may count "one and one and one" to a hundred may be to show off her enumerating skills in English, but it may also involve an effort to make each one of the hundred "count," have significance or value – something that is hard to do "in a foreign language." This enumeration, then, concerns counting *as* a speaker of English, or more precisely, counting *as* an American.

To be sure, the "ones" of Stein's list are also remarkably generic: machine-made ones, standardized ones; ones who are "all the same." Although a voice claims to be "tell[ing] their names," the name chosen ("one") is both variable and indeterminate. As Jennifer Ashton has argued about another of Stein's texts from this period, "the thing indicated by calling out 'one' is in no way determined or fixed by the act, as it might be if otherwise named. In fact, calling out 'one' can indicate virtually anything."[39] In other words, while the "value" of each individual "one" is asserted by this passage, so too is the variability of each "one." Here, as in "Wherein Iowa Differs from Kansas and Indiana," the text strives to keep in play both the integrity of the whole and the shifting differences of the parts. Yet the variability of these "parts" implies that the ranks of "a hundred prominent men" can include virtually anyone. Indeed, if this text outwardly purports to be a list of male geniuses, then Stein's notion of the shifting and variable "one" within the larger compositional "whole" is important in making room for others (including Stein herself) who might not conventionally fit into this list. "[W]ill you make me another one," the text ends, suggesting that there is no reason why the "me" (Stein? the reader?) could not as much be part of this list as the ninety-first ("The ninety-first who knows about this one").[40] No one, indeed, knows about any of the "ones" on the list, since the text makes only indeterminate associations and identifications. Hence any one could see themselves on this list; any one could be a genial "one."[41]

In the end, "An Instant Answer" serves as a particularly apt "answer" to the melancholic struggles of *The Making of Americans*. In the earlier text, as I have emphasized, Stein presents the American nation as the site of potentially crushing conformity, as a "whole" that threatens the existence of "queer singularity," yet contains within it, at the same time, the unique potential among nations to produce singularity as a vital thing, unhampered by conformist imperatives. "An Instant Answer," written over a decade later, rehabilitates the "unhappiness" of her earlier expatriate position by relocating this cultural problematic in textual space: the text *as* America, Stein's America, a sort of Lake Wobegone where "the children are all above average," an imaginative ideal where it "is natural to any one thinking that it is pleasant to be one."[42] In Stein's America, the abortive dream of *The Making of Americans* has at last come true: "Yes real singularity we have not made enough of yet so that any other one can really know it. I say vital singularity is as yet an unknown product with us." The knowledge that the reader takes from *Useful Knowledge* is that "genius" is not incompatible with "being an American"; indeed, to be an American "one" *is* to be a "genius," at least within the Steinian text. Having overcome her expatriate ambivalence, Stein, in her late writings about America, suggestively reworks the Romantic understanding of "genius" as what "reveals" to the nation its "immanent impulse." Nine years later, in *Everybody's Autobiography*, Stein would announce to the public that *her* American story was indeed the story of "everybody."

Notes

1. Williams, "The Work of Gertrude Stein," 350.
2. Hegel, *Lectures on Philosophy*, 76.
3. Schlegel, "Caesar and Alexander: An Historical Comparison," in his *A Course of Lectures*, 339.
4. Novalis, *Philosophical Writings*, 116.
5. Williams, "Metropolitan Perceptions and the Emergence of Modernism," in his *The Politics of Modernism*, 44.
6. Ibid., 45.
7. Stein, *Paris France*, 37.

8. Wald, *Constituting Americans*, 12.
9. Ibid., 242.
10. This chronology has been established by Leon Katz in his "Introduction" to Stein, *Fernhurst*, ix-xlii. See my Ch. 2, note 2.
11. See Ch. 2, 62.
12. Katz, "The First Making," 46.
13. As Shari Benstock has pointed out, educated American women of the late nineteenth century with intellectual inclinations invariably looked to Europe as a place where their aspirations might flourish, a place unconstrained by the gendered demands of their Victorian mothers and fathers; to become an ex-patriate was quite literally to leave the fatherland behind. In her own resistance to fathers and their injunctions, Stein's decision to take up permanent residence in Paris at the moment when she begins to imagine herself a serious writer can thus be seen as liberatory, and her case has often been an exemplary one in such narratives of feminist liberation. See Benstock, *Women of the Left Bank*; also Helle, "Speculative Subjects," ch. 3.
14. The class and gender freedoms that Paris seemed to offer turn-of-the-century Americans were also experienced by African-Americans, as a recent study has suggested. African-Americans in Paris "found that leaving their homeland made them feel more American," since it re-enacted "one of our cherished national myths, that of immigrant upward mobility... However, in this case those people were *leaving* the United States, not seeking it; America loomed as the obstacle to freedom not its attainment" (Stovall, *Paris Noir*, xvi).
15. Ruddick, *Reading*, 63.
16. Ibid., 65.
17. Seltzer, *Bodies and Machines*, 55.
18. See, for example, Hermann Graf von Keyserling: "It is far easier to define 'the' American than 'the' representative of any other nation simply because nowhere else are there more individuals true to type" (Graf von Keyserling, *America Set Free* ..., 456). Thanks to Michael Ermarth for providing me with this reference.
19. Nietzsche quoted in Kittler, *Discourse Networks*, 196.
20. Said, "Intellectual Exile: Expatriates and Marginals," in his *Representations of the Intellectual*, 36.
21. Renan, "What is a Nation?," 19.
22. Alice Toklas's notes, from Katz correspondence with the author.
23. Freud, "The Interpretation of Dreams," in his *Standard Edition*, vol. IV, 261–6.
24. Freud, "Mourning and Melancholia," in his *Standard Edition*, vol. XIV, 246.
25. Ibid., 249. Freud later makes explicit that this conflict is indeed foundational to the Oedipal phase; in *The Ego and the Id*, he regrets that in "Mourning and Melancholia" "we did not appreciate the full significance of this process and did not know how common and how typical it is. Since then we have come to understand that this kind of substitution [of ego for lost object] has a great share in determining the form taken by the ego and that it makes an essential contribution

towards building up what is called its 'character.'" "The Ego and the Id," in his *Standard Edition*, vol. XIX, 28.

26. Freud, "Mourning and Melancholia," in his *Standard Edition*, vol. XIV, 256.
27. Ibid., 245.
28. Said, *Representations*, 39.
29. Dubnick, *Structure of Obscurity*, 18.
30. Levinson, "Gertrude Stein," 127.
31. Kristeva, *Desire in Language*, 131.
32. Pease, "National Identities," 5.
33. Renan, "What Is a Nation?", 11.
34. Ibid., 11.
35. The Beinecke Rare Book and Manuscript Library, Yale University, has a list of the books that were found in the personal library of Stein and Toklas and delivered to Yale University at Toklas's death.
36. See Stavitsky, *Gertrude Stein*, 17.
37. Dubnick, *Structure of Obscurity*, 18.
38. DeKoven, "Gertrude Stein and Modern Painting: Beyond Literary Criticism," in Hoffman, *Critical Essays*, 180.
39. Ashton, "Gertrude Stein for Anyone," 324.
40. This logic of "variable singularity" is again emphasized in the aptly titled companion text to "An Instant Answer," "A Singular Addition. A Sequel to An Instant Answer or One Hundred Prominent Men" (composed 1922).
41. I am indebted in this analysis to Ashton's plotting of the "principle of substitutability" in Stein's late writings ("Gertrude Stein for Anyone"); see also Hejinian, "Grammar and Landscape."
42. This phrase appears in the "Advertisement" to *Useful Knowledge*.

5 From "Genius" to Celebrity: *The Autobiography of Alice B. Toklas* and *Everybody's Autobiography*

The idea of America is so wonderful because the more equal something is, the more American it is.

(Andy Warhol)[1]

In the 1920s, Gertrude Stein often adopted a stance of bafflement at the public assessment of her work as "difficult." For Stein, texts like *How to Write* or *Useful Knowledge* were self-evidently readable; and what is more, they allowed the reader to experience, through the process of reading, the "intuitions of genius." Yet few in fact saw it in these terms. By the 1920s Stein's work had found support among a small band of "disciples" (Carl Van Vechten's term) but had suffered widespread rejection in the Anglo-American press and publishing establishment. As Ellery Sedgwick, editor of the *Atlantic*, put it to Stein in 1919, "[Y]ou misjudge our public. Here there is no group of *literati* or *illuminati* or *cognoscenti* or *illustrissimi* of any kind, who could agree upon interpretations of your poetry. More than this, you could not find a handful even of careful readers who would think that it was a serious effort."[2] Stein's response to Sedgwick was telling: "I don't misjudge your public. I am not interested in their being literati, etc.," she writes.

> My work is legitimate literature and I amuse and interest myself in words as an expression of feeling as Shakespeare or anyone else writing did. This is entirely in the spirit of all that is first class in American letters whether it's newspapers, Walt Whitman or Henry James, or Poe.[3]

Fig. 5.1 *Carl Van Vechten, "Gertrude Stein, January 4, 1935"*

In bringing together Henry James with newspapers as various possible analogues to her work, Stein attempts to bridge the "great divide" between high modernism and mass culture by affiliating herself with both sides: her work is on a par with that of the canonical writers, but as readable as newspapers: no special interpretive tools required. Sedgwick remained unconvinced: "the simple truth is that not one of our readers in a thousand would understand your essay."[4]

In Chapter 3, I suggested that critiques like that of Sedgwick might be contrasted with another kind of reading of Stein – one attentive to multiple, open-ended interpretations, a kind of reading that would stress the availability of these texts to *any* reader. And in Chapter 4, I emphasized Stein's textual construction of "America" in which difference rather than hierarchy was the defining principle, a place in which every "one" could be seen as a "vitally singular" one. In both of these chapters, I have stressed not only the possibility of an audience for Stein's work, but also its necessity: "talking" necessitates someone "listening" and "talking back" in turn. In making her text the site where any "one" can have a voice, Stein reveals a central commitment to writing an enlightened audience into the very structure of her work. Yet the rejection of Stein's work by Sedgwick and other American editors on the grounds of elitism is important in identifying a larger "problem" within Stein's moment that I have also been attempting to trace throughout this book: the problem of high modernism and its investment in an exclusionary notion of artistic "genius," a problem of cultural and authorial positioning that is at odds with the radically democratic, anti-subjective, anti-essentialist tendencies in much of Stein's writing. On the other side of the aesthetic divide from Eliot, Pound, Loy, and their expatriate contemporaries, but sharing similar cultural assumptions, Sedgwick had stressed in his letter to Stein a central aesthetic opposition between the works of a foreign, highbrow "literati" on one hand and the tastes of a bemused American middlebrow public on the other, an opposition that Sedgwick felt to be unresolvable. Meanwhile, Sedgwick's critical opposition between Stein's writing and the tastes of the general public was being equally strongly iterated by Stein's defenders, those readers and "disciples" who had worked hard to secure her special status both in America and abroad. In the reverent tones of Sherwood Anderson, Stein's work was "of more importance to writers of English than the work of many of our more easily understood and more widely accepted word artists."[5]

"Genius" – a term both embedded in and generative of cultural hierarchies – was a key designation through which these social and economic oppositions between high and mass, individual artist and collectivity, creativity and mechanization could be asseverated on both sides of the great divide. Sedgwick, for one, could use the term "genius" toward Stein as a way both to flatter her and to render her work marginal to the mainstream.[6] Other more supportive readers like Anderson called Stein a "genius" as a way of underscoring the difficulty or highness of her work, its commitment to a heroic project of linguistic revitalization beyond the understanding of the masses. Stein herself often seemed to encourage this latter assessment, writing for example in *Four in America*:

> Clarity is of no importance because nobody listens and nobody knows what you mean no matter what you mean, nor how clearly you mean what you mean. But if you have vitality enough of knowing enough of what you mean, somebody and sometime and sometimes a great many will have to realise that you know what you mean and so they will agree that you mean what you know . . . (FIA, 127–8)

Whether spoken out of conviction or out of rejection, this kind of statement accompanies other of Stein's contemporaneous pronouncements about the threat of the masses (EA, 205) or the value of "the inside" as opposed to "the outside" (Narr, 39). Yet my point in this book has been to show how Stein was at once interpellated by the high modernist discourse of "genius," yet remained generally uncomfortable or even "bored" with this positioning on one side of the great divide, as her 1919 letter to Sedgwick makes clear. Or as she announced to *The New York Herald Tribune* in 1935: "I like ordinary people who don't bore me. Highbrows, you know, always do."[7] For Stein, both her texts and her claims to "genius" were part of a lifelong process of self-making and self-splitting that was at times a private enterprise occurring at the moment of composition, but was at many others a temporally and spatially flexible notion, directed toward an "outside," an "everybody" and an "anybody." Again, her double-edged aesthetic credo: "I write for myself *and* strangers."[8] If for Stein "genius" was ultimately not so much a type or "frozen conception" (James) as a dialogic process of "talking and listening," then it was finally descriptive of a form of expression that could flourish only through open and unrestricted exchange with a general collectivity, an expression that was always in excess of both the bounded "self" and the undifferentiated Other. Stein's description in 1934 of the "essence of genius, of being most intensely alive" as the divided process of "the motor going inside and the car moving" was one of many attempts to reconfigure the notion of "genius" as a process of simultaneity between two categories of universal human experience: the habitual or "automatic," and the unhabitual or unmechanizable. Another attempt was the composition in 1932 of *The Autobiography of Alice B. Toklas*, a remarkable thematic and stylistic departure from her earlier work which again emphasizes the importance of "genius" for Stein as a universal capacity and shared or democratic ideal.

Aware that her pleas to American publishers were falling on deaf ears, Stein in 1932 composed a text that would be an assured best-seller, as Sedgwick, Harcourt Brace, and many others immediately recognized. The difference between *The Autobiography of Alice B. Toklas* (1933) and Stein's earlier work was the apparent location of its voice in a unified and coherent "character" (the homespun and gossipy Alice Toklas) and in a relatively linear "plot" (the travails of a group of *avant-gardistes* in the heyday of modernism). Such standard devices of narration, Sedgwick felt sure, would allow Stein the dual function of pleasing a general audience and glamorizing a coterie of high modernist geniuses with herself at their center; perhaps, he suggested, this "easy" work might bring attention to the "difficult" manuscripts. Operating firmly within a high/low dichotomy, Sedgwick – like many of Stein's subsequent critics – worked to repress the way in which *The Autobiography* disrupts dominant modes of authority and representation through a queering of narrative agency at the very moment at which this agency becomes visible. As I argue in this chapter, *The Autobiography*, through this queering, extracts "genius" from the domain of the autonomous artist and relocates it in the shifting and polymorphous terrain of same-sex desire, explicitly making sexuality part of the equation of "talking and listening." To be sure, the challenge that this queering of "genius" poses to the autonomy of the authorial voice was not without anxiety for Stein; in the several years following the enormous success of *The Autobiography of Alice B. Toklas*, she claimed to have lost her voice, both literally and figuratively. Yet this did not stop her from crossing the "great divide" several years later in order to claim identity with a popular audience in the aptly named *Everybody's Autobiography* (1937), an account of her lecture tour in America during 1934–5. In the latter, Stein again works to queer the figure of the "genius" by constituting its voice through dialogue with an unnamed, general, and generic "you." Stein further disavows the uniqueness of this figure by claiming that her newfound fame in the

1930s is not so much a sign of genial superiority as of generic commonality, since in America "everybody is a public something." In the America to which Stein returns after thirty years' absence, "vital singularity" in the form of "celebrityhood" has become a mass-produced product, an identity to which everybody has claim thanks to an emergent mass-media culture industry. Only within such a context could Stein entitle a book about being a "genius" in America *Everybody's Autobiography*. In ending my analysis with this text, I argue that it represents for Stein an important occasion for reflection upon the shrinking importance of the high/low cultural dichotomy – particularly of the high modernist values of privacy, aesthetic autonomy, and authorial inwardness – in the face of an emergent popular culture of postmodernism.

I

As the work through which Gertrude Stein finally became a household name, *The Autobiography of Alice B. Toklas* has long been considered by Stein's most attentive readers as the least "Steinian" text she wrote – a book about "genius" but certainly not of it. Randa Dubnick writes that in relation to the "clarity" of *The Autobiography of Alice B. Toklas*, Stein's "more obscure work is more innovative, and on that account it is more interesting and more important." Richard Bridgman makes the broad claim that the book was in fact partially written by Toklas, since "it is natural to wonder if her companion was in any way responsible for the drastic stylistic metamorphosis." Janet Hobhouse argues that Stein's *Four in America*, "was, in a way, her defence of her 'difficult' style, in the face of the popularity of the easy, false style of *The Autobiography*." And for Bruce Kellner, *The Autobiography* "is so entirely uncharacteristic of Gertrude Stein's writing that it can serve only as a false, even detrimental, introduction."[9] Yet for at least one of her readers, Ellery Sedgwick, the editor with whom Stein had been carrying on a tense and largely unproductive exchange about her work for years, *The Autobiography* represented the emergence of the "true" Stein from behind the "false" obscurity of her more "difficult" style: "[W]hat a delightful book it is, and how glad I am to publish four installments of it! During our long correspondence, I think you felt my constant hope that the time would come when the real Miss Stein would pierce the smoke-screen with which she has always so mischievously surrounded herself."[10]

What emerges from these critical responses is an essential antinomy for her readers between two "Gertrude Steins": the true one and the false one, seen variously as either the writer of the popular *Autobiography* or the writer of everything *but* the *Autobiography.* Curiously, this dynamic is one that the text replicates within its own structure: by refusing to sign her text and attributing it to Alice, Stein creates a void at the very center of a genre dedicated to the primacy of authority and self-constitution in life as in writing. Within this void, questions of truth and falsity proliferate, with no apparent resolution. Who, indeed, is the "Gertrude Stein" of *The Autobiography of Alice B. Toklas*? As an author, she is nowhere to be seen: the title page of the first edition carries no authorial designation.[11] Moreover, as a character within the text, Stein is seen only through the gaze of another. "Alice," the text's "narrator," is equally elusive: her claim that "I like a view but I like to sit with my back turned to it" synthesizes her shifting textual role as voice, gaze, muse, object of desire and projection, as Stein's substitute, double, and informant. Hyperbolic, excessive, and queer, *The Autobiography of Alice B. Toklas* is in the end nothing if not a performance, an enactment of authority and all its privileges which in its excessive theatricalization is also a subversive undoing of both authority and identity. As such, attention to the relative truth or falsity of this text seems both critical and finally somewhat irrelevant: for what seems to dominate this text is less a hidden substance but rather "the *appearance* of substance."[12] More recently, critics like Catharine Stimpson, Sidonie Smith, and Leigh Gilmore have attempted to move beyond polarized debates over the book's merits and have stressed the "proto-pomo" concern of *The Autobiography* with notions of performativity, masking, and theatricality.[13] What I would add to this contemporary discussion is the suggestion that Stein's "performance" of identity in this text is to be found paradoxically in those moments where identity appears to be at its most stable and certain, moments which have often been cited by detractors as exemplary of Stein's "egotism," as textual mandates meant to "bully" her audience into appreciation of her work's singularity. The moments, in short, when "Alice" describes "Stein" as a "genius," a process which insistently foregrounds not subjective "essence" but "the appearance of substance."

In the opening pages of *The Autobiography of Alice B. Toklas*, "Alice" makes the following famous proclamation:

> I may say that only three times in my life have I met a genius and each time a bell within me rang and I was not mistaken, and I may say in each case it was before there was any general recognition of

> the quality of genius in them. The three geniuses of whom I wish to speak are Gertrude Stein, Pablo Picasso and Alfred Whitehead. (ABT, 6)

For Richard Bridgman, this passage manifests "the reverence of a disciple for a great literary figure," despite the fact that it is quite clearly Alice's capacity, not Gertrude's, that is here being celebrated. In fact, the capacities of this "I" precisely recall earlier definitions by Kant, Schlegel, or Nietzsche of the transmission of "genius," of a receptivity and sensitivity to greatness that enables one mind to "awaken" another.[14] If Gertrude is a "genius," therefore, then so too is Alice, whose "genius" is developed or awakened by engagement with Stein's own. To this extent, what appears to be an account of the singularity of Gertrude Stein comes to seem like an affirmation of the dialogic nature of the capacity of "genius" – as what can conceivably emerge, as Stein would put it, through the process of "talking and listening." "Genius," here, as in Stein's more obviously experimental texts, is not the capacity of a unique individual but a shared phenomenon.

Many other elements within the narrative emphasize this shifty double movement between, on the one hand, the presentation of the figure of "Gertrude Stein, genius," and, on the other, the deconstruction of this figure and of its authorial position along the dialogic lines established in the earlier, experimental writings. Even the text's frontispiece (Fig. 5.2), a photograph of Toklas and Stein by Man Ray which faces a title page without any signature, at once establishes a hierarchy between the author and her helpmate or between intellectual and domestic labor, and deforms the conventional trajectory of the portraitist's gaze through which this gendered hierarchy might be emphasized. Stein, in the dusky foreground, is seated at a desk, writing: the heavy shapes of the furniture and Stein's own hunched body seem to complement the darkened objects in the room which collectively signify "modern art": small, primitive figurines, oriental rugs, wrought iron candelabra, thick books piled on the table. Toklas, by contrast, appears in the background and off to the side, in an opened doorway from which light spills into the room. The iconography is rather conventional: Stein, wielding the pen, occupies the position of literary, cultural, and aesthetic power in this relationship, while Alice herself can only stand at the entrance to the sanctum of modern art, a visitor from the world of women whose voice must be heard through that of Stein in order to be made intelligible (or interesting). Yet Man Ray's photograph inverts the traditional power

Fig. 5.2 *Man Ray, "Alice B. Toklas at the Door"*

imbalance of this gendered division of labor. The light streaming from the door throws both Toklas and Stein into relief, so that both appear as darkened outlines or negative spaces in the room. As such, their difference is obscured: one holds a pen, one a doorknob, but each occupies space in a similar way, as an outline or border area which throws other objects into relief. The open door further suggests a free movement between the domestic spaces of the two women, between atelier and kitchen, from which Alice has perhaps emerged. But most central to the significance of this photograph for the text itself is the way in which the gaze is arranged. Alice is looking intently in the direction of either Stein or the camera, while

Stein appears absorbed in her writing. The camera's eye, on the other hand, is positioned from the perspective of neither, allowing for three major simultaneous points of view: Stein's, directed toward her writing; Alice's, directed toward Stein/the camera; and the camera's, directed toward the two figures in relation. Who is the eye/"I" in this image? With whose gaze are we meant to identify in this photograph, or in this text? Rather than establishing the author as "the subject of his own understanding" – Paul de Man's definition of autobiography[15] – this photograph proliferates and disseminates points of view, in the process unraveling fixed hierarchies of writer/reader, subject/object, genius/disciple.

In chapter one, "Alice" writes, "I like a view but I like to sit with my back turned to it." Again, here, "Alice" appears as the passive sitter and object of someone else's gaze – of Stein, the behind-the-scenes wizard of this text. Yet this sentence also parallels Alice's position in the Man Ray photograph by attributing to her a central agency even as it emphasizes her marginality from the sphere of authority and knowledge. Alice may indeed be at the doorway to Stein's atelier just as she is the object of someone's gaze when sitting in front of a view, but it is Alice to whom the "I" of the text ostensibly belongs; it is Alice who signifies "identity". The instability of Alice's position within the text, and the way in which this position unsettles conventional modalities of seeing and knowing, correlates with Jacques Lacan's notion of *le regard* (the gaze):

> In our relationship to things as it is constituted by the path of vision and ordered in the figures of representation, something glides, passes, transmits itself from stage to stage, in order always to be in some degree eluded there – it is that which is called the gaze.[16]

The Autobiography of Alice B. Toklas, through its invocation and subsequent deformation of a genre arguably dedicated to the uniqueness, self-evidence and autonomy of the authorial subject, acts out the "elision" of which Lacan speaks. The text both posits and prohibits the construction of "Alice" as the transcendental signified behind the text's "I," just as it nominates and negates the position of Gertrude Stein as a "genius." In foregrounding the gaze as well as what eludes the gaze, *The Autobiography* appropriates its genre's claims to authority, mastery, and by extension, "genius," and emphasizes their fictitiousness.

Such a rewriting of the autobiographical genre, to borrow

Houston A. Baker's suggestive inversion, works ultimately to "deform mastery" rather than to "master form."[17] Hardly the cloudless mirror of a creative writer's life, the Steinian autobiography stresses dialogue over monologue, mutual authorship over individual self-constitution, the performance of the self and of its Other. The contradictory movements within this text work to ensnare the reader within a textual economy in which the exchange between signifier and signified, author and audience, the "real" and the "imaginary," is always already disproportionate, in excess of any possible position of epistemological certainty. This signifying excess, of course, also helps explain why for countless readers *The Autobiography of Alice B. Toklas* has provided so much pleasure. The humor and playfulness of this verbal, visual, and generic game of surfaces lies precisely in its capacity to send-up privileged categories and hierarchies, even those that would seem central to Stein's ostensible effort at self-advertisement and self-glamorization. In *The Autobiography* this ludic process occurs through the wildly excessive descriptive gesture. By having the unremarkable, secretarial Alice receive intuitions of her lover's "genius" through the ringing of internal bells, for example, Stein thoroughly undercuts the high seriousness of this moment of authorial definition. The same could be said of Alice's professed desire to write a book entitled "The wives of geniuses I have sat with":

> I have sat with so many. I have sat with wives who were not wives, of geniuses who were real geniuses. I have sat with real wives of geniuses who were not real geniuses. I have sat with wives of geniuses, of near geniuses, of would be geniuses, in short I have sat very often and very long with many wives and wives of many geniuses. (ABT, 17)

Here, the pairing of genius/wife is "a parody of heterosexual segregation," emphasizing less the fixity of gender roles than their performability.[18] Again it is Alice/Stein's ironic focus on the difference between "real" wives/geniuses that foregrounds the artificiality, the constructedness of the categories "wife" and "genius." Within a text in which the "real" author is nowhere to be found, the deliberate emphasis upon an incontestable "real" creates an excess that cannot be assimilated by a "straight" reading; the result is a massive send-up of conventional norms of gender, identity, and discursivity within which genial male authority or wifely passivity can be articulated. In miming and mimicing these norms, the text transforms a seemingly conventional relationship of genius/wife into a butch/femme relationship that parodies dominant heterosexual modes as it unsettles the possibilities for point of view. The text performs a similar queering on the figures from the Parisian avant-garde through the mode of gossip, both forwarding salacious inside information about these figures (Madame Matisse's "firm large loosely hung mouth like a horse"; Fernande Olivier's "little ways"), and refusing to accept authorial attribution. That so many of Stein's contemporaries felt badly served by their representations in the text reveals, again, the peculiar power of this work at once to solicit the desiring gaze of the reader seeking historical "truth" and at the same time to deny the trajectory of this gaze.[19]

In its queering of the notion of "genius" as a category of high modernist singularity, in its emphasis upon identity as a performance constructed in the play of verbal and visual surfaces, and in the theatrical hyperbole of its characterizations, *The Autobiography of Alice B. Toklas* seems very close to the stylistic sensibility defined in Susan Sontag's famous 1964 essay, "Notes on 'Camp.'" For Sontag, "camp" is a "sensibility," a "way of seeing the world as an aesthetic phenomenon,"[20] whose modes encompass exaggeration, perversity, glamor, flamboyance, the embrace of both the esoteric and of "kitsch": in sum, a full-scale rejection of high modernism and its high seriousness. In privileging excess over restraint, sensuous frivolity over seriousness, mass-produced kitsch over high modernist "difficulty" – including the more restrained modes of irony and satire – the camp sensibility "introduces a new standard: artifice as an ideal, theatricality," as well as "detachment."[21] This standard contains its own contradictions: over-the-top playfulness and an aesthetic stance of boredom, affiliations with *both* the "theatrical" and the "banal." But camp works in the twentieth century, according to Sontag, precisely because it rejects any single affiliation or mode of identification, because it "refuses both the harmonies of traditional seriousness and the risks of fully identifying with extreme states of feeling."[22] In other words, camp works as a new standard because it stresses that identification or even identity itself is a form of performance, and that life conducts itself within a theater of representation.

One of the privileged perspectives of camp, Sontag writes, is that it

> sees everything in quotation marks. It's not a lamp, but a "lamp"; not a woman but a "woman." To perceive Camp in objects and persons is to understand Being-as-Playing-a-Role. It is the farthest extension, in sensibility, of the metaphor of life as theater.[23]

To cite something, or to put it between quotation marks, as Sontag and later Derrida remind us, is to suggest its "nonsaturability," its duplicatability, its "duplicity." That a term can be cited means that it can be articulated within a variety of different contexts; that a human being can be cited suggests that her "being" is a role, a performance, masquerade. The citationality of the mark or sign is also its duplicity, since it is what undermines the fiction of the word as the "center of absolute anchoring"; the citationality of a person, and particularly a woman, dupes the essentialist logic of the humanist subject.[24] The effect of this process is again, for Sontag, largely aesthetic, for "It goes without saying that the Camp sensibility is disengaged, depoliticized – or at least apolitical."[25] As many subsequent critics have pointed out, Sontag's failure to engage with the politically subversive aspects of camp – particularly as they concern queer practice – drastically limits her ability to pursue the implications of her analysis. In her effort to "edit . . . homosexuals out of camp" Sontag loses track of the most radical aspects of the phenomenon she describes,[26] in particular what Moe Meyer has called "its political validity as an ontological critique."[27] In response, Meyer, Esther Newton, Judith Butler, and many others have attempted to redress Sontag's "sanitization" of camp practice by relocating it within a queer context, as "a dissonant and denaturalized performance that reveals the performative status of the natural itself."[28]

Of course, one could argue for the campiness of an anxiously "heterosexual" text like Theodore Dreiser's 1915 novel *The "Genius"*, which cites the notion of "genius" only to underscore the failure of this notion as a meaningful designation for the modern artist, encoding this failure within the neurasthenic "effeminacy" of its oversexed protagonist, Eugene Witla.[29] In comparison, Gertrude Stein's less explicit but no less deconstructive citing of "genius" in *The Autobiography of Alice B. Toklas* is nevertheless more explicitly located in queer practice: in Stein's own lesbian relationship, as well as in her close relationships during this period with a number of gay men.[30] Stein's parody of herself as a "real genius" parallels her parody of a "heterosexual" relationship with Alice; both are acts of impersonation, of "being-as-playing-a-role," and of a role-playing that calls into question the "status of the natural." In fact, the two parodic performances are inextricable, since both are part of the text's larger effort at hyperbolically exposing the fallacy of a fixed and natural "original." For if the position of the "genius" (like that of the "wife") can be theatricalized, camped up, parodied, then it is no longer essential, natural, or fixed in a hierarchy of dominance and exclusion. Such deconstructive maneuvers unsettle generic expectations and the passive position of the reader, disrupt traditional canonical notions of literary value and authorial agency, and open the way for a more inclusive, shifting, and demotic understanding of textual engagement. In this, *The Autobiography of Alice B. Toklas* must be seen as part of the same aesthetic and political project as more clearly experimental texts by Stein.

II

"Alice B. Toklas did hers and now everybody will do theirs," reads the first line of *Everybody's Autobiography*, a text written four years after *The Autobiography of Alice B. Toklas*. As with its predecessor, *Everybody's Autobiography* from the outset foregrounds relationship: what Alice was to Stein in the earlier text will be a role now occupied by "everybody." The text is accordingly structured around the exchange between two, shifting entities: an "I" and a "you," between a first-person narrator usually taken to be Gertrude Stein and an unspecified "you" whose figuration is more slippery, as its presence is at once gestural ("you know") and generic ("you are never yourself to yourself" (EA, 68)). Although easy to overlook, the "you" in *Everybody's Autobiography* is as crucial to the text as "Alice" was to her *Autobiography*, serving a strategic purpose in working to fracture the presumed autonomy of the autobiographical "I." Although few critics have made note, Stein's text clearly wants us to register this pronominal slippage, even arresting itself at one point to "correct" itself: "you that is I" (EA, 12). Hence it is interesting that the "you" is figured in the text almost invariably at those moments where the autonomy, uniqueness, and difference of this "I" is being asserted, as in this seeming instance of authorial emergence:

> Slowly and in a way it was not astonishing but slowly I was knowing that I was a genius . . . It is funny this thing of being a genius, there is no reason for it, there is no reason that it should be you and should not have been him, no reason at all that it should have been you, no no reason at all. (EA, 76–7)

Stein's "knowing" that she is a "genius" here appears to arise in contradistinction to the capacities of someone else, a masculine subject implicitly figured in the text as Stein's older brother, Leo. "Being a genius" is rendered as a mark of individual difference – an odd or "funny" happenstance, given the likeness which family members are "reasonably" meant to share. But the tonal resonances of this passage call for a closer reading. In an account which is meant to be autobiographical, hence dominated by the reflections of an "I," and which is meant to assert the specificity of identity over collective similarity, the appearance of the second-person pronoun effects a strange shift in emphasis: "[T]here is no reason that it should be you and should not have been him, no reason at all that it should have been you." A generalized form of address, the "you" seems to be functioning here as a kind of appeal, encouraging the reader to identify with the "I" and her realization. But how can the "I" ask the "you" to participate in this account of the discovery of "genius"? How can the "I" at once predicate her claim to "genius" on the supposition of individual uniqueness, and subvert this claim in making "genius" *generic*?

As linguist Emile Benveniste writes, "discourse" comprises "the discrete and always unique acts by which the language is actualized in speech by a speaker," a conversion that takes place when a speaker identifies himself as "a unique person pronouncing *I*."[31] Yet crucially,

> [c]onsciousness of self is only possible if it is experienced by contrast. I use *I* only when I am speaking to someone who will be a *you* in my address. It is this condition of dialogue that is constitutive of *person*, for it implies that reciprocally *I* becomes *you* in the address of the one who in his turn designates himself as *I*.[32]

In the 1930s, Stein would refer to "being a genius" as "talking and listening" at the same time, locating genial "agency" within a conversational dynamic similar to what Benveniste describes. For Stein, language is not a vehicle through which an extra-linguistic "genius" expresses a self, but a site of discursive exchange through which the open-ended, processual notion of "genius" emerges. The Steinian text and the notion of "genius" are thus synonyms, equivalent categories of "being" constituted by the mutual exchange of two or more voices: in *Everybody's Autobiography*, the "I" and the "you."

Moreover, this pronominal slippage that constitutes the narrative "voice" of *Everybody's Autobiography* can also be situated within the queer context that I have traced in this chapter. In *The Autobiography of Alice B. Toklas*, as I have tried to suggest, Stein employs the hallmarks of "camp" – hyperbole and gestural excess – to invert traditional autobiographical notions of narrativity and to foreground the performance and constructedness of identity. A similar process could be said to take place in *Everybody's Autobiography*. Recently, critic David Bergman has argued that "pronoun substitutions are an essential part of the grammar of gay language and an important part of camp"; he cites as an example the practice of referring to a drag queen as "she."[33] Although this practice has a complex history all its own, representing both slander and ridicule as well as approbation, it is clear that the power of this pronominal substitution lies potentially in its recognition that "sex-role behavior," as Newton classically put it, "can be manipulated at will."[34] Stein's manipulations of authority, identity, and heterosexual "role behavior" contribute to the campy self-presentation of *The Autobiography of Alice B. Toklas*; *Everybody's Autobiography* extends this project onto the most general level by making the "being" of which Stein writes substitutable with "everybody." In so doing, the text parodies and reverses its own hierarchical strategies, foregrounding the radical inessentialism of the authority embedded in the "I." And while *Everybody's Autobiography* does not make explicit the dynamics of gender parodied in the slippage between "I"/"you" and "genius"/"everybody," it retains the "subversive laughter" of camp in its extravagant, excessive, and hyperbolic assertions of "being":

> What is a genius . . . Really inside you if you are a genius there is nothing inside you that makes you really different to yourself inside you than those are to themselves inside them who are not a genius. That is so. (EA, 84)

This statement of seeming identity ("a genius is X") works primarily as an expression of *anti*-essentialism ("a genius is nothing") and as an instance of subjective leveling ("there is nothing inside you that makes you really different" from non-geniuses). "A genius" – here equivalent to the "you" – is nothing, an idea that reflects the generic status of the "you"; furthermore, the "genius" is no different "inside" from anyone else, as Stein both states and exemplifies in the pronominal play of this passage. In the same text, Stein again defines "genius" as an essential "nothingness": "It takes a lot of time to be a genius, you have to sit around so much doing nothing, really doing nothing" (EA, 70). While "being a genius" is time-consuming, this state of "being" is "filled" with "nothing": inaction and stasis. The shock and humor of this statement lie in the "incongruous juxtaposition" between the presumably full presence of a "genius" and its ontological "nothingness."[35] This incongruity is further borne out by the use of pronouns in this passage, which again emphasize that the "genius" is no different from the general public, from everybody, from an infinitely variable "you" that serves as its double and its mirror. Substitution takes place not only on the micro level of the text – in the slippage between "I" and "you" – but also structurally, within the very form of autobiography: the authorial self as "every" self. To this extent, *Everybody's Autobiography*, like *The Autobiography of Alice B. Toklas*, lays claim to the autobiographical mode and its grounding in the unique, inviolable and autonomous self only to disable its own generic mechanisms by de-essentializing this self, revealing it to be variable, substitutable, and contingent: "genius" as generic.

III

So far, I have attempted to explore the complex and subversive textual strategies deployed within Stein's "popular" writings, and to suggest ways in which the disruptive possibilities of these texts might initiate critical rereadings. Just as Stein's "experimental" work can be seen offering a "model of genius" to the reader willing to follow Stein along its bewildering paths, so too do Stein's "popular" autobiographies of the 1930s operate through a recursive model of "talking and listening" that holds out a complex lure, soliciting the reader's complicity in the performance of textual authority while appearing to ground this authority in a seemingly monolithic notion of authorial "genius."

On another, more historical level, however, Stein's popular autobiographies of the 1930s are fascinating as culminating gestures within an aesthetic career at once embedded in the hierarchies and exclusions of high modernism and perched on the cusp of a more properly postmodern cultural moment. By postmodern, here, I am referring to a certain "cultural logic," in the words of Fredric Jameson, that is reflective of late capitalism and that represents both the extension and the repositioning of certain tenets of aesthetic modernism. For Jameson, postmodernism emerges out of new economic dynamics of consumption and commodification (including fetishization) which in turn restructure the way in which both the aesthetic object and the modern subject can be thought: as a set of texts or simulacra characterized by "a new kind of flatness or depthlessness, a new kind of superficiality in the most literal sense."[36] In juxtaposing the work of Van Gogh to that of Andy Warhol (particularly the latter's serialized "portraits" of celebrities like Monroe or Elvis), Jameson suggests that the difference between the two lies in the "compensatory" gesture within the high modernist work, which creates out of the material of life "a whole new Utopian realm of the senses," as opposed to the "affectless" treatment of the subject (the celebrity or "star") in the postmodernist work, which not only emphasizes the mechanical reproducibility of the image but is itself complicit with this "serial" logic. For Jameson, the essence of this logic lies in the relationship between new cultural "intensities" – the primacy of the image and the signifier over "depth" – and new technologies, themselves figures for "a whole new economic world system."[37] Postmodernism, then, is "related to notions of the waning or extinction of the hundred-year-old modern movement"; "the force field in which very different kinds of cultural impulses . . . must make their way."[38]

This is not to suggest that postmodernist features are not to be seen, in various stages of emergence, within the works of an earlier high modernism; indeed, many critics have contended that Gertrude Stein herself "wrote texts whose features and aesthetic assumptions mark them as decidedly postmodern."[39] As we have seen in chapters 3 and 4, Stein's most obviously experimental writing seems to resonate deeply with late twentieth-century modes of textual engagement that foreground linguistic fragmentation, the dissemination of authority, and the indeterminacy of textual "meaning." But what interests me here is the possibility that the writing Stein produces after her most experimental period – in particular, *Everybody's Autobiography* – might represent another kind of nascent yet somehow reluctant postmodernism, uncertain about the emerging "cultural logic" that it both addresses and expresses. To the extent that *Everybody's Autobiography* attempts to reproduce the intimacy of "talking and listening" through structuring itself around the dialogic exchange of an "I" and a "you" (and hence making "everybody" into a "genius") it can be seen as extending the most radical textual implications of the experimental writing. But insofar as the text also registers a *historical* recognition of the way modern forms of representation and mediation (particularly film, public relations, and advertising) have forever changed the structure of subjectivity, authority, and textuality, it represents a crucial counter-vision to the more "utopian" experimental writings of the 1910s and 1920s. And in light of this latter recognition the modernist notion of "genius," even Stein's effort to deconstruct this notion, becomes particularly problematic.

As Michael André Bernstein has recently written:

At its most radical, postmodernism throws into doubt the category

> of the genius, which from Immanuel Kant to Marcel Duchamp, and especially in Marcel Proust, Pound, Stein, and Joyce, grounded and justified the artist's exempla whose universality was guaranteed precisely and tautologically because they were discovered by a genius.[40]

In fact, *Everybody's Autobiography* both justifies itself and guarantees its "universality" not so much through the claim that Gertrude Stein is a "genius," but through the claim that "everybody" is one as well: the "I" as well as the "you." This claim is in a sense "postmodern" in that it registers a new kind of serialization of persons, a new reproducibility in the category of "everybody" that effectively levels distinctions and differences, including those upon which the very notion of "genius" is founded. Yet the crucial point to be made about Gertrude Stein is that in opening up the category of "genius" to "everybody" in *Everybody's Autobiography* she is both voiding this category of individual distinction *and* affirming its validity. Hers is not a fully postmodern aesthetic in the Warholian sense: there is less stress, in Stein, upon the flattening or "death" of the subject in the face of new technologies, and more upon its proliferation within a bounded textual or national landscape. One need only recall Stein's vision of an ideal American nation, articulated in *The Making of Americans* and in later works like *Useful Knowledge*: a modernist utopia in which the production line of the modern factory has been geared up to produce "vitally singular ones." Within this paradoxical utopia lies the desire to merge the transcendent dimensions of "genius" with the movement, energy, and shocking potentialities – including those of mechanization and technology – of the modern nation, i.e., America.

Stein articulates this vision in *Everybody's Autobiography* through blurring the difference between "genius" and "celebrity." In stressing the changes that have taken place in America during her thirty years' absence, Stein attests to the seeming proliferation of distinct "personalities" that she meets on her lecture tour, a proliferation that the text itself contributes to both in its name-dropping and in its eight-page index of individual names at the back of the book. Curiously, however, Stein refers to these fellow Americans not in the terms through which she had long described individual distinction – as "geniuses" or as "vitally singular" – but rather as "celebrities." As we have seen above, Stein's remarks about "genius" in the text only arise in reference to an "I" and "you." The "names" whom she meets on her lecture tour (and her own "name" which she sees on "an electric sign moving around a building" in New York) are "celebrities," public subjects, subjects constructed through the gaze of a collectivity or mass. That Stein recognizes in *Everybody's Autobiography* that "celebrityhood" can and perhaps should be the natural extension of individual "genius" is evident from a statement that she arguably lifted from a contemporaneous book on genius and creative intelligence: "one does not in one's heart believe in mute inglorious Miltons."[41] Yet the celebrities she meets on her tour – Dashiell Hammett, Mary Pickford, William Saroyan, among others – seem rather more like "everybody" than like "Milton," and they even seem different from the modernist "geniuses" she both described and ridiculed in *The Autobiography of Alice B. Toklas*. The latter's containment within a marginal space of expatriate otherness and within the intimate or at times hermetic space of the modernist text seems qualitatively different from the celebrity's emergence within the public discourses and institutions of American mass culture. One has the sense in *Everybody's Autobiography* that Stein embraces the leveling of individual distinction into mass celebrityhood in America, as it represents the fulfillment of her early vision of mass-produced "vital singularity"; at the same time, it is clear that Stein finds this cultural shift in favor of "the masses" to be troubling.

In discussing the celebrity phenomenon, Stein reveals a remarkable prescience toward American culture of the 1930s. By the time of her lecture tour in 1934–5, a new force field was beginning to affect American modes of production and cultural representation, as well as habits of consumption. According to popular culture critic Joshua Gamson, during the 1930s advertising or public relations, the development of film technology, and the rise of modern American consumer culture "had entered a period of industrialization"; the result was the development of "an engine of publicity such as the world ha[d] never known before."[42] The Hollywood film industry and its stable of "stars" were at the white-hot center of this engine, not only generating enormous domestic revenues but also creating one of the most important "industries of desire" in the twentieth century.[43] Celebrities became the most potent commodities to emerge out of this system, transcending individual film texts and representing for audiences an alluring and elusive mix of glamor, wealth and frivolity: the qualities that most fed the fantasies of Depression-era audiences. Hollywood further perfected celebrity appeal in the 1930s by "de-divinising" stars, presenting them as "people like you and me – embodiments of *typical* ways of behaving."[44] The widely popularized myth of "discovery," disseminated in fan magazines and other venues of publicity, in which an unknown "nobody" was transformed overnight into a celebrated "somebody," helped to secure the role of the star as both celestial and generic. And this role was also constructed in relation to the potentialities of the new media themselves – film, radio, advertising – all of which made images of individual transcendence "widely available to a heterogeneous audience and capable of unlimited reproducibility."[45] In the relentless productivity of the publicity machine, as Walter Benjamin writes, "stars" are manufactured "as any article made in a factory."[46]

For Gertrude Stein, returning to America after more than thirty years abroad, the cultural dominance of this "engine of publicity" seemed to have produced a change in the very structure of human subjectivity and relationality that was at once thrilling and somewhat unnerving. On the one hand, film and publicity had made it possible for *anyone* to achieve individual distinction, for everybody to be a "public something." This, again, would seem to suggest the confirmation of Stein's early ideal of a great national machine or system manufacturing singular personalities as efficiently as any other standardized, machine-made, national product. The massification of "vital singularity" that Stein notes in the American celebrity system, and in which she sees herself implicated, clearly represents for her a new kind of cultural formation that unites the realm of the "normal" with that of the "extraordinary" – the cultural apotheosis of her lifelong effort to democratize the notion of "genius" and make it the province of "everybody." On the other hand, Stein writes, in a world in which individual exceptionality has become generic – a public commodity – there is a threat that "a person is so publicized that there isn't any personality left." This is of course the threat articulated by postmodernism, as Jameson suggests in his description of the Warholian celebrity as "flat" and "depthless," a figure in which "there is no longer a self present to do the feeling."[47] It is a threat that *Everybody's Autobiography* registers in economic terms, noting the commodity status of the celebrity "self" ("if the outside puts a value on you then all your inside gets to be outside" (EA, 47); "how once you know that the buyer is there can you go on knowing that the buyer is not there" (EA, 65)). And it is a threat that Stein also perceives in the predominance of autobiographical writing in modernity, and in the corresponding decline of the novel:

> It is funny about novels and the way novels now cannot be written. They cannot be written because actually all the things that are

> being said about any one is what is remembered about that one or decided about that one. And since there is so much publicity so many characters are being created every minute of every day that nobody is really interested in personality enough to dream about personalities . . . now well now how can you dream about a personality when it is always being created for you by a publicity. . . (EA, 69)

The change registered in this passage is from a time when the self was not created or "decided about" by an outside force ("publicity") but generated by an inside one (the "dream" of the nineteenth-century novelist). Stein goes on to note that "autobiography is written which is in a way a way to say that publicity is right, they are as the public sees them" (EA, 69): autobiography being the privileged genre of this newly mediated world because it offers a narrative construction of the self created for an "outside" and its modes of circulation and dissemination, like the star image in a media text. Stein's point is clear: that modern autobiography and its sister forms – film, radio, and advertising – not only entertain and fascinate but reconfigure the divide between private and public, individual and mass, turning "personality" from something inherent or given into something that can be made and manipulated by an "outside." Faced with a popular audience for the first time, Stein both welcomes the contingencies of a community of readers and laments the loss of interiority: "I who had always lived within myself and my writing" (HWIW, 63).

The irony is that both *The Autobiography of Alice B. Toklas* and *Everybody's Autobiography*, as I have argued in this chapter, attempt to replicate this process of relationality between "inside" and "outside" within the very structure of the seemingly "autobiographical" text. Yet *Everybody's Autobiography* also registers Stein's contradictory concerns about both autobiography and about her newfound role as celebrity: that both threaten to "flatten" and proliferate the subject through the public circulation of image rather than to encourage the subject's dynamic rearticulation within the intimate and vital space of the modernist text. Despite her desire to write the story of "everybody," to present her experience as a universal American experience, to make the "I" infinitely substitutable with a generic "you," and to deform and delegitimize claims to authority and mastery, *Everybody's Autobiography* also records moments of anxiety about the de-personalizing and de-hierarchizing effects of the story which it is engaged in telling. As Stein writes of celebrityhood, "In America everybody is but some are more than others. I was more than others" (EA, 168). Within the "I"'s claim to "more," finally, lies the fading refrain of high modernism and its attendant notion of "genius" – however deconstructed – in the face of a new popular credo that Stein herself both welcomed and feared – a credo embedded in the more properly, or perhaps more queerly, postmodern comments of an Andy Warhol: "Everybody looks alike and acts alike, and we're getting more and more that way. I think everybody should be a machine."[48]

As with Warhol's pronouncements, there is, of course, something very funny about Stein's statement that "[i]n America everybody is but some are more than others. I was more than others." The humor lies in the incongruous juxtaposition of opposing claims to a democratic truth ("everybody is a celebrity") and to an elitist one ("some are more than others. I was more than others"). Such a statement registers both a residual anxiety and the pleasures to be had from foregrounding the multiple affiliations which had always determined her sense of herself as an artist, as an American, and as a "genius." Both like everyone and "more than" everyone, both typical and transcendent, the product of standardized American manufacture while also expatriate and queer, Stein had always negotiated the boundaries between opposing authorial affiliations – largely, as I have suggested throughout this book, through her claims to "genius." In a statement that might be taken as indicative of her entire aesthetic, she writes at the end of *Everybody's Autobiography*, "I had always wanted it all to be commonplace and simple anything that I am writing and then I get worried lest I have succeeded . . . I have always all the time thought it was so and hoped it was so and then worried lest it was so" (EA, 310). In its desiring, shifting, comic, campy self-presentation, *Everybody's Autobiography* represents an important statement of aesthetic uncertainty that captures a moment of mixed pleasure in the historical and cultural transition from modernism to postmodernism.

Notes

1. Warhol, *Philosophy*, 101.
2. Sedgwick quoted in Gallup (ed.), "Stein and *Atlantic*," 111. The Sedgwick–Stein correspondence is reprinted in Gallup's text, along with introductory notes.
3. Ibid., 112.
4. Ibid., 117.
5. Anderson quoted in White (ed.), *Sherwood Anderson/Gertrude Stein*, 25.

6. "We live in different worlds. Yours may hold the good, the beautiful, and the true, but if it does their guise is not for us to recognize. Those vedettes who lead the vanguard of pictorial arts are understood, or partly understood, over here by a reasonably compact following, but that following cannot translate their loyalties into a corresponding literature, and it would really be hopeless for us to set up this new standard." (Letter from Sedgwick to Stein (26 Feb. 1932), quoted in Gallup (ed.), "Stein and *Atlantic*," 125).
7. Stein quoted in Mellow, *Charmed Circle*, 409. Of course, Stein herself would appear to subscribe to this opposition by generating a distinction in the 1930s between "entity" and "identity" writing: the former an expression of the autonomous "human mind," the latter the product of the relational "human nature." Apparently originating out of the dislocation she felt upon the sudden commercial success of *The Autobiography of Alice B. Toklas* in 1933, the entity/identity distinction finds its fullest expression in the 1936 text entitled *The Geographical History of America: Or, the Relation of Human Nature to the Human Mind*. "On one side there was genius, the masterpiece, the present, entity, the human mind," as one critic summarizes Stein's main points in this work, "and on the other, society, newspaper writing, memory, identity, human nature." (Perelman, *Trouble with Genius*, 154). The popular autobiographies of the 1930s – *The Autobiography of Alice B. Toklas* and *Everybody's Autobiography*, along with such memoirs as *Picasso* (1938) and *Paris France* (1940) – would appear to belong firmly to the latter, to the public, to identity and to human nature; a "difficult" work like *The Geographical History* would belong to the former, to the private, to the human mind, to "genius." But such a claim reduces Stein's work to a set of stable binary distinctions that she herself was continually destabilizing in the texts at hand. Just as *The Geographical History of America: Or, the Relation of Human Nature to the Human Mind* is as much a text of "relation" as it is of "entity" (as its title makes clear), so too are the "popular" texts as disruptive to the presentation of public identity as they are productive of it (as their titles likewise suggest). As I argue in this chapter, Stein herself problematizes the effort either to privilege a "difficult" work like *The Geographical History of America* or to dismiss the "popular" writings out of hand without attending to the rhetorical strategies and subversions of each.
8. MOA, 289 (emphasis mine).
9. Dubnick, *Structure of Obscurity*, 68; Bridgman, *Stein in Pieces*, 209; Hobhouse, *Everybody Who Was Anybody*, 148; Kellner, *Stein Companion*, 21.
10. Letter from Sedgwick to Stein (11 Feb. 1933), quoted in Gallup (ed.), "Stein and *Atlantic*," 126.
11. It is interesting that Sedgwick would refuse to serialize *The Autobiography of Alice B. Toklas* in the *Atlantic* without using Stein's name, writing to Harcourt Brace that "It is . . . obviously impossible for a magazine to get readers for it and keep them, unless the authorship is disclosed" (unpublished correspondence, Gertrude Stein and

Alice B. Toklas Collection, Yale Collection of American Literature. Beinecke Rare Book and Manuscript Library).

12. Butler, *Gender Trouble*, 33 (emphasis mine).
13. Gilmore, for example, has brilliantly emphasized the overdetermined nature of the "I" in *The Autobiography of Alice B. Toklas*, as it bespeaks "Stein's ambivalence about the self as a unified figure" (Gilmore, "Signature," 59). See also Smith, "Performativity," 28–9; Stimpson, "Gertrude Stein and the Lesbian Lie." The term "proto-pomo" is Gayle Rubin's ("Sexual Traffic," 66).
14. See Ch. 3, 83–4.
15. For de Man, all writing is structured around the differentiation of two elements, "the two subjects involved in the process of reading." Yet autobiography purports to be univocal: "[t]his specular structure is interiorized in a text in which the author declares himself the subject of his own understanding" (de Man, "Autobiography as De-Facement," 922).
16. "Dans notre rapport aux choses, tel qu'il est constitué par la voie de la vision, et ordonné dans les figures de la représentation, quelque chose glisse, passe, se transmet, d'étage en étage, pour y être toujours à quelque degré élidé – c'est ça qui s'appelle le regard" (Lacan, *Séminaire XI*, 70).
17. Houston A. Baker Jr., quoted in Chay, "Reconstructing Essentialism," 141.
18. Gilmore, "Gertrice/Altrude," 65.
19. As Patricia Meyer Spacks points out, "gossip," like literature itself, "possesses a double valence: enemy and agent of desire" (Spacks, *Gossip*, 262). Several years after the publication of *The Autobiography of Alice B. Toklas*, several detractors published a rebuttal in *transition*, "Supplement: Testimony against Gertrude Stein by Henri Matisse, Tristan Tzara, Maria Jolas, Georges Braque, Eugene Jolas, André Salmon": "*transition* has opened its pages to several of those she [Stein] mentions who, like ourselves, find that the book often lacks accuracy. This fact and the regrettable possibility that many less informed readers might accept Miss Stein's testimony about her contemporaries, make it wiser to straighten out those points with which we are familiar before the book has had time to assume the character of historic authenticity... These documents invalidate the claim of the Toklas–Stein memorial that Miss Stein was in any way concerned with the shaping of the epoch she attempts to describe. There is a unanimity of opinion that she had no understanding of what really was happening around her" (2).
20. Sontag, "Notes on 'Camp,'" 105–6.
21. Ibid., 116.
22. Ibid., 115.
23. Ibid., 109.
24. Derrida, "Signature Event Context," 320. On the particular function of femininity as dissimulation or "masquerade," as the veil that hides a (phallic) lack, see Riviere, "Womanliness as a Masquerade"; Lacan, "The Signification of the Phallus," 289–90.
25. Sontag, "Notes on 'Camp,'" 107.

26. Newton, *Mother Camp*, 106.
27. M. Meyer, "Introduction," in his *Politics and Poetics of Camp*, 2.
28. Butler, *Gender Trouble*, 146.
29. In a letter to H. L. Mencken, Dreiser notes his decision during the final stages of his novel's composition to put quotation marks around the central term in his title in order "to convey the exact question which I mean to imply" (letter from Dreiser to Mencken, 30 November 1914, in Riggio (ed.), *Dreiser–Mencken Letters*, 166). Many of Dreiser's stereotypes in this novel about the ambiguous figure of the artistic "genius" are drawn from late nineteenth-century discourses of degeneracy; see Introduction, note 14.
30. Stein's close gay male friends during this period included Virgil Thomson, Thornton Wilder, Paul Bowles, and Carl Van Vechten; for a history, see Kaiser, *The Gay Metropolis*; Summers (ed.), *The Gay and Lesbian Literary Heritage*, esp. 30–9.
31. Benveniste, "The Nature of Pronouns," in his *Problems in General Linguistics*, 217; 220.
32. Benveniste, "Subjectivity in Language," in his *Problems in General Linguistics*, 224–5.
33. Bergman, "Introduction," in his *Camp Grounds*, 6. See also Marty Roth's essay in the same volume, "Homosexual Expression and Homophobic Censorship: The Situation of the Text" (268–81), which discusses pronoun substitutions as "cross-writing" (270).
34. Newton, "Role Models," in Bergman (ed.), *Camp Grounds*, 44.
35. Newton writes that "Camp usually depends on the perception or creation of *incongruous juxtapositions*. Either way, the homosexual 'creates' the camp, by pointing out the incongruity or devising it" (Newton, *Mother Camp*, 106).
36. Jameson, "Postmodernism," 60. For a dissenting view, see Perloff, "Postmodernism/Fin de Siècle: Defining 'Difference' in Late Twentieth-Century Poetics," in her *Poetry On & Off the Page*, 3–33.
37. Ibid., 58–9.
38. Ibid., 57.
39. Berry, *Curved Thought*, 4.
40. Bernstein, "Making Modernist Masterpieces," 12.
41. In arguing for the necessary containment of "genius" within a circumscribed social space, Nathaniel Hirsch writes, "The environment of genius is genius; when it is not so, mute, inglorious Miltons and functionless Newtons further darken 'Cities of Dreadful Night'" (Hirsch, *Genius and Creative Intelligence*, 331). In 1932, Hirsch sent Stein a copy of his book, along with an adulatory letter proclaiming her "a genius of the first mark . . . a pythoness . . . a priestess upon the tripod" (letter from Nathaniel D. M. Hirsch to Gertrude Stein (17 June 1932), unpublished correspondence, Gertrude Stein and Alice B. Toklas Papers, Yale Collection of American Literature. Beinecke Rare Book and Manuscript Library). To be sure, Stein's interest in the relation between "genius" and "celebrityhood" was longstanding: many of her earliest word portraits, for example, reveal an intense interest in the potential of certain artists for "going on succeeding" (see "Four

Protégés"; "Five or Six Men"; "A Kind of Women," in Stein, *Two*).

42. Gamson, *Claims to Fame*, 28; 33.
43. For a discussion, see Gledhill (ed.), *Stardom: Industry of Desire*.
44. Dyer, *Stars*, 24. Gamson concurs with Dyer, writing that in the 1930s, Hollywood worked to present its celebrities as "blown-up version[s] of the typical." This development was also fueled by the phenomenon of "discovery," where successful stars and starlets were presented as ordinary people who had happened upon a "lucky break." See Gamson, *Claims to Fame*, 29–31.
45. Berry, *Curved Thought*, 143.
46. Benjamin, "The Work of Art in the Age of Mechanical Reproduction," 231. In this essay, Benjamin suggests how new media technologies themselves had made available the possibility for everyone to become a "singular" one: "[T]he newsreel offers everyone the opportunity to rise from passer-by to movie extra . . . Any man today can lay claim to being filmed" (ibid., 231).
47. Jameson, "Postmodernism," 64.
48. Warhol quoted in Huyssen, *After the Great Divide*, 148. For an insightful comparison of Stein and Warhol, see Wendy Steiner, "Introduction," in Stein's *Lectures in America*, ix–xxvii.

Coda: Warhol's Stein

Gertrude Stein's anticipation of postmodern notions of the authorial subject as decentered and fragmented, as processual, multiple, and indeterminate, has been one of the issues of this book. Her insistence upon the proliferation of this subject through explicit strategies of dialogic address or through modes of textual defamiliarization that make potential room for anyone allow Stein to be perceived as a fellow-traveler for a contemporary age. Yet as I have also argued here, Stein's "need to think of [herself] as special," her investment in modernist discourses of aesthetic withdrawal and in a poetics of interiority, and the unresolved contradictions between her profound affiliation with American "democratic" culture and her inscription within European high culture, all demand that we see Stein's project as one located both within and against the specific historical moment of high modernism. The shifting, complex notion of "genius" has provided the focus through which to examine the exigencies, constraints, and possibilities of Stein's authorial positions, and their necessary imbrication in textual practice.

Stein's proximity to and distance from certain postmodern notions of the subject can be seen once again through reference to the work of Andy Warhol, who indeed forces the issue when in 1980 he produces a portrait of Stein for his silk-screen series *Ten Portraits of Jews of the Twentieth Century* (Fig. C.1). I end with this portrait, not only for the relevance of its subject (Warhol referred to the series casually as his "Jewish Geniuses" project), but for the way it both extends and departs from some of Stein's more pressing aesthetic and subjective concerns. Warhol reads Gertrude Stein as a "genius," but refuses to ascribe to her the kind of interiority that would traditionally be associated with this name; his Stein is literally the copy of a copy, a silk-screened print of a photograph from the 1930s to which Warhol or one of his Factory assistants has added variously a few dark outlines or some collage-like blocks of color.[1] A found object or appropriated image, Warhol's Stein is unoriginal, simulated,

Fig. C.1 *Andy Warhol, "Gertrude Stein" (1980)*
(Ten Portraits of Jews of the Twentieth Century)

depthless; even when the "artisanal" flourishes of tracing and color appended to the image serve less to heighten than to deface or erase their subject: graffiti marks on a screened image of a photographic negative of a celebrity. Stein might well have appreciated this defacement, given her own playful, camp, self-fracturing presentation in *The Autobiography of Alice B. Toklas*, as well as her recognition in *Everybody's Autobiography* that having one's image freed into public circulation is, in a sense, like becoming estranged from one's own face and name, like having "a little shock of recognition and non-recognition" (EA, 175). Warhol's Stein can thus be seen as an extension of Stein's own self-construction in the 1930s: both exceptional and generic in a world where everybody is a celebrity (or as Warhol would put it, where everybody is "world famous for fifteen minutes"); both located within a hierarchy of cultural meaning (a "genius," or, in Warhol's portrait, a "Jewish genius"[2]) and a copy without an original, an image circulating in depthless public space.

The "post" in Warhol's postmodernism – and the arguable point of difference between his own portrait of Gertrude Stein and the many and varied portraits of herself throughout her literary career – lies in the patent indifference of his work and of his "philosophy" toward the "great divide" within which notions of aesthetic value, quality, originality, autonomy, appropriation and plaigiarism operate as significant categories. As I suggested in Chapter 5, Stein's texts from the 1930s write out her ambivalence toward the spectacle of American culture within which she finds herself circulating as the image of a "genius": both like everybody and "more than" everybody, she is drawn to the aesthetic and subjective possibilities of an emerging popular culture yet also fears the effect of this "outside" upon the transcendent, "high," arguably hermetic voice of "the inside." Warhol's disavowal of transcendence (of his subject, of the projections and limitations of Art, of his own artistic position) represents an interesting transformation of Stein's concerns in *Everybody's Autobiography*. After early efforts in the 1950s to establish himself as both a commercial and a fine artist, Warhol in the 1960s abandoned this twofold pursuit for a Pop-ulist project that would align itself with a new social leveling of hierarchies and differences: "Everybody looks alike and acts alike, and we're getting more and more that way. I think everybody should be a machine"; "I think everybody should be like everybody. That seems to be what is happening now."[3] As Andreas Huyssen has argued, the emergence of Pop art appeared to represent "the beginning of a far reaching democratization of art and art appreciation,"[4] replacing the seemingly intractable cultural opposition of an earlier modernist moment between a coterie of artistic "highbrows" with their intensely personal styles and a debased, redundant, mechanized mass culture. In the place of this opposition Pop art offered a new celebration of "the popular," that repository of fantasy and desire refracted through the workings of mechanical reproduction and inscribed in the free-floating economic circuits of late capitalism. Warhol's screenprints and paintings – especially the early portraits of celebrities (Marilyn and Elvis); cartoon characters (Superman and Nancy); and commodities (Campbell's soup cans and Brillo boxes) – partake in this celebration through a camp recycling or plagiarism of popular culture. Part of this project is a disavowal of what Warhol calls the "hand gesture" in favor of a "noncommittal, anonymous" art:[5] "I really don't believe in signing my work. Anyone could do the things I am doing, and I don't feel they should be signed"[6] – for "signing," like the notion of "plagiarism," is located within a cultural logic of the "master" and of the "masterpiece," as in a literal correspondence between name and self, "figure" and "ground." Rather, Warhol's aesthetic claim is to *likeness*: his Marilyns and Supermans and Jackies are the generic, serial images or simulacra of everyday, post-war American culture, "figures" without "ground," which also serve as "the calling into question of the possibility of ground."[7] Reproducible, fungible, displayed in a series of ten, or one hundred, these images emphasize not the unique and discrete "reality" of Monroe or Elvis or Liz Taylor but the deferral of presence in a potentially infinite chain of similar and simulated figures. Most radically, these images also inscribe the spectator within their Pop-ulist vision: just as one Elvis is like another Elvis, so is Elvis like Marilyn like Jackie, and so also is the spectator like the celebrity: "Everybody looks alike and acts alike, and we're getting more and more that way."

Warhol's repudiation of the artist's "signature" and his emphasis upon the generic qualities of both his subjects and his prints is similar to Gertrude Stein's refusal of the author-function in *The Autobiography of Alice B. Toklas* – with its unsigned title page – and her construction of the reproducible subject in such texts as "An Instant Answer or A Hundred Prominent Men" and *Everybody's Autobiography*. Yet while in the latter Stein had thrilled at the possibility that popular American culture had made "everybody" into a "celebrity," she had also registered a concern about the loss of interiority that such developments entailed, since "if the outside puts a value on you then all your inside gets to be outside" (EA, 47). Interestingly, Warhol's own ludic "autobiography" *POPism* (1980) also locates his work within a dichotomy of inside/outside: "Pop Art took the inside and put it outside, took the outside and put it inside."[8] Yet the point of this statement is clearly upheaval, disruption, inversion: a debunking of Romantic and modernist pieties favoring the integrity of the "inside" over the values of the "outside." If anything, Warhol clearly privileges the "outside" over any residual "inside": the public and the publicized, the visible, replicable, surface ephemera of a rapidly expanding American consumerist culture. Being "out" – in all senses of the term – carries for Warhol none of the anxiety that Stein displays in *Everybody's Autobiography*: "If you want to know all about Andy Warhol, just look at the surface: of my paintings and films and me, and there I am. There's nothing behind it."[9] The lack of a "behind," of a "bottom nature," of an inside or of an original that "grounds" the copy circulating in public space does not particularly concern Warhol; what matters is the camp, performative gesture, the gesture that parodies and disrupts the "authentic" and the "original," that calls into question the very possibility of "highness" and "depth."

In his insistence upon a mode of likeness that includes all aspects of the experience of "art" (from its Factory-made production to its serial conception to its public consumption), and thus in his refusal to establish differentiating boundaries between high and low, good and bad, artist and audience, Warhol extends Stein's recognition in *Everybody's Autobiography* that her story is "everybody's" story; that there is no difference between "one" and "anyone"; that the "ground" through which differentiating oppositions can be maintained and policed via notions of aesthetic and subjective "highness" is no longer either solid or sharply defined. Yet in his desire to privilege the spectacle of "the outside" over any possibility of an "inside" – or finally, arguably, to refuse this binary logic altogether – Warhol departs from Stein's own contradictory investment in the boundaries and exclusions of artistic "genius." Of course, Warhol's Stein is not the only postmodern Stein, and there are other ways to tell the story of Stein's relationship to high modernism and of her continual, vital significance to contemporary art, literature, music, and theory.[10] The terms with which she provides us, like her shifting, complex claims to "being a genius," make this story as ever an open-ended one.

Notes

1. Warhol screenprinted 200 portfolios of the series, which included portraits of Stein, Kafka, Martin Buber, Einstein, Brandeis, Gershwin, the Marx brothers, Golda Meir, Sarah Bernhardt, and Freud. Several trial proofs of this portfolio also exist, as well as paintings (prints executed upon canvas rather than on paper), including the ones of Stein reproduced in this book, which show variations from the screenprint series in color and outlining. In a reversal of the priority traditionally assigned painting as a medium, the images in this series "were first conceptualized as prints and then later produced as paintings" (de Salvo, "Prints of Andy Warhol," 26). For more on Warhol's production of this series, see ibid. 26–7; Bourdon, *Warhol*, 384–5.
2. Warhol's effort to "out" Stein as a "Jewish genius" says more about his own anxieties toward Jewish cultural authority than it does about Stein's sense of the parameters of her identity, which, as I have argued earlier, were always drawn in complex ways outside issues of race. Brian Selsky has offered some suggestive comments on the potentially "anti-Semitic logic" at work in this series (Selsky, "I Dream of

Genius . . .," in Doyle, Flatley, and Muñoz (eds), *Pop Out: Queer Warhol*, 188–9). For a provocative response to Warhol from a Jewish feminist perspective, see Kass, *The Warhol Project*; also note 10 below.

3. Warhol quote from an unsigned 1964 *Newsweek* article, in Madoff (ed.), *Pop Art*, 279; also in Huyssen, *After the Great Divide*, 148.
4. Huyssen, *After the Great Divide*, 142.
5. Warhol, *POPism*, 7.
6. Warhol quoted in Roger Vaughan, "Superpop or A Night at the Factory," in Madoff (ed.), *Pop Art*, 284.
7. Marjorie Garber, *Vested Interests*, 150. For further discussion, see Mandy Merck, "Figuring Out Warhol," in Doyle, Flatley, and Muñoz (eds), *Pop Out*, 234–5.
8. Warhol, *POPism*, 3.
9. Berg, "Andy: My True Story," 3.
10. At least one place to begin is with the work of contemporary American visual artist Deborah Kass, who "repeats" Warhol's own work but in patently contradictory ways. In "The Warhol Project" (1992–8), Kass appropriates Warhol's silk-screen technique and use of the serialized image in order to represent lesbian or Jewish subjects occluded in traditional modernism and even in the work of Warhol himself. Her own erxtensive work on Stein (including the "Chairman Ma" series, which appropriates both Warhol's Mao images and his "Gertrude Stein" portrait) has an intensity of presence and feminist meaning missing in the Warhol work; at the same time, she complicates Warhol's cool celebration of the "out"side by problematizing the issue of lesbian visibility. See Kass, *The Warhol Project*, which includes critical essays by Linda Nochlin and others. An equally powerful contemporary artistic engagement with Stein can also be seen in the work of Faith Ringgold, whose story quilt entitled "Dinner at Gertrude Stein's" (1991) directly confronts the relays between gender, "genius," and race in high modernism. Like Kass, Ringgold places Stein at the genial center of her work but also raises the question of Stein's implication in the primitivist and elitist modernist gaze. In ways that move beyond the work of Kass, Ringgold complicates Stein's relationship to racial difference by portraying Stein's visible discomfort at the subversive "folk" dialect and laughter of Zora Neale Hurston, who occupies a marginal position at the dinner party. Yet in the text that circles around the frame of the quilt, Ringgold presents an interesting fusion of black dialect and Steinian repetition which suggest once again the elasticity of Stein's work and its availability to different voices, even (or especially) to those that fall outside the traditional frame of the high modernist work and social circle. See Cameron et al., *Dancing at the Louvre*.

Selected Bibliography

Adams, Brooks. *The Law of Civilization and Decay: An Essay on History* [1896]. New York: Vintage, 1955.

Adorno, Theodor. *Aesthetic Theory* [1970]. Trans. C. Lenhardt. London: Routledge, 1984.

Althusser, Louis. *Lenin and Philosophy and Other Essays*. Trans. Ben Brewster. New York: Monthly Review Press, 1971.

Armstrong, Tim. *Modernism, Technology, and the Body: A Cultural Study*. Cambridge: Cambridge UP, 1998.

Ashton, Jennifer. "Gertrude Stein for Anyone." *ELH* 64 (Spring 1997), 289–331.

Bakhtin, M. M. *The Dialogic Imagination* [1975]. Trans. Caryl Emerson and Michael Holquist. Austin: University of Texas Press, 1981.

Battersby, Christine. *Gender and Genius: Towards a Feminist Aesthetics*. London: The Women's Press, 1989.

Benjamin, Walter. "The Work of Art in the Age of Mechanical Reproduction." *Illuminations: Essays and Reflections*, ed. H. Arendt, trans. Harry Zohn. New York: Schocken, 1969, 217–51.

Benstock, Shari. *Women of the Left Bank: Paris 1900–1940*. Austin: University of Texas Press, 1986.

Benveniste, Emile. *Problems in General Linguistics* [1966]. Trans. Mary Elizabeth Meek. Coral Gables: University of Miami Press, 1971.

Berg, Gretchen. "Andy Warhol: My True Story," *Los Angeles Free Press* 6:11 (1967).

Bergman, David (ed.). *Camp Grounds: Style and Homosexuality*. Amherst: University of Massachusetts Press, 1993.

Bernstein, Michael André. "Making Modernist Masterpieces." *Modernism/Modernity* 5:3 (September 1998), 1–17.

Berry, Ellen E. *Curved Thought and Textual Wandering: Gertrude Stein's Postmodernism*. Ann Arbor: University of Michigan Press, 1992.

Bohrer, Karl Heinz. *Suddenness: On the Moment of Aesthetic Appearance* [1981]. Trans. Ruth Crowley. New York: Columbia UP, 1994.

Booth, Alison. *Greatness Engendered: George Eliot and Virginia Woolf*. Ithaca: Cornell UP, 1992.

Bourdon, David. *Warhol*. New York: Henry N. Abrams, 1989.

Bridgman, Richard. *Gertrude Stein in Pieces*. New York: Oxford UP, 1970.

Brinnin, John Malcolm. *The Third Rose: Gertrude Stein and Her World* [1959]. Reading, Massachusetts: Addison-Wesley, 1987.

Bürger, Peter. *Theory of the Avant-Garde* [1974]. Trans. Michael Shaw. Minneapolis: University of Minnesota Press, 1984.

Butler, Judith. *Bodies that Matter: On the Discursive Limits of Sex*. New York: Routledge, 1993.

——. *Gender Trouble: Feminism and the Subversion of Identity*. New York: Routledge, 1990.

Cameron, Dan, Richard J. Powell, Michele Wallace, Patrick Hill, Thalia Gouma-Peterson, Moira Roth, and Ann Gibson (eds). *Dancing at the Louvre: Faith Ringgold's French Collection and Other Story Quilts*. New York: New Museum of Contemporary Art, 1998.

Carby, Hazel. *Reconstructing Womanhood: The Emergence of the Afro-American Woman Novelist*. New York: Oxford UP, 1987.

Carey, John. *The Intellectuals and the Masses: Pride and Prejudice among the Literary Intelligentsia 1880–1939*. New York: St Martin's Press, 1992.

Chay, Deborah. "Reconstructing Essentialism." *Diacritics* (Summer–Fall 1991), 135–47.

Chessman, Harriet. *The Public Is Invited to Dance: Representation, the Body, and Dialogue in Gertrude Stein*. Stanford: Stanford UP, 1989.

Cheyette, Bryan, and Laura Marcus (eds). *Modernity, Culture and 'the Jew'*. Stanford: Stanford UP, 1998.

Coburn, Alvin Langdon. *Men of Mark*. New York: M. Kennerley, 1913.

Cohen, Milton A. "Black Brutes and Mulatto Saints: The Racial Hierarchy of Stein's 'Melanctha'." *Black American Literature Forum* 18:3 (Fall 1984), 119–21.

Conrad, Bryce. "Gertrude Stein in the American Marketplace." *Journal of Modern Literature* xix:2 (Fall 1995), 215–33.

Cook, Albert. "Some Notes on Gertrude Stein and Deixis." *Arizona Quarterly* 53:1 (Spring 1997), 91–102.

Cooley, Charles H. "Genius, Fame, and the Comparison of Races." *Annals of the American Academy of Political and Social Science* (May 1897), 1–42.

Cope, Karin. "'Moral Deviancy' and Contemporary Feminism: The Judgment of Gertrude Stein." *Feminism Beside Itself*, ed. Diane Elam and Robyn Wiegman. New York: Routledge, 1995, 155–78.

Curnutt, Kirk. "Parody and Pedagogy: Teaching Style, Voice, and Authorial Intent in the Works of Gertrude Stein." *College Literature* 23:2 (June 1996), 1–24.

Currie, Robert. Genius: *An Ideology in Literature*. New York: Schocken, 1974.

Damon, Maria. "Gertrude Stein's Jewishness, Jewish Social Scientists, and the 'Jewish Question'." *MFS* 42:3 (Fall 1996), 489–506.

DeKoven, Marianne. *A Different Language: Gertrude Stein's Experimental Writing*. Madison: University of Wisconsin Press, 1983.

——. "Introduction" to Gertrude Stein entry. *The Gender of Modernism*, ed. Bonnie Kime Scott. Bloomington: Indiana UP, 1990, 479–88.

de Man, Paul. "Autobiography as De-Facement." *MLN* 94:5 (December 1979), 919–30.

Derrida, Jacques. "Signature Event Context" [1971]. *Margins of Philosophy*, trans. Alan Bass. Chicago: University of Chicago Press, 1982, 309–30.

de Salvo, Donna. "God Is in the Details: The Prints of Andy Warhol." *Andy Warhol Prints: A Catalogue Raisonné 1962–1987*, ed. Frayda Feldman and Claudia Defendi. New York: Distributed Art Publishers, 1997, 16–31.

de Staël, Madame. *Corrine ou l'Italie* [1806]. Paris: Editions Gallimard, 1985.

Diner, Hasia R. *In the Almost Promised Land: American Jews and Blacks, 1915–1935*. Westport, CT: Greenwood Press, 1977.

Doyle, Jennifer, Jonathan Flatley, and José Esteban Muñoz (eds). *Pop Out: Queer Warhol*. Durham: Duke UP, 1996.

Dreiser, Theodore. *The "Genius"*. New York: John Lane, 1915.

Dubnick, Randa. *The Structure of Obscurity: Gertrude Stein, Language, and Cubism*. Urbana: University of Illinois Press, 1984.

Dydo, Ulla. "To Have the Winning Language: Texts and Contexts of Gertrude Stein." *Coming to Light: American Women Poets in the Twentieth Century*, ed. Diane Wood Middlebrook and Marilyn Yalom. Ann Arbor: University of Michigan Press, 1985, 58–73.

Dyer, Richard. *Stars*. London: British Film Institute, 1986.

Eliot, T. S. "Charleston, Hey! Hey!" *The Nation & Athenaeum* xl:17 (29 January 1927), 595.

——. *The Sacred Wood: Essays on Poetry and Criticism* [1920]. London: Faber & Faber, 1997.

Everett, Patricia R. (ed.). *A History of Having a Great Many Times not Continued to be Friends: The Correspondence between Mabel Dodge and Gertrude Stein, 1911–1934*. Albuquerque: University of New Mexico Press, 1996.

Fisher, George. *The American instructor: or, Young Man's best companion*. Philadelphia: B. Franklin and D. Hall, 1748.

Fitch, Noel Riley. *Sylvia Beach and the Lost Generation: A History of Literary Paris in the Twenties and Thirties*. New York: W. W. Norton, 1983.

Fitzgerald, F. Scott. *The Great Gatsby* [1925]. New York: Scribner, 1995.

Foucault, Michel. *Discipline and Punish: The Birth of the Prison* [1975]. Trans. Alan Sheridan. London: Penguin, 1977.

Franklin, Benjamin. *The Autobiography and Other Writings*. New York: Penguin, 1986.

Freud, Sigmund. *The Standard Edition of the Complete Psychological Works of Sigmund Freud*. Trans. and ed. James Strachey. London: The Hogarth Press, 1957.

Friedman, Ellen G., and Miriam Fuchs (eds). *Breaking the Sequence: Women's Experimental Fiction*. Princeton: Princeton UP, 1989.

Gallup, Donald (ed.). "Gertrude Stein and the *Atlantic*." *Yale University Library Gazette* xxviii (1954), 109–28.

Galton, Francis. *Hereditary Genius: An Inquiry into Its Laws and Consequences*. London: Macmillan, 1869.

Gamson, Joshua. *Claims to Fame: Celebrity in Contemporary America*. Berkeley: University of California Press, 1994.
Garber, Marjorie. *Vested Interests: Cross-Dressing & Cultural Anxiety*. New York: Routledge, 1992.
Gilbert, Roger. "Review of *The Trouble with Genius. Reading Pound, Joyce, Stein, and Zukovsky*. By Bob Perelman." *American Literature* 67 (September 1995), 600–1.
Gilman, Sander L. *Smart Jews: The Construction of the Image of Jewish Superior Intelligence*. Lincoln: University of Nebraska Press, 1996.
Gilmore, Leigh. "A Signature of Lesbian Autobiography: 'Gertrice/Altrude'." *Autobiography and Questions of Gender*, ed. Shirley Neuman. London: Frank Cass, 1991, 56–75.
Gledhill, Christine (ed.). *Stardom: Industry of Desire*. New York: Routledge, 1991.
Graf von Keyserling, Hermann. *America Set Free . . .* New York: Harper & Brothers, 1929.
Greenberg, Clement. "Avant-Garde and Kitsch" [1939]. *The Collected Essays and Criticism*, vol. I, ed. John O'Brian. Chicago: Chicago UP, 1986, 5–22.
Grosz, Elizabeth. *Volatile Bodies: Toward a Corporeal Feminism*. Bloomington: Indiana UP, 1994.
Harrowitz, Nancy A., and Barbara Hyams (eds). *Jews & Gender: Responses to Otto Weininger*. Philadelphia: Temple UP, 1995.
Hawthorn, Jeremy. *A Concise Glossary of Contemporary Literary Theory*. London: Edward Arnold, 1992.
Hegel, G. W. F. *Aesthetics* [1835]. Trans. and ed. T. M. Knox. Oxford: Oxford UP, 1991.
——. *Encyclopädie der Philosophischen Wissenschaften* [1830]. Vol. 53 of *Sämtliche Werke*. Ed. Georg Lasson. Leipzig: Meiner, 1930.
——. *Lectures on the Philosophy of World History* [1830]. Trans. H. B. Nisbet. Cambridge: Cambridge UP, 1975.
Hejinian, Lyn. "Grammar and Landscape." *Temblor* 3 (1986), 134–9.
Helle, Anita Plath. "Speculative Subjects: The Uses of Exile to the Imagination of Djuna Barnes, Gertrude Stein, and Mina Loy." Unpublished Dissertation, University of Oregon, 1986.
Herrnstein, Richard J., and Charles Murray. *The Bell Curve: Intelligence and Class Structure in American Life*. New York: Free Press, 1994.
Hindus, Milton. "Ethnicity and Sexuality in Gertrude Stein." *Midstream* 20:1 (January 1974), 69–76.
Hirsch, Nathaniel D. Mttron. *Genius and Creative Intelligence*. Cambridge, MA: Sci-Art, 1931.
Hobhouse, Janet. *Everybody Who Was Anybody: A Biography of Gertrude Stein*. New York: Doubleday, 1975.
Hoffman, Michael J. (ed.). *Critical Essays on Gertrude Stein*. Boston: G. K. Hall, 1986.
Hovey, Jamie. "Sapphic Primitivism in Gertrude Stein's *Q.E.D.*". *MFS* 42:3 (Fall 1996), 547–68.
Huyssen, Andreas. *After the Great Divide: Modernism, Mass Culture, Postmodernism*. Bloomington: Indiana UP, 1986.

Jain, Manju. *T. S. Eliot and American Philosophy: The Harvard Years*. Cambridge: Cambridge UP, 1992.

James, William. *The Principles of Psychology* [1890]. Cambridge, MA: Harvard UP, 1983.

——. *The Varieties of Religious Experience* [1903]. Ed. Martin E. Marty. New York: Penguin, 1985.

——. "The Will to Believe" [1896]. *Essays in Pragmatism*, ed. Alburey Castell. New York: Hafner, 1948, 88–109.

Jameson, Fredric. *Fables of Aggression: Wyndham Lewis, the Modernist as Fascist*. Berkeley: University of California Press, 1979.

——. "The Ideology of the Text." *The Ideologies of Theory: Essays 1971–1986*. Vol. 1: *Situations of Theory*. Minneapolis: University of Minnesota Press, 1988, 17–71.

——. "Postmodernism, or, The Cultural Logic of Late Capitalism." *New Left Review* 146 (July/August 1984), 53–92.

Kaiser, Charles. *The Gay Metropolis: 1940–1996*. New York: Harcourt Brace, 1997.

Kant, Immanuel. "On Genius" [1790]. *Philosophical Writings*, ed. Ernst Behler. New York: Continuum, 1986, 224–37.

Kass, Deborah. *The Warhol Project*. Ed. Michael Plante. New York: Distributed Art Publishers, 1999.

Katz, Leon. "The First Making of *The Making of Americans*: A Study Based on Gertrude Stein's Notebooks and Early Versions of Her Novel (1902–1908)." Unpublished Dissertation, Columbia University, 1963.

Kellner, Bruce (ed.). *A Gertrude Stein Companion: Content with the Example*. Westport, CT: Greenwood Press, 1988.

Kennedy, J. Gerald. *Imagining Paris: Exile, Writing, and American Identity*. New Haven: Yale UP, 1993.

Kern, Stephen. *The Culture of Time and Space 1880–1918*. Cambridge, MA: Harvard UP, 1983.

Kittler, Friedrich. *Discourse Networks 1800/1900* [1985]. Trans. Michael Metteer, with Chris Cullens. Stanford: Stanford UP, 1990.

Koestenbaum, Wayne. "Stein is Nice." *Parnassus: Poetry in Review* 20 (1995), 297–319.

Kohlschmidt, Werner, and Wolfgang Mohr (eds). *Reallexikon der deutschen Literaturgeschichte*. Berlin: Walter de Gruyter & Co., 1958.

Krauss, Rosalind E. *The Originality of the Avant-Garde and Other Modernist Myths*. Cambridge, MA: MIT Press, 1988.

Kretschmer, Ernst. *The Psychology of Men of Genius*. New York: Harcourt Brace, 1931.

Kristeva, Julia. *Desire in Language: A Semiotic Approach to Literature and Art* [1969]. Trans. Thomas Gora, Alice Jardine, and Leon S. Roudiez. New York: Columbia UP, 1980.

Lacan, Jacques. *Le Séminaire, livre XI: les quatre concepts fondamentaux de la psychanalyse*. Paris: Editions du Seuil, 1973.

——. "The Signification of the Phallus" [1958]. *Ecrits: A Selection*, trans. Alan Sheridan. New York: W. W. Norton, 1977, 281–91.

Lee, Hermione. *Virginia Woolf*. London: Random House, 1996.

Lentricchia, Frank. *Modernist Quartet*. Cambridge: Cambridge UP, 1994.

Levinson, Ronald Bartlett. "Gertrude Stein, William James, and Grammar." *American Journal of Psychology* 54 (January 1941), 124–8.

Lezra, Jacques. "How to Read How to Write." *Modernism/Modernity* 5:1 (January 1998), 117–29.

Lombroso, Cesare. *The Man of Genius*. London: W. Scott, 1891.

Loy, Mina. "Apology of Genius" [1922]. *The Lost Lunar Baedeker*, ed. Roger L. Conover. New York: Farrar, Straus, & Giroux, 1997, 77–8.

Lyotard, Jean-François. *The Differend: Phrases in Dispute*. Trans. George Van Den Abbeele. Minneapolis: University of Minnesota Press, 1988.

Madoff, Steven Henry (ed.). *Pop Art: A Critical History*. Berkeley: University of California Press, 1997.

Mayo, Louise A. *The Ambivalent Image: Nineteenth-Century America's Perception of the Jew*. Cranbury, NJ: Associated University Press, 1988.

Mellow, James R. *Charmed Circle: Gertrude Stein & Company*. Boston: Houghton Mifflin, 1974.

Meyer, Moe (ed.). *The Politics and Poetics of Camp*. New York: Routledge, 1994.

Meyer, Steven. "Writing Psychology Over: Gertrude Stein and William James." *The Yale Journal of Criticism* 8 (1995), 133–63.

Mill, John Stuart. "On Liberty" [1859]. *Mill: Texts, Commentaries*, ed. Alan Ryan. New York: Norton, 1997, 41–131.

Miller, Rosalind S. *Gertrude Stein: Form and Intelligibility*. New York: Exposition Press, 1949.

Moore, George B. *Gertrude Stein's* The Making of Americans: *Repetition and the Emergence of Modernism*. New York: Peter Lang, 1998.

Murray, Penelope. *Genius: The History of an Idea*. London: Basil Blackwell, 1989.

Nahm, Milton. *The Artist as Creator: An Essay of Human Freedom*. Baltimore: Johns Hopkins Press, 1956.

Neuman, Shirley, and Ira B. Nadel (eds). *Gertrude Stein and the Making of Literature*. Boston: Northeastern UP, 1988.

Newton, Esther. *Mother Camp: Female Impersonators in America*. Chicago: University of Chicago Press, 1972.

——. "The Mythic Mannish Lesbian: Radclyffe Hall and the New Woman." *Signs* 9:4 (Summer 1984), 557–75.

Nietzsche, Friedrich. "Schopenhauer as Educator" [1874]. *Unfashionable Observations*, trans. Richard T. Gray. Stanford: Stanford UP, 1995, 169–255.

Nisbet, J. F. *The Insanity of Genius; and the General Inequality of Human Faculty Physiologically Considered*. London: Ward and Downey, 1891.

Nitzsche, Jane Chance. *The Genius Figure in Antiquity and the Middle Ages*. New York: Columbia UP, 1975.

North, Michael. *The Dialect of Modernism: Race, Language, and Twentieth-Century Literature*. New York: Oxford UP, 1994.

Novalis (Friedrich von Hardenberg). *Philosophical Writings*. Trans. Margaret Mahony Stoljar. Albany: SUNY Press, 1997.

——. *Pollen and Fragments*. Trans. Arthur Versluis. Grand Rapids, MI: Phanes Press, 1989.
Ortega y Gasset, José. *The Dehumanization of Art and Other Essays on Art, Culture, and Literature* [1925]. Princeton: Princeton UP, 1968.
Oxford English Dictionary, 2nd edn. Oxford: Clarendon Press, 1992.
Pease, Donald E. "National Identities, Postmodern Artifacts, and Postnational Narratives." *National Identities and Post-Americanist Narratives*, ed. Donald E. Pease. Durham: Duke UP, 1994, 1–13.
Perelman, Bob. *The Trouble with Genius: Reading Pound, Joyce, Stein, and Zukovsky*. Berkeley: University of California Press, 1994.
Perkins, Priscilla. "'A Little Body with a Very Large Head': Composition, Psychopathology, and the Making of Stein's Normal Self." *MFS* 42:3 (Fall 1996), 529–46.
Perloff, Marjorie. *Poetry On & Off the Page: Essays for Emergent Occasions*. Evanston: Northwestern UP, 1998.
Petersen, William. "Jews as a Race." *Midstream* 34:2 (February–March 1988), 35–7.
Quartermain, Peter. *Disjunctive Poetics: From Gertrude Stein and Louis Zukovsky to Susan Howe*. Cambridge: Cambridge UP, 1992.
Radway, Janice A. *A Feeling for Books: The Book-of-the-Month Club, Literary Taste, and Middle-Class Desire*. Chapel Hill: University of North Carolina Press, 1997.
Renan, Ernest. "What Is a Nation?" [1882]. *Nation and Narration*, ed. Homi K. Bhabha. London: Routledge, 1990, 8–22.
Riggio, Thomas P. (ed.). *Dreiser–Mencken Letters: The Correspondence of Theodore Dreiser & H. L. Mencken 1907–1945*, vol. I. Philadelphia: University of Pennsylvania Press, 1986.
Riviere, Joan. "Womanliness as a Masquerade" [1929]. *Formations of Fantasy*, ed. Victor Burgin, James Donald, and Cora Kaplan. London: Methuen, 1986, 35–44.
Rogin, Michael. *Blackface, White Noise: Jewish Immigrants in the Hollywood Melting Pot*. Berkeley: University of California Press, 1996.
Rubin, Gayle, with Judith Butler. "Sexual Traffic: Interview." *differences* 6:2–3 (1994), 62–99.
Ruddick, Lisa. *Reading Gertrude Stein*. Ithaca: Cornell UP, 1990.
Ryan, Judith. *The Vanishing Subject: Early Psychology and Literary Modernism*. Chicago: University of Chicago Press, 1991.
Said, Edward. *Representations of the Intellectual: The 1993 Reich Lectures*. London: Vintage, 1994.
Saldivar-Hull, Sonia. "Wrestling Your Ally: Stein, Racism, and Feminist Critical Practice." *Women's Writing in Exile*, ed. Mary Lynn Broe and Angela Ingram. Chapel Hill: University of North Carolina Press, 1989, 189–98.
Schlegel, Friedrich. *A Course of Lectures on Modern History* [1810]. Trans. L. Purcell and R. H. Whitelock. London: Henry Bohn, 1849.
——. *Philosophische Vorlesungen*, vol. XII. Munich: Thomas-Verlag, 1964.
Schopenhauer, Arthur. *The Works of Schopenhauer*. Ed. Will Durant. New York: Frederick Ungar Publishing, 1955.

Schultz, Susan M. "Gertrude Stein's Self-Advertisement." *Raritan* 12:2 (Fall 1992), 71–87.

Schwartz, Sanford. *The Matrix of Modernism: Pound, Eliot, and Early Twentieth-Century Thought*. Princeton: Princeton UP, 1985.

Schwarz, Osias L. *General Types of Superior Men*. Boston: Richard G. Badger, 1916.

Scott, Bonnie Kime (ed.). *The Gender of Modernism*. Bloomington: Indiana UP, 1990.

Seltzer, Mark. *Bodies and Machines*. New York: Routledge, 1992.

Sengoopta, Chandak. "Science, Sexuality, and Gender in the *Fin de Siècle*: Otto Weininger as Baedeker." *History of Science* xxx (1992), 249–79.

Shklovsky, Victor. "Art as Technique" [1917]. *Russian Formalist Criticism: Four Essays*, trans. Lee T. Lemon and Marion J. Reis. Lincoln: University of Nebraska Press, 1965, 3–24.

Simpson, David (ed.). *The Origins of Modern Critical Thought: German Aesthetic and Literary Criticism from Lessing to Hegel*. Cambridge: Cambridge UP, 1988.

Smith, Dinitia. "Another Top 100 List: Now It's Nonfiction." *The New York Times* E:2 (30 April 1999), 45.

Smith, Sidonie. "Performativity, Autobiographical Practice, Resistance." *a/b:Auto/Biography Studies* 10:1 (Spring 1995), 17–33.

Sontag, Susan. "Notes on 'Camp'" [1964]. *A Susan Sontag Reader*. New York: Farrar, Straus & Giroux, 1982, 105–19.

Spacks, Patricia Meyer. *Gossip*. Chicago: University of Chicago Press, 1986.

Stavitsky, Gail. *Gertrude Stein: The American Connection*. New York: Sid Deutsch Gallery, 1990.

Stein, Gertrude. *The Autobiography of Alice B. Toklas*. New York: Harcourt Brace, 1933.

——. Carnets (unpublished). Gertrude Stein and Alice B. Toklas Papers, Yale Collection of American Literature. Beinecke Rare Book and Manuscript Library.

——. Correspondence (unpublished). Gertrude Stein and Alice B. Toklas Papers, Yale Collection of American Literature. Beinecke Rare Book and Manuscript Library.

——. "Cultivated Motor Automatism" [1898]. *Motor Automatism*. New York: The Phoenix Book Shop, 1969.

——. *Everybody's Autobiography* [1937]. New York: Vintage, 1973.

——. *Fernhurst, Q.E.D., and Other Early Writings*. Introduction by Leon Katz. New York: Liveright, 1983.

——. *Four in America* [1933]. Introduction by Thornton Wilder. New Haven: Yale UP, 1947.

——. *Geography and Plays* [1922]. Introduction by Cyrena N. Pondrom. Madison: University of Wisconsin Press, 1993.

——. *How to Write* [1931]. Preface and Introduction by Patricia Meyerowitz. New York: Dover, 1975.

——. *How Writing Is Written. Vol. 2 of the Previously Uncollected Writings of Gertrude Stein*. Ed. Robert Bartlett Haas. Los Angeles: Black Sparrow Press, 1974.

——. *Lectures in America* [1935]. Introduction by Wendy Steiner. London: Virago, 1988.
——. *The Making of Americans: Being a History of a Family's Progress* [1925]. Introduction by Steven Meyer. Normal, IL: Dalkey Archive Press, 1995.
——. *Matisse Picasso and Gertrude Stein with Two Shorter Stories* [1933]. Barton, Berlin, Middleton: Something Else Press, 1972.
——. *Narration* [1935]. Chicago: University of Chicago Press, 1969.
——. (with Leon M. Solomons). "Normal Motor Automatism" [1896]. *Motor Automatism*. New York: The Phoenix Book Shop, 1969.
——. Notebooks to *The Making of Americans* (unpublished). Gertrude Stein and Alice B. Toklas Papers, Yale Collection of American Literature. Beinecke Rare Book and Manuscript Library.
——. *Operas and Plays* [1932]. Barrytown, NY: Station Hill, 1987.
——. *Paris France* [1940]. New York: Liveright, 1970.
——. *Picasso* [1938]. New York: Dover, 1984.
——. *Portraits and Prayers*. New York: Random House, 1934.
——. *A Stein Reader*. Ed. Ulla E. Dydo. Evanston, IL: Northwestern UP, 1993.
——. *Three Lives* [1909]. New York: Penguin, 1990.
——. "To Call It a Day." *Painted Lace and Other Pieces (1914–1937)*. New Haven: Yale UP, 1955, 243–50.
——. "A Transatlantic Interview 1946." *The Gender of Modernism*, ed. Bonnie Kime Scott. Bloomington: Indiana UP, 1990, 502–16.
——. *Two: Gertrude Stein and Her Brother and Other Early Portraits (1908–1912)*. New Haven: Yale UP, 1951.
——. *Useful Knowledge*. New York: Payson & Clarke, 1928.
——. "What Are Master-pieces and Why Are There So Few of Them." *Look at Me Now and Here I Am: Writings and Lectures 1909–45*, ed. Patricia Meyerowitz. London: Penguin, 1967.
Steiner, Wendy. *Exact Resemblance to Exact Resemblance: the Literary Portraiture of Gertrude Stein*. New Haven: Yale UP, 1978.
Stillinger, Jack. *Multiple Authorship and the Myth of Solitary Genius*. Oxford: Oxford UP, 1991.
Stimpson, Catharine R. "Gertrude Stein and the Lesbian Lie." *American Women's Autobiography*, ed. Margo Culley. Madison: University of Wisconsin Press, 1992, 152–66.
——. "The Mind, the Body, and Gertrude Stein." *Critical Inquiry* 3 (Spring 1977), 489–506.
Stovall, Tyler. *Paris Noir: African-Americans in the City of Light*. Boston: Houghton Mifflin, 1996.
Summers, Claude J. (ed.). *The Gay and Lesbian Literary Heritage*. New York: Henry Holt & Co., 1995.
Sundquist, Eric J. *To Wake the Nations: Race in the Making of American Literature*. Cambridge, MA: Harvard UP, 1993.
"Supplement: Testimony against Gertrude Stein by Henri Matisse, Tristan Tzara, Maria Jolas, Georges Braque, Eugene Jolas, André Salmon." *transition* 23 (July 1935).

Sutherland, Donald. *Gertrude Stein: A Biography of Her Work*. New Haven: Yale UP, 1951.
Synnott, Marcia Graham. *The Half-Opened Door: Discrimination and Admissions at Harvard, Yale, and Princeton, 1900–1970*. Westport, CT: Greenwood Press, 1979.
Terman, Lewis M. *Genetic Studies of Genius*. Stanford: Stanford UP, 1925.
Toklas, Alice B. *What is Remembered*. New York: Holt, Rinehart & Winston, 1963.
Townsend, Kim. *Manhood at Harvard: William James and Others*. New York: W. W. Norton, 1996.
Van Dusen, Wanda. "Portrait of a National Fetish: Gertrude Stein's 'Introduction to the Speeches of Maréchal Pétain' (1942)." *Modernism/Modernity* 3:3 (September 1996), 69–96.
Wagner-Martin, Linda. *"Favored Strangers": Gertrude Stein and Her Family*. New Brunswick, NJ: Rutgers UP, 1995.
——. "Gertrude Stein." *Jewish American Women Writers: A Bio-Bibliographical and Critical Sourcebook*, ed. Ann Shapiro. London: Greenday Press, 1994, 431–9.
Wald, Priscilla. *Constituting Americans: Cultural Anxiety and Narrative Form*. Durham: Duke UP, 1995.
Walker, Jayne. *The Making of a Modernist: Gertrude Stein from* Three Lives *to* Tender Buttons. Amherst: University of Massachusetts Press, 1984.
Warhol, Andy. *The Philosophy of Andy Warhol*. New York: Harcourt Brace, 1975.
Warhol, Andy, and Pat Hackett. *POPism: The Warhol '60s*. New York: Harcourt Brace, 1980.
Weininger, Otto. *Sex and Character* [1903]. London: Heinemann, 1906.
Werner, Marta L. "'Most Arrows': Autonomy and Intertextuality in Emily Dickinson's Late Fragments." *Text* 10 (1997), 41–72.
White, Ray Lewis (ed.). *Sherwood Anderson/Gertrude Stein: Correspondence and Personal Essays*. Chapel Hill: University of North Carolina Press, 1972.
Williams, Raymond. *The Politics of Modernism: Against the New Conformists*. London: Verso, 1989.
Williams, William Carlos. "The Work of Gertrude Stein" [1930]. *Imaginations*. New York: New Directions, 1970, 344–51.
Wineapple, Brenda. *Sister Brother: Gertrude and Leo Stein*. New York: G. P. Putnam's Sons, 1996.
Woolf, Virginia. "Middlebrow" [n.d.]. *Collected Essays*, vol. 2. New York: Harcourt, Brace & World, 1966, 196–203.
——. "The War from the Street" [1919]. *The Essays of Virginia Woolf*, vol. 3, ed. Andrew McNeillie. New York: Harcourt Brace, 1988, 3–4.

Index

Numbers in *italics* indicate illustrations.